SPECIAL LIST NO. 29

List of Selected Maps of States and Territories

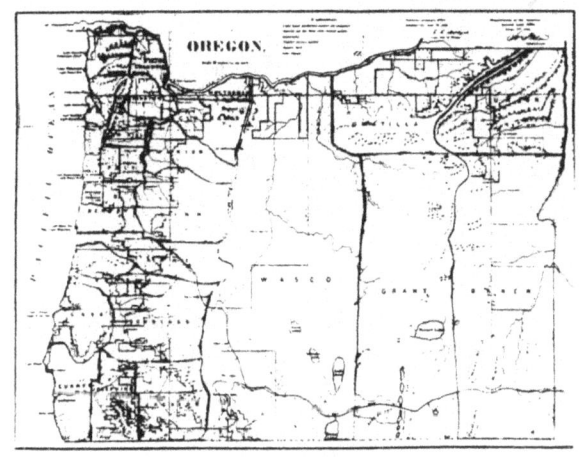

COMPILED BY
Janet L. Hargett

THE NATIONAL ARCHIVES
NATIONAL ARCHIVES AND RECORDS SERVICE
GENERAL SERVICES ADMINISTRATION
WASHINGTON: 1971

HERITAGE BOOKS
2011

HERITAGE BOOKS
AN IMPRINT OF HERITAGE BOOKS, INC.

Books, CDs, and more—Worldwide

For our listing of thousands of titles see our website
at
www.HeritageBooks.com

A Facsimile Reprint
Published 2011 by
HERITAGE BOOKS, INC.
Publishing Division
100 Railroad Ave. #104
Westminster, Maryland 21157

Originally published
The National Archives
National Archives and Records Service
General Services Administration
Washington: 1971

Library of Congress Catalog Card No. 78-183183

— Publisher's Notice —
In reprints such as this, it is often not possible to remove blemishes from the original. We feel the contents of this book warrant its reissue despite these blemishes and hope you will agree and read it with pleasure.

International Standard Book Numbers
Paperbound: 978-1-888265-16-3
Clothbound: 978-0-7884-8920-4

Foreword

The General Services Administration, through the National Archives and Records Service, is responsible for administering the permanent noncurrent records of the Federal Government. These archival holdings, now amounting to more than 900,000 cubic feet, date from the days of the First Continental Congress and consist of the basic records of the legislative, judicial, and executive branches of our Government. The Presidential libraries of Herbert Hoover, Franklin D. Roosevelt, Harry S. Truman, Dwight D. Eisenhower, John F. Kennedy, and Lyndon B. Johnson contain the papers of those Presidents and many of their associates in office. While many of the archival holdings document events of great moment in our Nation's history, most of them are preserved because of their continuing practical use in the ordinary processes of government, for the protection of private rights, and for the research use of scholars and students.

To facilitate the use of the records and to describe their nature and content, archivists prepare various kinds of finding aids. The present work is one such publication. We believe that it will prove valuable to anyone who wishes to use the records it describes.

Preface

Special lists are published by the National Archives as part of its records description program. The special list describes in detail the contents of certain important records series; that is, units of records of the same form or that deal with the same subject or activity or that are arranged serially. Its form and style are not fixed but vary according to the nature of the records to which it relates. Its distinguishing characteristic is that it goes beyond the general description contained in a record group registration statement, a preliminary inventory, or an inventory and describes records in terms of individual record items.

In addition to lists and other finding aids that relate to particular record groups, the National Archives issues publications that give an overall picture of materials in its custody. A new, comprehensive *Guide to the National Archives of the United States* will be issued in 1972. A guide devoted to one geographical area—*Guide to Materials on Latin America in the National Archives* (1961)—has been published. Reference information papers analyze records in the National Archives on such subjects as transportation, small business, and the Middle East. Records of the Civil War are described in *Guide to Federal Archives Relating to the Civil War* (1962), *Guide to the Archives of the Government of the Confederate States of America* (1968), and *Civil War Maps in the National Archives* (1961); those of World War I in *Handbook of Federal World War Agencies and Their Records, 1917-1921* (1943); and those of World War II in the two-volume guide, *Federal Records of World War II* (1950-51). Genealogical records are described in *Guide to Genealogical Records in the National Archives* (1964). Among the holdings of the National Archives are large quantities of audiovisual materials received from all sources: Government, private, and commercial. The *Guide to the Ford Film Collection in the National Archives* (1970) describes one of the largest private gift collections. The extensive body of maps and charts is described in the *Guide to Cartographic Records in the National Archives* (1971).

Many bodies of records of high research value have been microfilmed by the National Archives as a form of publication. Positive prints of these microfilm publications, many of which are described in the current *List of National Archives Microfilm Publications,* are available for purchase. For other publications, see the most recent *Select List of Publications of the National Archives and Records Service,* General Information Leaflet No. 3.

JAMES B. RHOADS
Archivist of the United States

Contents

	Page
Introduction	1

List

Alabama	3
Alaska	4
Arizona	7
Arkansas	10
California	12
Colorado	16
Connecticut	20
Delaware	21
Florida	21
Georgia	24
Hawaii	26
Idaho	27
Illinois	29
Indiana	32
Iowa	34
Kansas	36
Kentucky	39
Louisiana	41
Maine	44
Maryland	46
Massachusetts	47
Michigan	48
Minnesota	50
Mississippi	53
Missouri	55
Montana	57
Nebraska	61
Nevada	63
New Hampshire	65
New Jersey	67
New Mexico	67
New York	72
North Carolina	74
North Dakota (including Dakota Territory)	76
Ohio	79
Oklahoma (including Indian Territory)	80
Oregon	84
Pennsylvania	87
South Carolina	90

	Page
South Dakota	91
Tennessee	92
Texas	92
Utah	95
Vermont	97
Virginia	98
Washington	100
West Virginia	102
Wisconsin	103
Wyoming	105
Index	109

Introduction

This publication describes approximately 900 State maps selected from the holdings of the Cartographic Archives Division of the National Archives and Records Service. The maps date from the late 18th century to 1920. Maps of the Territories are included to provide early coverage of areas which later became States. The list is intended primarily for use by researchers seeking general maps of States and Territories. Because of the general nature of the maps, their arrangement alphabetically by State and chronologically thereunder, and their relative uniformity of content, no subject index has been prepared for this publication. Variations in content, however, have been indicated in the descriptive entries. The accompanying index gives the names of cartographers, surveyors, publishers, and other persons connected with the production of the maps.

Most of the maps cover an entire State or a major part of one; some include several States or Territories. Basic information shown on the maps selected, however, applies to the State or Territory as a whole rather than to any one particular area. The maps are listed alphabetically by State and chronologically within each State listing. Maps including more than one State or Territory are listed under the name of the first State mentioned in the title and are cross-referenced under the other States.

Maps described in this list were selected from 12 record groups and the Reference Map Collection (referred to in this publication as Ref. Coll.). Record groups usually consist of the records of a single Federal agency, typically at the bureau level. The Reference Map Collection is a small group of published maps that are not a part of any record group. The Records of the Post Office Department (RG 28), the Bureau of Land Management (RG 49; formerly the General Land Office), and the Office of the Chief of Engineers (RG 77) account for about two-thirds of the maps listed. Other record groups from which maps were selected are Records of the Coast and Geodetic Survey (RG 23), Records of the United States Senate (RG 46), Records of the Geological Survey (RG 57), Records of the Bureau of Indian Affairs (RG 75), Records of Boundary and Claims Commissions and Arbitrations (RG 76), Records of the Office of Territories (RG 126), Records of the United States House of Representatives (RG 233), and Records of United States Army Continental Commands, 1821-1920 (RG 393).

Most entries include the following information: map title; name of compiler, draftsman or originating Federal agency, and publisher, if any; date; scale; dimensions to the nearest half inch (from edge to edge of sheet, vertical dimension first); brief description of contents; and file designation. When appropriate, cross-references to related entries are included.

In this publication a "manuscript" map is defined as one made with pencil, ink, watercolors, or some similar hand-applied medium, usually on paper or tracing cloth. Blueprints are identified as such, but other photographically reproduced records are referred to as "photoprocessed." A "published" map is one that is issued for general distribution, usually in print or near print. An "annotated" map is a published or photoprocessed map that includes information added by hand.

Map titles shown in the entries, unless enclosed in brackets, are taken directly from the maps; but they do not always appear on the maps in title blocks or with the wording in consecutive order. Spelling, abbreviations, and capitalization in the titles and in quoted remarks in the entries are as they appear on the maps. Punctuation, however, has at times been changed or supplied in the interest of clarity. Information enclosed in brackets has been supplied by the compiler. Undated maps are indicated by "n.d." In some instances, a comparison with dated maps has enabled the compiler to establish an approximate date.

INTRODUCTION

The number of maps listed for a given State often is indicative of Federal activity in that State. Those States that were part of the public domain and within which the Federal Government holds much of the land, therefore, are better represented than the States that were parts of the Thirteen Original Colonies.

Cartographic records described in this publication may be examined in the Research Room of the Cartographic Archives Division in accordance with regulations issued by the Administrator of General Services. The National Archives and Records Service is equipped to provide photocopies of the maps in its custody, for a fee. Information concerning the cost of reproductions will be provided upon request.

Preliminary descriptions for this list were prepared under the direction of Ralph E. Ehrenberg by archivist trainees during assignments in the Cartographic Archives Division, and they were compiled for publication by Janet L. Hargett.

ALABAMA

1. A Diagram of the State of Alabama. [Issued by the Office of the Surveyor General, Florence, Ala., n.d.]

   1 inch to ca. 20 miles. 25 x 14½. Published. Extent of public land surveys, Indian land cessions, and information concerning location of survey records. Filed as RG 49: Alabama 4, Pub.

2. Map of Alabama Constructed From The Surveys in the General Land Office and other Documents By John Melish.... Published by John Melish 1818.

   1 inch to 15 miles. 28 x 20. Annotated published. County names and boundaries, Cherokee and Creek lands, Indian villages, towns, trails, and roads. Filed as RG 77: US 32-1.

3. Map of Alabama Constructed From The Surveys in the General Land Office and other Documents By John Melish.... Published by John Melish. Improved to 1819.

   1 inch to 15 miles. 28½ x 20½. Annotated published. County names and boundaries, Cherokee and Creek lands, Indian villages, towns, trails, and roads. Annotated to show additional roads. Filed as RG 77: US 32-2.

4. Map of the States of Alabama, and Georgia.... Published Oct. 15, 1831, by I. T. Hinton & Simpkin & Marshall.

   1 inch to ca. 38 miles. 11½ x 17. Published. County names and boundaries, settlements, and military posts. Small-scale inset plan of Savannah, Ga. Filed as Ref. Coll.: Alabama 1831.

5. An Accurate Map of the State of Alabama and West Florida: Carefully Compiled from the original Surveys of the General Government... By John La Tourette... 1837.

   1 inch to 6 miles. 4 sections, each 34 x 28. Published. County names and boundaries, roads, towns, and township and range numbers. Inset plans of Montgomery, Wetumpka, Huntsville, Pensacola, Mobile, Florence, Tuscaloosa, and Tuscumbia. Scales of inset maps not given. Filed as RG 77: US 86.

6. A Diagram of the State of Alabama... Exhibiting the situation of the Public Surveys... [Issued by the Surveyor's Office, Florence, Ala., Jan. 25, 1840].

   1 inch to ca. 18 miles. 26 x 13. Published. Shows the extent and status of public land surveys and boundaries of Indian cessions and of "Old Madison County." Boundaries of Indian cessions and of "Old Madison County" are shown in color. A copy of this map is published in S. Doc. 61, 26th Cong., 2d sess. Filed as RG 46: 26th Cong., 2d sess.

7. No. 9 [Map of] Alabama.

   1 inch to ca. 40 miles. 11 x 9. Published. Names and boundaries of land districts in 1828 and 1841. An explanation of the map and 1828 land district boundaries is given in S. Doc. 92, 26th Cong., 2d sess. Filed as RG 49: Alabama 3, Pub.

8. [Map of] Alabama... Entered according to Act of Congress in the year 1842 by Sidney E. Morse and Samuel Breese.

   1 inch to ca. 25 miles. 17½ x 14. Published. County names and boundaries, towns, township and range numbers, roads, canals, and railroad lines. Filed as Ref. Coll.: Alabama 1842.

9. A Diagram of the State of Alabama. Issued by the Office of the Surveyor General, Florence, Ala., October 10, 1844.

   1 inch to ca. 20 miles. 24 x 13½. Published. Extent of public land surveys, information concerning the location of survey records, and township surveys under contract and those proposed to be surveyed by June 30, 1846. Also shows Indian land cessions. Filed as RG 49: Alabama 5, Pub.

10. La Tourette's Map of the State of Alabama and West Florida: Carefully Compiled from the original Surveys of the General Government; Revised, Corrected, and Published with the Approval of the Governor and other State Officers By D. H. Cram, Civil Engineer, Montgomery, Ala., 1856.

MAPS OF STATES AND TERRITORIES

1 inch to 6 miles. 4 sections, each 34 x 29. Published. County names and boundaries, cities and towns, railroad lines, roads, and physical features. Inset maps of Montgomery, Huntsville, Pensacola, Mobile, Florence, Tuscaloosa, and Tuscumbia. Scales of inset maps not given. Filed as Ref. Coll.: Alabama 1856.

11. Gray's New Map of Alabama by Frank A. Gray...Copyright, 1878, by O. W. Gray & Son.

1 inch to ca. 14 miles. 27 x 17. Published. Counties (in color), railroads, canals, cities and towns, township and range numbers, and physical features. Also shows lighthouses and lightships. Inset map "Entrance to Mobile Bay from Charts of the U. S. Coast Survey." Filed as RG 77: US 373-55.

12. [Map of the] State of Alabama. 1878. Compiled from the official Records of the General Land Office.

1 inch to 12 miles. 34 x 27. Published. County names and boundaries, cities and towns, railroad lines, and extent of public land surveys. Filed as RG 49: Alabama 1878, Pub.

13. [Map of the] State of Alabama. 1882. Compiled from the official Records of the General Land Office.

1 inch to 12 miles. 32 x 24½. Published. County names and boundaries, cities and towns, railroad lines, and extent of public land surveys. Filed as RG 49: Alabama 1882, Pub.

14. [Map of the] State of Alabama. 1889. Compiled from the official Records of the General Land Office.

1 inch to 10 miles. 40 x 26. Published. County names and boundaries, cities and towns, railroad lines, military reservations, and extent of public land surveys. Also a black and white base map for this date. Filed as RG 49: Alabama 1889, Pub.

15. [Map of the] State of Alabama. Compiled from the official Records of the General Land Office...1895.

1 inch to 12 miles. 36 x 25. Published. County names and boundaries, cities and towns, railroad lines, military reservations, and extent of public land surveys. Relief is shown in color. Also a black and white base map for this date. Drainage in blue. Filed as RG 49: Alabama 1895, Pub.

16. State of Alabama Compiled from official Records of the General Land Office...1915....Compiled and Drawn by Daniel O'Hare. Traced and Lettered by George A. Daidy.

1 inch to 12 miles. 34 x 23. Published. County names and boundaries, towns and cities, military reservations, and public land surveys. Relief is shown in color. Also a black and white base map for this date. Filed as RG 49: Alabama 1915, Pub.

See also entry 201.

ALASKA

17. [Map of] North Western America Showing the Territory Ceded by Russia to the United States. Compiled for the Department of State at the U.S. Coast Survey Office...1867.

1 inch to 80 miles. 25 x 38. Published. Physical features, "Russian Settlements" (names underlined in red), and "Esquimaux [sic] Settlements" (names underlined in blue). Filed as RG 75: map 970.

18. Map of the (Alaska) Territory of the United States Including Islands on the North Pacific, Accompanying the Annual Report of Commissioner of the General Land Office for 1869.

1 inch to ca. 80 miles. 2 sections, each 24 x 31. Photoprocessed. Settlements and physical features. Map also includes information on the climatology of Alaska. Filed as RG 49: Alaska 2, Pub.

19. Map Showing the Distribution of the Native Tribes of Alaska and Adjoining Territory. Compiled from the latest authorities by W. H. Dall, U.S. Coast Survey, 1875.

ALASKA 5

1 inch to ca. 60 miles. 23 x 31. Published. Also shows settlements, forts, and physical features. Filed as RG 75: maps 823 and 469.

20. Sketch Map of Alaska Furnished by the U.S. Coast and Geodetic Survey To accompany Report by Sheldon Jackson, D.D., U.S. General Agent of Education in Alaska, 1885.
Small scale. 17 x 20. Annotated published. Annotated with symbols to show locations of "schools ordered" and "schools in operation." Also shows a few place names. A published copy of this map without the annotations appears in S. Ex. Doc. 85, 49th Cong., 1st sess. See also entry 21. Filed as RG 75: map CA 1.

21. Sketch Map of Alaska, Furnished by the U.S. Coast and Geodetic Survey To accompany Report by Sheldon Jackson, D.D., U.S. General Agent of Education in Alaska, 1885.
Small scale. 17 x 20. Annotated published. Alaska shaded red. Symbols indicate locations of schools. These locations differ somewhat from those shown in entry 20. Marked "B" on the reverse of map. Filed as RG 75: map CA 618.

22. General Chart of Alaska ... Coast and Geodetic Survey Report for 1890. No. 3. ... Compiled and drawn by A. & H. Lindenkohl.
1 inch to ca. 60 miles. 29½ x 53. Published. Nautical chart. Also shows topographical features and settlements. Filed as RG 75: map 1395.

23. Sketch Map of Alaska Prepared for U.S. Bureau of Education By the U.S. Coast and Geodetic Survey To accompany Reindeer Report by Sheldon Jackson, D.D., U.S. General Agent of Education in Alaska, 1893.
1 inch to ca. 100 miles. 17 x 24. Published. Shows areas of good pasturage for reindeer, military posts, settlements, and missions. Filed as RG 75: map CA 620.

24. [Map of Alaska compiled in the General Land Office, 1894. Compiled and drawn by Robert H. Morton.]
1 inch to ca. 58 miles. 29½ x 35½. Manuscript. Shows settlements and other place names. Relief shown by hachures. Inset map of "Continuation of the Aleutian Islands." Filed as RG 49: Alaska 2.

25. Map of Alaska and a Portion of the Northwest Territory Showing the New Gold Fields and the Route of the North American Transportation and Trading Company ... Compiled and drawn by I. P. Berthong ... Copyright, 1897, North American Transportation and Trading Company.
1 inch to 140 miles. 21 x 26. Published. Also shows general topography and some place names. Filed as Ref. Coll.: Alaska 1897.

26. General Chart of Alaska To Accompany Reindeer Report of Sheldon Jackson, General Agent of Education in Alaska. 1897.
1 inch to ca. 60 miles. 27½ x 40½. Published. Settlements, missions, military reservations, and locations of reindeer stations including "Reindeer Purchasing Station" in Eastern Siberia. Copy of this map appears with report in S. Doc. 30, 55th Cong., 2d sess. Filed as RG 46: 55th Cong., 2d sess.

27. Map of Alaska ... 1898 [Compiled by the General Land Office].
1 inch to 48 miles. 2 sections, each 38 x 24. Published. Map includes a table of "Distances" and shows overland and water routes to the interior, proposed railroads, mineral deposits, land district boundaries, locations of land offices, and church missions. Inset map "From Juneau to Forty Mile Creek" at a scale of 1 inch to 24 miles. Filed as RG 49: Alaska 3, Pub.

28. Map of Alaska Showing Explorations by U.S. Geological Survey in 1898, Together with Principal Previous Routes of Exploration.
1 inch to ca. 57 miles. 25½ x 34½. Published. Also shows settlements and other place names. Relief is shown by hachures. "Report, Public Resolution No. 25, 55th Cong., 3d Session." Filed as RG 46: 55th Cong., 3d sess.

29. Post Route Map of the Territory of Alaska Showing Post Offices with the intermediate distances on mail routes in operation on the list of December, 1901.
1 inch to 40 miles. 2 sections, each 36 x 26. Published. Frequency and type of mail service, post offices, "settlements and offices discontinued," missions, railroad lines, and railroad stations. Frequency of service shown by colors. Map includes "List of Post Offices in Alaska Territory" and inset maps of Aleutian Islands and Southeastern Alaska. Filed as RG 28: Alaska 1901.

30. Map of Alaska [Published by the U.S. Geological Survey, 1904].

   1 inch to ca. 40 miles. 36 x 48. Annotated published. Settlements and other place names. Annotated apparently to show trails and a few corrections to shoreline. Drainage in blue; contour lines in brown. "Issued as a Supplement to the National Geographic Magazine, May, 1904." Filed as RG 49: Alaska 3.

31. General Chart of Alaska To Accompany Reindeer Report by Sheldon Jackson, LL.D., General Agent of Education in Alaska, 1905.

   1 inch to 40 miles. 34½ x 50½. Published. Shows locations of public schools, reindeer stations, and missions. Post route map was used as a base map. Inset maps of Southeastern Alaska and Aleutian Islands. Filed as RG 46: S. Doc. 61, 58th Cong., 3d sess.

32. [Map of] Alaska ... Compiled [in the General Land Office] by M. Hendges and revised and drawn by Charles J. Helm. 1906.

   1 inch to 60 miles. 31 x 40. Published. Forest reserves, military and Indian reservations, and reindeer station reserves are shown in color. Also shows towns and telegraph lines. Small inset plans of Sitka, Juneau, and Nome. Relief is shown in color. Also a black and white base map (drainage in blue) for the same date. Filed as RG 49: Alaska 1906, Pub.

33. Alaskan Exhibit Alaska-Yukon-Pacific Exposition Seattle, Washington. 1909 [map of] Alaska. [Compiled by the General Land Office.]

   1 inch to ca. 70 miles. 28 x 40. Published. Land district boundaries, national forests, Indian reservations, and military reservations are shown in color. Also shows settlements, bird reserves, and public school reserves. Relief is shown in color. Filed as RG 49: Alaska 4, Pub.

34. [Map of] Alaska [Compiled in the General Land Office by Daniel O'Hare] ... 1909.

   1 inch to 60 miles. 33 x 44. Published. Land district boundaries, military and Indian reservations, national forests, and wildlife reservations are shown in color. Also a black and white base map for this date. Filed as RG 49: Alaska 1909, Pub.

35. Map of Alaska Showing the Known Distribution of Mineral Resources. Compiled under the direction of Alfred H. Brooks ... Division of Alaskan Mineral Resources. [Issued by U.S. Geological Survey.] 1910.

   1 inch to ca. 80 miles. 19 x 26. Published. Also shows some settlements. Filed as RG 46: S. Doc. 77, 62d Cong., 1st sess.

36. [Map of Alaska showing locations of reindeer stations and public schools for natives of Alaska. Issued by the U.S. Bureau of Education, Department of the Interior. 1910.]

   1 inch to ca. 80 miles. 19 x 26. Published. Also shows military telegraph lines, wireless stations, settlements, and drainage features. Filed as RG 75: map CA 621.

37. Post Route Map of the Territory of Alaska Showing Post Offices, with the intermediate distances on mail routes in operation on the 1st of January, 1915.

   1 inch to 40 miles. 2 sections, each 36½ x 25. Published. Frequency and type of mail service, post offices, "settlements and offices discontinued," missions, railroad lines, and railroad stations. Frequency of service shown by different colors. Map includes "List of Post Offices in Alaska Territory" and inset maps of Tanana District, Aleutian Islands, and Southeastern Alaska. Field as RG 28: Alaska 1915.

38. Map of Alaska By the Alaska Road Commission, 1916.

   1 inch to 27.62 miles. 36 x 50. Published. Towns, wireless stations, wagon and sled roads, pack trails, railroads, and telegraph and telephone lines. Drainage in blue; contour lines in brown. Inset maps of the Aleutian Islands, Bering Sea Islands, and part of the Arctic shore. (See also entry 41.) Filed as RG 126: Alaska 1916.

39. Post Route Map of the Territory of Alaska Showing Post Offices with the intermediate distances on mail routes in operation on the 1st of January, 1917.

   1 inch to 40 miles. 2 sections, each 36 x 25½. Published. Frequency and type of mail service, post offices, "settlements and offices discontinued," missions, railroad lines, and railroad stations. Map includes "List of Post Offices in Alaska Territory" and inset maps of Tanana District, Aleutian Islands, and southeastern Alaska. Filed as RG 28: Alaska 1917.

ARIZONA

40. [Map of] Alaska [Compiled in the General Land Office] ... 1917.
 1 inch to 40 miles. 38 x 48½. Published. Land district boundaries, military and Indian reservations, national forests, and wildlife reservations are shown in color. Also shows U.S. Government schools, towns, and telegraph lines. Relief is shown in color. Inset map of the Aleutian Islands. Filed as RG 49: Alaska 1917, Pub.

41. Map of Alaska By the Alaska Road Commission 1916 ... [Corrected to Jan. 1, 1919].
 1 inch to 27.62 miles. 36 x 50. Annotated published. Annotated to show military roads and military posts. Other areas outlined in green without explanation are apparently national forests. Noted: "Map Corrected to Jan. 1, 1919." Filed as RG 126: Alaska 1919.

ARIZONA

42. Official Map of the Territory of Arizona with all the Recent Explorations Compiled by Richard Gird, C.E., Commissioner. Approved by John N. Goodwin, Governor. In Accordance with an Act of the Legislature, Approved Oct. 23d, 1864. Certified October 12, 1865.
 1 inch to 15 miles. 35½ x 37. Published. Wagon roads, trails, proposed railroad routes, towns, Indian villages, mines, and military posts. Filed as RG 77: W 86

43. Hartley's Map of Arizona from Official Documents. Drawn & Eng. by J. C. Smith, N. Y., ca. 1865.
 1 inch to ca. 26 miles. 31 x 37. Towns, military posts, roads, physical features, and mines. Shows adjacent parts of Nevada, Utah, Colorado, New Mexico, California, and Mexico, including western Sonora south to Guaymas. Filed as RG 77: W 84.

44. Map of the Territory of Arizona Accompanying The Annual Report of the Commissioner of the General Land Office for 1869.
 1 inch to ca. 14 miles. 39½ x 30. Manuscript. County names and boundaries, mining districts, principal mail routes, and locations of mineral deposits. Filed as RG 49: Arizona 1.

45. Map of Public Surveys in Arizona To Accompany Surveyor General's Report, 1871.
 1 inch to 12 miles. 2 sections, 36 x 22½ and 36½ x 26. Manuscript. Map shows extent of public land surveys, towns, roads, military posts, and Indian reservations in the general area of the Salt and Gila River Valleys in the central part of Arizona and along the Santa Cruz River Valley. The rest of Arizona on this map is essentially blank except Fort Yuma and Arizona City on the Colorado River. Filed as RG 49: Arizona 5.

46. Map of Arizona Showing Progress of Public Surveys To Accompany Surveyor General's Report, 1874.
 1 inch to 12 miles. 2 sections, 36½ x 22 and 37 x 25½. Manuscript. County and land district boundaries, Indian and military reservations, and railroad land-grant limits are added in color. Also shows towns, roads, some mining districts, and railroad lines. Filed as RG 49: Arizona 6.

47. Map of Arizona Showing Progress of Public Surveys To Accompany Surveyor General's Report, 1875.
 1 inch to 12 miles. 2 sections, 37 x 23 and 36½ x 24. Manuscript. Also shows towns and military posts. Filed as RG 49: Arizona 7.

48. [Map of the] Territory of Arizona. ... 1876. Compiled from the official Records of the General Land Office.
 1 inch to 18 miles. 24½ x 29½. Published. Public land surveys, towns, counties, land district boundaries, railroad lines, railroad land-grant limits, military reservations, Indian reservations, and locations of land offices. Relief shown by hachures. Filed as RG 49: Arizona 1876, Pub.

49. [Map of the] Territory of Arizona. ... 1879. Compiled from the official Records of the General Land Office.

1 inch to 18 miles. 26½ x 33½. Annotated published. County boundaries, Indian reservations, and military reservations are shown in color. Also shows public land surveys, cities and towns, railroad lines, and railroad land-grant limits. Relief is shown by hachures. Annotated to show the Prescott and Tucson land districts. Filed as RG 49: Arizona 12.

50. Map of Arizona Territory Prepared by Authority of Bvt. Major General O. B. Willcox ... Under the Direction of 1st Lieut. Fred A. Smith ... Engineer Officer, D. A., 1879.... Compiled and Drawn by Paul Riecker.

   1 inch to 18 miles. 28 x 23. Published. Settlements, military posts, roads, railroad lines, mining districts, Indian reservations, and physical features. Filed as RG 393: Department of Arizona 3.

51. [Map of the] Territory of Arizona.... 1887. Compiled from the official Records of the General Land Office.... Compiled and drawn by A. F. Dinsmore.

   1 inch to 12 miles. 37 x 31. Published. County boundaries, railroad land-grant limits, private land claims, and Indian reservations shown in color. Also shows public land surveys, cities and towns, railroad lines, and locations of U.S. land offices. Relief shown by hachures. Filed as RG 49: Arizona 1887, Pub.

52. Heliograph Lines and Stations in Arizona & New Mexico, Prepared from reports and reconnaissances of Acting Signal Officers ... July 1st, 1890.

   1 inch to ca. 11 miles. 30 x 42. Blueprint. Lines and stations proposed and in operation. Also shows U.S. military telegraph lines. Filed as RG 393: Dept. of Arizona 13.

53. [Map of the] Territory of Arizona.... 1892. Compiled from the official Records of the General Land Office.... Compiled and drawn by A. F. Dinsmore. Traced and lettered by M. Hendges.

   1 inch to 13 miles. 36 x 29. Published. County boundaries, military reservations, Indian reservation boundaries, and private land claim boundaries in color. Also shows public land surveys, county names, towns and cities, railroad lines, railroad land-grant limits, and locations of U.S. land offices. Relief also shown in color. Also a base map in black and white with drainage shown in blue for this date. 36 x 29½. Filed as RG 49: Arizona 1892, Pub.

54. [Map of the] Territory of Arizona.... 1896. Compiled from the official Records of the General Land Office.... Revised and Reconstructed by R. H. Morton.... Lettered by M. Hendges and R. M. Towson.

   1 inch to 25 miles. 21¾ x 17¾. Published. County boundaries, military reservations, Indian reservation boundaries, private land claim boundaries, and boundaries of national forests shown in color. Also shows public land surveys, county names, towns and cities, railroad lines, railroad land-grant limits, and locations of U.S. land offices. Relief shown in color. Filed as RG 49: Arizona 1896, Pub.

55. [Map of the] Territory of Arizona. Compiled from the official Records of the General Land Office ... 1897.

   1 inch to 12 miles. 39 x 32. Published. County boundaries, private land claims, national forests, Indian reservations, and military reservations shown in color. For this date there also is a black and white base map with drainage shown in blue. 39½ x 32½. Filed as RG 49: Arizona 1897, Pub.

56. [Map of the] Territory of Arizona. Compiled from the official Records of the General Land Office ... 1902.

   1 inch to 22 miles. 22 x 18. Published. County boundaries, private land claims, national forests, Indian reservations, and military reservations shown in color. Also shows public land surveys, towns, and cities, roads, and railroad lines. Relief is shown in color. Filed as RG 49: Arizona 1902, Pub.

57. [Map of the] Territory of Arizona. Compiled from the official Records of the General Land Office ... 1903.... Compiled and Drawn by Daniel O'Hare.

   2 maps, 1 inch to 12 miles and 1 inch to 22 miles. 40 x 34 and 21 x 18. Published. County boundaries, land district boundaries, private land claims, national forests, Indian reservations, and military reservations shown in color. Also shows public land surveys, towns and cities, locations of U.S. land offices, and railroad lines. Relief is shown in color. For this date there also is a black and white base map. 39 x 31. Filed as RG 49: Arizona 1903, Pub.

58. [Map of the] Territory of Arizona. Compiled from the official Records of the General Land Office . . . 1903. . . . Compiled and Drawn by Daniel O'Hare.
1 inch to 12 miles. 39½ x 32½. Black and white copy annotated to show mineral monuments and mining districts. Stamped "92703." Filed as RG 49: Arizona 39.

59. [Map of the] Territory of Arizona. Compiled from the official Records of the General Land Office . . . 1908. . . . Compiled and Drawn by Daniel O'Hare.
1 inch to 22 miles. 22½ x 18. Published. County boundaries, private land claims, national forests, national monuments, Indian reservations, and military reservations. Also shows public land surveys, towns and cities, and railroad lines. Relief shown in color. Filed as RG 49: Arizona 1908, Pub.

60. [Map of the] Territory of Arizona. Compiled from the official Records of the General Land Office . . . 1909. Compiled and drawn by Daniel O'Hare . . . Lettering by Wm. Bauman, Jr.
1 inch to 12 miles. 39½ x 33. Published. County boundaries, private land claim boundaries, national forests, national monuments, Indian reservations, military reservation boundaries, and Federal reclamation projects shown in color. Also shows public land surveys, towns and cities, and railroad lines. Relief is shown in color. For this date there also is a black and white base map. 39 x 33. Filed as RG 49: Arizona 1909, Pub.

61. [Map of the] Territory of Arizona. [Showing] Lands designated by the Secretary of the Interior, April 27, 1909, under the Enlarged Homestead Act of Feb. 19, 1909. [Issued by the Department of the Interior.]
1 inch to 24 miles. 20½ x 17. Published. Areas designated are shaded red. Also public land surveys. Filed as RG 49: Arizona 4, Pub.

62. [Map of the] State of Arizona Compiled from the official Records of the General Land Office . . . 1912. . . . Compiled and drawn by Daniel O'Hare . . . Lettering by Wm. Bauman, Jr.
1 inch to 12 miles. 39½ x 33. Published. County boundaries, private land claim boundaries, national forests, national monuments, Indian reservations, military reservation boundaries, and Federal reclamation projects shown in color. Also shows public land surveys, towns and cities, and railroad lines. Relief is shown in color. There is also a black and white base map for this date. 38½ x 33. Filed as RG 49: Arizona 1912, Pub.

63. [Map of the] State of Arizona [showing] Lands designated by the Secretary of the Interior Under the provisions of the Enlarged Homestead Acts. Edition of June 30, 1916. [Issued by the Department of the Interior.]
1 inch to 24 miles. 20½ x 17½. Published. Areas designated are shaded red. Also shows public land surveys Filed as RG 49: Arizona 6, Pub.

64. Post Route Map of the State of Arizona showing post offices with the intermediate distances on mail routes in operation on the 1st of January, 1917.
1 inch to 12 miles. 40 x 32. Published. Frequency and types of mail service, counties, towns, national monuments, railroads, discontinued post offices, and parts of adjoining States. Filed as RG 28: Arizona 1917.

See also entries 101, 567, 568, 570, 572-578, 584, and 587.

10   MAPS OF STATES AND TERRITORIES

ARKANSAS

65. [Map of] Arkansas [Issued by Surveyor's Office, Little Rock, Oct. 31, 1837].
1 inch to ca. 19 miles. 15 x 18. Published. Shows status of public land surveys. Filed as RG 46: S. Doc. 11, No. 5, 25th Cong., 2d sess.

66. A (1) [Map of] Arkansas [Issued by the Surveyor's Office, Little Rock, Sept. 30, 1839].
1 inch to ca. 20 miles. 19 x 24. Published. Shows extent of public land surveys. Map includes an explanation of the colors and symbols used to indicate the status of township surveys. Filed as RG 46: 26th Cong., 1st sess.

67. A (1) [Map of] Arkansas. [Issued by the Surveyor's Office, Little Rock, Sept. 30, 1840.]
1 inch to ca. 20 miles. 18 x 19. Published. Shows the extent and status of public land surveys. Map includes an explanation of the colors and symbols used to indicate the status of township surveys. A copy of this map is published in S. Doc. 61, 26th Cong., 2d sess., Serial 377. Filed as RG 46: 26th Cong., 2d sess.

68. [Map of] Arkansas ... Entered according to Act of Congress in the year 1844 by Sidney E. Morse and Samuel Breese.
1 inch to ca. 22 miles. 18 x 14. Published. Counties, township and range numbers, towns, mills, ferries, roads, an area in Mississippi County "Sunk by the Earthquake of 1811," and physical features. Parts of adjoining States and Territories also shown. Filed as Ref. Coll.: Arkansas 1844.

69. No. 6 [Map of] Arkansas.
1 inch to ca. 40 miles. 8½ x 9½. Published. Shows names and boundaries of land districts and locations of land offices in 1841. For an explanation of map and 1828 land district boundaries see S. Doc. 92, 26th Cong., 2d sess., Serial 377. Filed as RG 49: Arkansas 1, Pub.

70. A (1) [Map of] Arkansas. [Issued by the Surveyor's Office, Little Rock, Sept. 30, 1844.]
1 inch to ca. 20 miles. 17 x 18½. Published. Shows the extent and status of public land surveys. Filed as RG 49: Arkansas 2, Pub.

71. Langtree's New Sectional Map of the State of Arkansas. Showing the Sections, and Fractional Sections, on all Navigable Streams, the Military Land District in which are located all those Forfeited Lands which are now subject to Donation to Actual Settlers.... Drawn and Published by C. Langtree, Draughtsman, Surveyor's Office, Little Rock, 1850.
1 inch to 8 miles. 37½ x 41. Annotated published. Counties (in color), public land surveys, towns, land districts, locations of land offices, drainage features, and roads. Annotated to show additional roads. Filed as RG 77: MD 50.

72. A (1) [Map of] Arkansas. [Dated Oct. 20, 1852, Surveyor's Office, Little Rock.]
1 inch to ca. 20 miles. 17 x 19. Annotated published. Annotated to show land district boundaries and the location of land offices. Filed as RG 49: Arkansas 5.

73. A (1) [Map of] Arkansas. [Issued by the Surveyor's Office, Little Rock, Oct. 12, 1853.]
1 inch to ca. 20 miles. 18 x 18½. Published. Shows the extent and status of public land surveys. Filed as RG 49: Arkansas 3, Pub.

74. A (1) [Map of] Arkansas. [Issued by the Surveyor's Office, Little Rock, Oct. 18, 1854.]
1 inch to ca. 20 miles. 17½ x 18. Published. Shows the extent and status of public land surveys and "boundaries of the principal bodies of Swamp and overflowed lands." A copy of this map also is filed as S. Ex. Doc. 1, Pt. 3, 33d Cong., 2d sess., in RG 46. Filed as RG 49: Arkansas 4, Pub.

75. A (1) [Map of] Arkansas. [Issued by the Surveyor's Office, Little Rock, Oct. 28, 1856.]
1 inch to ca. 20 miles. 18 x 18½. Published. Shows extent and status of public land surveys, locations of land offices, and "boundaries of the principal bodies of Swamp and overflowed Lands." A copy of this map is filed also as S. Ex. Doc. 5, 34th Cong., 3d sess., in RG 46. Filed as RG 49: Arkansas 5, Pub.

76. Langtree's New Sectional Map of the State of Arkansas. Showing the Sections, and Fractional Sections, on all Navigable Streams, the Military

ARKANSAS

Land District in which are located all these Forfeited Lands which are now subject to Donation to Actual Settlers ... Drawn and Published By C. Langtree, Draughtsman, Surveyor's Office, Little Rock, Arks. 1859. Engraved by Edwin O. Reed.

1 inch to ca. 20 miles. 2 sections, each 39 x 21½. Counties (in color), township and section lines, land districts and locations of land offices, towns, roads, railroads, and physical features. Also shows numbers and boundaries of what appear to be congressional districts. Filed as RG 77: Q 81.

77. Map of the District [State] of Arkansas Compiled from Surveys and Military Reconnoissances [sic] by order of Lieut. Col. H. T. Douglas, Chief, Engineer Dept., Richard M. Venable, Capt. and Chief of Topographical Engineers, Dist. West La. and Arks. [1864-5]

1 inch to 4 miles. 2 sections, each 35 x 77. Manuscript. Roads shown in red were reconnoitered; roads shown in blue were taken from township maps and other sources. Double, dotted, and broken lines differentiate between public or main roads, settlement roads, and trails. County boundaries and prairies are shown in color. Also shows swamp or overflowed lands, drainage features, railroad lines, and names of some residents. Some relief is indicated by hachures. Noted "Engineer Department, Washington, July 17, 1865. Received with Maj. McAlester's letter of July 5, 1865." Title is preceded by "Dep't. Trans. Miss., Topographical Bureau." Map also has the emblem of the "Topographical Bureau, Dist. Arks., Mar. 21st, 1864." Filed as RG 77: drawer 123, sheet 15.

78. Map of Arkansas. [Issued by the General Land Office on Oct. 2, 1866.]

1 inch to ca. 20 miles. 17½ x 21½. Published. County boundaries, railroad land-grant limits, and coal regions are shown in color. Also shows public surveys, county seats, and physical features. Filed as RG 49: Arkansas 6, Pub.

79. [Map of] Arkansas By Frank A. Gray ... Copyright, 1876, by O. W. Gray & Son.

1 inch to 15 miles. 31½ x 19. Published. Counties (in color), towns, township and range numbers, roads, railroads, battle sites and dates, and physical features. Filed as RG 77: US 373-53.

80. [Map of the] State of Arkansas. ... 1878. Compiled from the official Records of the General Land Office.

1 inch to 12 miles. 27 x 34. Published. Public land surveys, counties, towns, railroad lines, railroad land-grant limits, locations of land offices, and physical features. County boundaries in color. Filed as RG 49: Arkansas 1878, Pub.

81. [Map of the] State of Arkansas. ... 1886. Compiled from the official Records of the General Land Office. ... Compiled and Drawn by A. F. Dinsmore.

1 inch to 10 miles. 28¾ x 36½. Published. Public land surveys, counties, towns, railroad lines, railroad land-grant limits, locations of land offices, and physical features. County boundaries in color. Also a black and white copy of this map. 26 x 36. Filed as RG 49: Arkansas 1886, Pub.

82. Post Route Map of the State of Arkansas and of Indian and Oklahoma Territories with adjacent portions of Mississippi, Tennessee, Missouri, Kansas, Texas, and Louisiana. Showing post offices with the intermediate distances and mail routes in operation on the 1st of August 1891. ... Published ... under the direction of C. Roeser Jr., Topographer, P. O. Dept.

1 inch to 10 miles. 2 sections, each 44 x 28½. Published. Frequency and types of mail service, mileages between post offices, discontinued post offices, counties, towns, railroads, Indian reservations, and physical features. Post routes in color to show frequency of service. Filed as RG 28: series 1, folder XXVI.

83. Map of the State of Arkansas Compiled from the official Records of the General Land Office ... 1901. Compiled and Drawn by E. B. Olney. Lettered by Wm. Bauman, Jr.

1 inch to 12 miles. 26 x 31. Published. Public land surveys, counties, towns, railroad lines, railroad land-grant limits, locations of U.S. land offices, and physical features. County boundaries in color. Also a black and white copy of this map. 25 x 29½. Filed as RG 49: Arkansas 1901, Pub.

84. [Map of the] State of Arkansas ... Compiled [in the U.S. Geological Survey] in 1912 and 1913.

1 inch to ca. 8 miles. 34 x 40. Published. County names and boundaries, towns and cities,

township and range numbers, steam and electric railroad lines, and drainage features. Noted: "Advance sheet. Subject to corrections." Filed as RG 57: Arkansas 1913, Pub.

85. [Map of the] State of Arkansas Compiled from the official Records of the General Land Office . . . 1914.
1 inch to 12 miles. 21 x 26. Published. County boundaries, land district boundaries, national forests, U.S. reservations, and relief in color. Also shows county names, public land surveys, towns, and locations of U.S. land offices. 2 copies; 1 copy also in black and white. 25 x 29½. Filed as RG 49: Arkansas 1914, Pub.

86. [Map of Arkansas compiled in 1912-13 and issued by the U.S. Geological Survey, 1916.]
1 inch to ca. 16 miles. 18 x 20. Published. County names and boundaries, township and range numbers, towns and cities, steam and electric railroad lines, and drainage features. Filed as RG 57: Arkansas 1916, Pub.

See also entries 443 and 450.

CALIFORNIA

87. Map of the Californias by T. J. Farnham. . . . Entered according to Act of Congress in the year 1845.
1 inch to ca. 55 miles. 18 x 14. Published. Towns, missions, roads, and physical features. Shows State of California, Baja California, and area east to Santa Fe, N. Mex., and south to Mazatlan, Sonora, Mexico. Filed as Ref. Coll.; California 1845.

88. A Newly Constructed and Improved Map of the State of California Shewing The extent and Boundary of the different Counties according to an Act passed by the Legislature, April 25th, 1851. With a corrected and improved delineation of the Gold Region Compiled from the best and most recent Surveys by J. B. Tassin . . . Published by Cooke and Lecourt.
.1 inch to 25 miles. 26 x 20. Published. County names and boundaries, settlements, and roads. Relief is shown by hachures. Filed as RG 75: map 37.

89. Approved & Declared to be the Official Map of the State of California by an Act of the Legislature Passed March 25th 1853. Compiled by W. M. Eddy, State Surveyor General. Published for R. A. Eddy . . . by J. H. Colton . . . 1854.
1 inch to ca. 19 miles. 2 sections, each 22 x 39. Counties (in color), towns, roads, railroads, and physical features. Inset map of "San Francisco and Adjoining Bays" at a scale of 1 inch to ca. 2½ miles. Table shows population of entire State and of individual counties in 1852. Filed as RG 77: W26.

90. Map of Public Surveys in California to accompany Report of Surveyor Genl., 1854.
1 inch to 16 miles. 21 x 48. Annotated published. Annotated apparently to show land districts and locations of land offices. Also shows extent of public land surveys and a few towns. Filed as RG 49: California 5.

91. [Map of] California, Published by J. H. Colton & Co. . . . 1855.
1 inch to ca. 50 miles. 17 x 14. Counties (in color), towns, railroads, and physical features. Inset map of San Francisco. 1 inch to ½ mile. Filed as RG 77: W 601.

92. Map of Public Surveys in California to accompany Report of Surveyor Genl., 1856.
1 inch to 18 miles. 39 x 34. Annotated published. Annotated to show land districts, locations of land offices, and names and boundaries of a few counties. Also shows extent of public land surveys and towns and cities. Relief is shown by hachures. A published copy of the map without annotations is filed as 34th Cong., 3d sess, in RG 46. Filed as RG 49: California 7.

CALIFORNIA 13

93. Map of Public Surveys in California to Accompany Report of Surveyor Genl., 1857.

1 inch to 18 miles. 36 x 31. Annotated published. Annotated in different colors to show: (1) "Surveys of public lands contracted for previous to July 1st 1857 . . ." (2) areas of "Contracts for public work entered into by J. W. Mandeville, U.S. Survr. Genl., Cala.," (3) "Surveys made under these Contracts . . ." (4) "Ranchos surveyed under instructions issued previous to 1st of July 1857 . . ." and (5) "Ranchos surveyed under instructions issued during the fiscal year 1857-1858 . . . ." Also shows a few towns and cities and private land claims. Private land claims surveyed are numbered and keyed to a list appearing on the map. Relief is shown by hachures. A published copy of the map without annotations is filed as 35th Cong., 1st sess., in RG 46. Filed as RG 49: California 9.

94. [Map of the] State of California compiled in the Bureau of Topogl. Engrs., 1859.

1 inch to ca. 24 miles. 34 x 30. Manuscript. Shows towns, roads, military posts, and drainage features. Annotated to show additional military posts, railroad lines, proposed route of the Southern Pacific Railroad, and the Butterfield Route. Filed as RG 77: W 49-1.

95. Atlas of the United States. California and Nevada. [ca. 1860.]

1 inch to ca. 50 miles. 17 x 14. Counties (in color), towns, roads, railroads, military posts, "U.S. Mail Route," and physical features. Filed as Ref. Coll.: California 1860.

96. Map of Public Surveys in California to Accompany Report of Surveyor Genl., 1860.

1 inch to 18 miles. 36 x 31. Published. Status of public land surveys, towns, and private land claims. Private land claims are numbered and keyed to a list appearing on the map. Relief is shown by hachures. Filed as RG 46: 36th Cong., 1st sess.

97. Map of Public Surveys in California to accompany Report of Surveyor Genl., 1861.

1 inch to 18 miles. 38½ x 33. Annotated published. Annotated to show assigned numbers in each private land claim. Part of map showing list of private land claims is missing. Also shows towns and cities. Relief is shown by hachures. A published copy of this map without annotations is filed as 36th Cong., 2d sess., in RG 46. Filed as RG 49: California 16.

98. Map of Public Surveys in California to accompany Report of Surveyor Genl., 1862.

1 inch to 18 miles. 36½ x 31. Annotated published. Shows status of public land surveys, towns, and private land claims. List of private land claims appears on map. Annotated to show locations of lighthouses and military reservations. Also shown are some private land claims in different colors, but there is no key to the colors. Filed as RG 49: California 17.

99. Map of Public Surveys in California & Nevada to Accompany Report of Surveyor Genl., 1864-5.

1 inch to 18 miles. 36 x 31. Annotated published. Annotated apparently to show land district boundaries and land offices. Only a small portion of public surveys in Nevada is shown. Map also shows private land claims in California. List of private land claims appears in lower left portion of map. Filed as RG 49: California 23.

100. Map of Public Surveys in California and Nevada to accompany Report of Commissioner of the General Land Office, 1866.

1 inch to ca. 20 miles. 38 x 31. Published. County boundaries, locations of land offices, lighthouse reservations, boundaries of mining districts, and mineral deposits are shown in color. Also shows settlements and private land claims. Very little information shown about Nevada. Filed as RG 233: H. Ex. Doc. 1, 38th Cong., 1st sess.

101. Skeleton Map of the Military Department of California showing the Location of Military Posts and Stations. [1868.]

1 inch to 45 miles. 20 x 22½. Manuscript. Also shows railroad lines, wagon roads, and a few towns. Map includes States of California, Utah, and Arizona. Inset map of San Francisco area showing location of military posts. Shown on emblem: "Engineer Office, Military Division of the Pacific. Henry M. Robert, Major of Engineers. San Francisco, California. August. 1868." Filed as RG 77: Z 469.

102. Map of the State of California Showing the U.S. Land Districts, the County Boundaries, and what Townships have been Surveyed by the U.S. Government. Prepared Under the Direction of John Mullan . . . 1870. . . . The Original drawn by R. Gibbons, draughtsman, U.S. Surveyor General's office, S. F.

1 inch to ca. 24 miles. 30½ x 26. Annotated published. Annotated to show additional township and range numbers and locations of land offices. Filed as RG 49: California 29.

103. Map of Public Surveys in California to accompany Report of Surveyor Genl., 1871 [?].

1 inch to 18 miles. 35½ x 30½. Annotated published. Annotated to show, in color, land district boundaries; locations of land offices; lighthouse reservations; and mineral deposits. Also shows extent of public land surveys, towns and cities, completed and projected railroad lines, railroad land-grant limits, and private land claims which are numbered and keyed to a list on the map. Relief is shown by hachures. Date in title has been added in ink. Note on map states "Map accompanying Commissioner's Annual Report for 1869," but this date has been corrected in pencil to 1870. Filed as RG 49: California 30.

104. State Geological Survey of California. . . . Map of California and Nevada . . . 1873. Drawn by F. v. Leicht and A. Craven.

1 inch to 18 miles. 43½ x 34½. Published. Settlements and roads. Relief is shown by shading. Filed as RG 77: W 170-7.

105. Post Route Map of the States of California and Nevada . . . Dec. 1, 1876.

1 inch to 12 miles. 56½ x 49. Annotated photoprocessed. Settlements, post offices, railroad lines, and types of mail service. Annotated to show additional post offices. filed as RG 75: map 278.

106. [Map of the] State of California. . . . 1876. Compiled from the official Records of the General Land Office.

1 inch to 20 miles. 35½ x 31½. Published. Boundaries of private land claims, counties, land districts, military reservations, and Indian reservations. Also shows public land surveys, towns and cities, locations of U.S. land offices, railroad lines, and railroad land-grant limits. List of private land claims by name, with the numbers used to designate them. Filed as RG 49: California 1876, Pub.

107. [Map of the] State of California. . . . 1876. Compiled from the official Records of the General Land Office.

1 inch to 20 miles. 43 x 33. Annotated to give a history of the land districts of California from 1853 to 1878, and the locations of land offices in 1878. Filed in RG 49: California 42.

108. Map of Public Surveys in California to accompany the Report of the U.S. Surveyor General, 1878.

1 inch to 12 miles. 2 sections, each 29 x 52½. Annotated photoprocessed. Annotated in various colors to show townships and smaller areas surveyed from 1872 to 1881. Filed as RG 49: California 44.

109. Map of California and Nevada with parts of Utah & Arizona. Prepared in the Office of the Chief of Engineers, U.S.A., 1879.

1 inch to ca. 25 miles. 37½ x 31. Published. Map includes California, Nevada, parts of adjoining States and Territories, and adjacent areas in Mexico. Towns, roads, railroads, military posts, and physical features. Relief shown by hachures. Filed as RG 77: 1879, Pub.

110. [Map of the] State of California. . . . 1879. Compiled from the official Records of the General Land Office.

1 inch to 18 miles. 2 sections, each 27 x 34. Annotated published. Status of public land surveys, towns and cities, military and Indian reservations, railroad lines and land-grant limits, and private land claims are numbered and keyed to a list on the map. Annotated to emphasize the Southern Pacific Railroad route from the towns of Greenwich in Kern County to the Arizona-California boundary. Filed as RG 49: California 48.

111. [Map of the] State of California. . . . 1879. Compiled from the official Records of the General Land Office.

1 inch to 18 miles. 2 sections, each 26½ x 33½. Annotated published. Annotated to show land districts. Basic information same as that shown on entry 110. Filed as RG 49: California 49.

112. Map of the Military Department of California Prepared in the Engineer Office, Hdqrs., Mil. Div. of the Pac. and Dept. of Cal. . . . May, 1881. . . . Drawn by Thomas H. Humphreys & C. Winstanley, Top. Assists.

1 inch to ca. 24 miles. 32½ x 29. Blueprint. Map includes present States of California and Nevada. County names, towns, military posts, roads, railroad lines, and drainage features. Filed as RG 77: US 390.

CALIFORNIA   15

113. [Map of the] State of California. ... 1885. Compiled from the official Records of the General Land Office.
 1 inch to 15 miles. 2 sections, each 27 x 45½. Published. County boundaries, military reservations, Indian reservations, railroad land-grant limits, and boundaries of private land claims are shown in red. Also shows public land surveys, towns and cities, railroad lines, and locations of U.S. land offices. Relief is shown by hachures. List of private land claims by name, with numbers assigned them. Filed as RG 49: California 1885, Pub.

114. Post Route Map of the States of California and Nevada showing post offices with the intermediate distances and mail routes in operation on the 1st of October 1885.
 1 inch to 12 miles. 4 sections, each 31 x 27. Published. Frequency and types of service, mileages between post offices, discontinued post offices, counties, towns, railroads, military posts, and physical features. Post routes in color to show frequency of service. Inset map of San Francisco Bay area. 1 inch to ca. 7 miles. Filed as RG 28: series 1, folder IX.

115. [Map of the] State of California. ... 1891. Compiled from the official Records of the General Land Office.
 1 inch to 15 miles. 2 sections, each 26 x 41. Published. County boundaries, military reservations, Indian reservations, and private land claim boundaries are shown in color. Also shown are locations of U.S. land offices, public land surveys, towns and cities, and railroad lines. Relief is shown in color. Map also contains a list of private land claims by name, with numbers used to designate them. Filed as RG 49: California 1891, Pub.

116. Map of the State of California Showing the Three Principal Factors in the Water Supply ... Compiled for the California Water and Forest Association By Fletcher F. S. Kelsey. Directed by Marsden Manson, C. E., PhD. ... September 1900.
 1 inch to 36 miles. 21 x 18. Published. Counties, watersheds, mean annual rainfall distribution, timber and brush areas, and forest reserves. Filed as Ref. Coll.: California 1900.

117. [Map of the] State of California Compiled from the official Records of the General Land Office ... 1900 ... Compiled by A. F. Dinsmore. Revised and Drawn by Daniel O'Hare.
 1 inch to 12 miles. 2 sections, each 31 x 50. Published. County names, military reservations, Indian reservations, railroad lines, railroad land-grant limits, public land surveys, towns and cities, and private land claims. Drainage is shown in blue. List of private land claims by name, with numbers assigned them. Filed as RG 49: California 1900, Pub.

118. Commissioners' Official Railway Map of California. Approved by the Board of Railroad Commissioners, November 1st 1903.
 No scale indicated. 37 x 28. Published. Railroad lines in color. There is a color key. Also shows counties, towns, and physical features. Filed as RG 77: General Staff Map Collection, California.

119. [Map of the] State of California Compiled from the official Records of the General Land Office ... 1907. ... Compiled by A. F. Dinsmore ... Traced and lettered by Wm. Bauman, Jr.
 1 inch to 12 miles. 61 x 50. Published. County boundaries, military reservations, Indian reservations, land district boundaries, national forests, and private land claim boundaries are shown in color. Also shown are public land surveys, towns and cities, locations of U.S. land offices, and U.S. lighthouses. Relief is shown in color. Inset maps of San Francisco (city and county), Los Angeles, and San Diego. List of private land claims by name, with assigned numbers. For this date there also is a black and white base map in 2 sections, each 31½ x 50. Filed as RG 49: California 1907, Pub.

120. Map of California Showing location of Indians. ... C. E. Kelsey, Special Agent for the California Indians. July 1st, 1910.
 Large scale. 62 x 50. Manuscript. Indian reservations, Indian population figures, Indian boarding and day schools, Indian rancherias, and national parks and forests. Also shows counties, railroad lines, and Indian treaty information. Filed as RG 75: map 6541.

121. [Map of the] State of California Compiled from the official Records of the General Land Office ... 1913. ... Compiled by A. F. Dinsmore ... Traced and lettered by Wm. Bauman, Jr.
 1 inch to 12 miles. 61 x 50. Published. County

boundaries, military reservations, Indian reservations, land district boundaries, national forests, and private land claim boundaries are shown in color. Also shown are public land surveys, towns and cities, locations of U.S. land offices, and U.S. lighthouses. Relief is shown in color. Inset maps of San Francisco (city and county), Los Angeles, and San Diego. List of private land claims by name, with numbers assigned. For this date there is also a black and white base map in 2 sections, each 31½ x 50. Filed as RG 49: California 1913, Pub.

122. [Map of the] State of California [showing] Lands designated by the Secretary of the Interior Under the provisions of the Enlarged Homestead Acts. Edition of June 30, 1916. [Issued by the Department of the Interior.]
    1 inch to 24 miles. 31 x 25. Published. Areas designated are shaded red. Also shows public land surveys. Filed as RG 49: California 15, Pub.

123. Post Route Map of the States of California and Nevada showing post offices with the intermediate distances on mail routes in operation on the 1st of January, 1917.
    1 inch to 10 miles. 4 sections, each 36 x 31. Published. Frequency and types of mail service, counties, towns, railroads, discontinued post offices, physical features, and parts of adjoining States. Inset maps of San Francisco and Los Angeles areas at scales of 1 inch to 6 miles and 1 inch to 4½ miles, respectively. Filed as RG 28: California 1917.

124. [Map of the] State of California [showing] Lands designated as nonirrigable by the Secretary of the Interior under the provisions of the Enlarged Homestead Acts... Edition of June 30, 1920. [Issued by the Department of the Interior.]
    1 inch to 24 miles. 31 x 26. Published. Areas designated are shaded red. Also shows public land surveys. Filed as RG 49: California 16, Pub.

COLORADO

125. Map of Colorado Territory, Compiled from Government Maps & actual Surveys. Made in 1861.
    1 inch to ca. 20 miles. 19 x 23. Published. Status of public land surveys, towns, military posts, and Indian reservations. Relief is shown by hachures. Filed as RG 46: S. Ex. Doc. 1, 37th Cong., 2d sess.

126. Map of Colorado Territory, Embracing the Central Gold Region. Drawn by Frederick J. Ebert under direction of the Governor, Wm. Gilpin. Published by Jacob Monk . . . 1862.
    1 inch to 12 miles. 32½ x 36½. Counties (in color), towns, roads, and military posts. Relief shown by hachures. Note states "Presented to the U.S. Topographical Bureau By the Publisher." Filed as RG 77: W 75.

127. Map of Public Surveys in Colorado Territory. [Map] to accompany report of the Surr. Genl., 1865.
    1 inch to ca. 18 miles. 18½ x 22. Annotated published. Annotated with information relating to contracts with surveyors, appropriations, costs, and deposits for the survey of public lands from 1866 to 1868. Also information about the Cheyenne and Arapaho Indian Reservation. Map also shows status of public land surveys, towns, military posts, and private land claims. Relief is shown by hachures. Filed as RG 49: Colorado 2.

128. Map of Public Surveys in Colorado Territory. [Map] to accompany report of the Surr. Genl., 1866. [Issued by the General Land Office on Oct. 2, 1866.]
    1 inch to 18 miles. 18 x 26. Published. County boundaries and mineral regions shown in color. Status shown of public surveys, county names, military posts, towns, railroad lines, and physical features. Filed as RG 49: Colorado 2, Pub.

129. Map of Colorado Territory, showing the System of Parks. Drawn under direction of the Governor, Wm. Gilpin, 1866.
    1 inch to "13 miles." Corrected: 1 inch to 18 miles. 19 x 22. Annotated published. Annotated evi-

dently to show approximate boundaries of parks and the location of Poncho Pass. Also shows status of public land surveys, military posts, and towns. Filed as RG 49: Colorado 3.

130. Map of Public Surveys in Colorado Territory. [Map] to accompany the Report of the Sur'vr. Gen'l., 1868.
 1 inch to 12 miles. 25 x 35. Manuscript. Shows county boundaries and mineral regions (gold, silver, copper, iron, coal, and oil), in color. Also shows status of public land surveys, towns, locations of U.S. land offices, military posts, and Indian reservation for Cheyennes and Arapahoes. Relief is shown by hachures. Filed as RG 49: Colorado 5.

131. Map of Utah and Colorado ... Compiled under direction of Bvt. Col. Wm. E. Merrill, Maj. Engrs., St. Louis, 1869. Drawn by H. De Werthern.
 1 inch to 18.94 miles. 28½ x 46. Published. Includes portions of adjoining States and Territories. Settlements, military posts, roads, and routes of expeditions and railroad surveys. Relief shown by hachures. Filed as RG 393: Division of Missouri 2.

132. Map of the Territory of Colorado Showing the Extent of the Public Surveys. [Map] to accompany the Annual Report for 1871. Compiled under the direction of the Surveyor General.
 1 inch to 12 miles. 30 x 38½. Manuscript. Counties (in color), towns, military posts, and private land claims. Filed as RG 49: Colorado 7.

133. [Map of the] Territory of Colorado. ... 1876. Compiled from the official Records of the General Land Office.
 1 inch to 16 miles. 24½ x 31. Published. Boundaries of private land claims, counties, land districts, military reservations, and Indian reservations. Also shows status of public land surveys, towns and cities, locations of U.S. land offices, roads, railroad lines, and railroad land-grant limits. Relief shown by hachures. Filed as RG 49: Pub.

134. Williams' Tourist's Map of Colorado and the San Juan Mines. Engraved from Surveys by the Hayden U.S. Geological Expedition. Henry W. Troy, Designer, N.Y. [1877]
 1 inch to 12 miles. 25½ x 32. Annotated published. Counties (in color), settlements, military posts, roads, and drainage features. Annotated to show railroad lines completed and under construction. Noted: "Copyright 1877 By Henry T. Williams." Filed as RG 77: W 320.

135. Post Route Map of the State of Colorado.... Drawn by A. P. Dinsmore ... up to date of October 1, 1879.
 1 inch to 11 miles. 32½ x 43¼. Published. Frequency and types of mail service, mileages between post offices, discontinued post offices, counties, towns, railroads, military posts, and physical features. Post routes in colors to show frequency of service. Continental Divide is identified and shaded green. Filed as RG 28: series 1, folder IV.

136. Map of Colorado Prepared in the Office of the Chief of Engineers, U.S.A., 1879.
 1 inch to ca. 25 miles. 29 x 25½. Published. Map includes Colorado and parts of adjoining States and Territories. Towns, roads, railroads, military posts, and physical features. Relief shown by hachures. Filed as RG 77: 1879, Pub.

137. Thayer's Map of Colorado. Published by H. L. Thayer, Denver, Col., 1880. ... From Surveys of the General Land Office, used by permission, revised & corrected to date by the Publisher.
 1 inch to 15 miles. 26½ x 33. Annotated published. Counties (boundaries in color), towns and cities, principal railroad stations, status of public land surveys, military and Indian reservations, private land grants, and railroad lines. Relief is shown by hachures. Filed as RG 75: map 1232.

138. Nell's New Topographical & Township Map of the State of Colorado. Compiled from U.S. Government Surveys & other authentic Sources ... 1881.
 1 inch to 12 miles. 30½ x 41½. Counties (in color), towns, railroads in operation and in progress, wagon roads existing and proposed, trails, extent of public land surveys, private land grants, military posts and reservations, elevations shown by contour lines (contour interval, 1,000 feet), and physical features. Annotated to show route of Denver and New Orleans Railroad from Denver to Pueblo. Filed as RG 77: W 352.

139. Nell's New Topographical & Township Map prepared expressly for Crofutt's Grip-Sack Guide of Colorado. Compiled from U.S.

Government Surveys & other authentic Sources... 1881. The Overland Publishing Company.

1 inch to 16 miles. 20½ x 26. Counties (in color), towns, post offices, railroads in operation and in progress, wagon roads and wagon roads proposed, trails, extent of public land surveys, private land grants, military posts and reservations, elevation shown by contour lines (contour interval, 1,000 feet), and physical features. Filed as Ref. Coll.: Colorado 1881.

140. [Map of the] State of Colorado. ... 1881. Compiled from the official Records of the General Land Office.

1 inch to 15 miles. 26½ x 30. Published. Boundaries of counties, private land claims, military reservations, and Indian reservations shown in color. Also shows public land surveys, towns and cities, principal railroad stations, locations of U.S. land offices, railroad lines, and railroad land-grant limits. Relief shown by hachures. Filed as RG 49: Colorado 1881, Pub.

141. [Map of the] State of Colorado. ... 1885. Compiled from the official Records of the General Land Office.... Compiled and drawn by M. Hendges.

1 inch to 12 miles. 32½ x 36½. Published. County boundaries, private land claims, military reservations, Indian reservations, and railroad land-grant limits are shown in color. Also shows public land surveys, towns and cities, locations of U.S. land offices, and railroad lines. Relief shown by hachures. Filed as RG 49: Colorado, 1885, Pub.

142. Post Route Map of the State of Colorado showing post offices with the intermediate distances and mail routes in operation on the 1st of October 1885.

1 inch to 10 miles. 34 x 46. Published. Frequency and types of mail service, mileages between post offices, discontinued post offices, counties, towns, railroads, military posts, and physical features. Post routes are shown in color to show frequency of service. Filed as RG 28: series 1, folder XI.

143. [Map of the] State of Colorado. ... 1887. Compiled from the official Records of the General Land Office ... Compiled and Drawn by A. F. Dinsmore.

1 inch to 12 miles. 32 x 36. Published. County boundaries, private land claims, military reservations, and Indian reservations are shown in color. Also shows public land surveys, towns and cities, locations of U.S. land offices, railroad lines, proposed railroad lines, and railroad land-grant limits. Relief shown by hachures. Also a black and white base map for this date. 31 x 36. Filed as RG 49: Colorado 1887, Pub.

144. Nell's Topographical Map of the State of Colorado, 1887. E. Besly & Co., Publishers, Denver.

1 inch to 10 miles. 33 x 45. Counties (in color), towns, post offices, railroads, extent of public land surveys, private land grants, military reservations, roads, land district boundaries, locations of land offices, and physical features. Annotated without explanation—certain cities are underlined and certain mountain peaks are circled. Filed as Ref. Coll.: Colorado 1887.

145. [Map of the] State of Colorado ... 1892. Compiled from the official Records of the General Land Office ... Compiled and Drawn by A. F. Dinsmore ... Traced and Lettered by Wm. Naylor.

1 inch to 12 miles. 29½ x 36. Published. County, Indian reservation, timberland reserve, and private land claim boundaries shown in color. Also shows public land surveys, towns and cities, military posts, locations of U.S. land offices, railroad lines, and reservoir sites. Relief shown in color. For this date there also is a black and white base map, with drainage shown in blue. 30 x 35½. Filed as RG 49: Colorado. 1892, Pub.

146. [Map of the] State of Colorado. Compiled from the official Records of the General Land Office ... 1897. ... Compiled by A. F. Dinsmore ... Revised and corrected for reissue by M. Hendges.

1 inch to 12 miles. 29½ x 35½. Published. County names and boundaries, Indian reservations, military posts, private land claims, locations of U.S. land offices, railroad lines, public land surveys, and reservoir sites. Drainage in blue. Field as RG 49: Colorado 1897, Pub.

147. [Map of the] State of Colorado Compiled from the official Records of the General Land Office ... 1897. ... Compiled by A. F. Dinsmore ... Revised and corrected for reissue by M. Hendges.

1 inch to 12 miles. 32 x 36. Annotated published. Annotated to show land district boundaries. Basic information same as that shown on entry 146. Filed as RG 49: Colorado 24.

148. [Map of the] State of Colorado. Compiled from the official Records of the General Land Office ... 1905. ... Compiled by A. F. Dinsmore ... Traced and Lettered by Wm. Bauman, Jr.
 1 inch to 12 miles. 31½ x 37. Published. County and land district boundaries, Indian reservations, forest reserves, and private land claims are shown in color. Also shown are public land surveys, towns and cities, railroads, military reservations, and locations of U.S. land offices. Relief shown in color. For this date there also is a black and white base map. 31½ x 37. Filed as RG 49: Colorado 1905, Pub.

149. [Map of the] State of Colorado. [Showing] Lands designated by the Secretary of the Interior, April 27, 1909, under the Enlarged Homestead Act of Feb. 19, 1909. [Issued by the Department of the Interior.]
 1 inch to 24 miles. 16 x 19. Published. Areas designated are shaded red. Also shows public land surveys. Filed as RG 49: Colorado 10, Pub.

150. [Map of the] State of Colorado. Compiled from the official Records of the General Land Office ... 1910. ... Compiled by A. F. Dinsmore ... Traced and Lettered by Wm. Bauman, Jr.
 1 inch to 12 miles. 31 x 36. Published. County and land district boundaries, Indian and military reservations, national forests, national parks, and Federal reclamation projects are shown in color. Also shows towns, public land surveys, and railroad lines. Relief is shown in color. Also a black and white base map for this date. 31 x 36. Filed as RG 49: Colorado 1910, Pub.

151. [Map of the] State of Colorado [showing] Lands designated by the Secretary of the Interior Under the provisions of the Enlarged Homestead Acts. [Issued by the Department of the Interior.] Edition of June 30, 1916.
 1 inch to 24 miles. 16½ x 19. Published. Areas designated are shaded red. Also shows public land surveys. Filed as RG 49: Colorado 12, Pub.

152. Post Route Map of the State of Colorado showing post offices with the intermediate distances on mail routes in operation on the 1st of January, 1917.
 1 inch to 10 miles. 2 sections, each 36 x 25½. Published. Frequency and types of mail service, counties, discontinued post offices, towns, railroads, physical features, and parts of adjoining States. Inset map of "Denver and Vicinity." Scale 1 inch to ca. 2½ miles. Filed as RG 28: Colo. 1917.

153. [Map of the] State of Colorado [showing] Lands designated as nonirrigable by the Secretary of the Interior under the provisions of the Enlarged Homestead Acts. Includes Patented and Entered as well as Vacant land. [Issued by the Department of the Interior.] Edition of June 30, 1920.
 1 inch to 24 miles. 16½ x 19. Published. Areas designated are shaded red. Also shows public land surveys. Filed as RG 49: Colorado 13, Pub.

MAPS OF STATES AND TERRITORIES

CONNECTICUT

(Including general maps of New England)

154. Post Route Map. Supposed Date A.D. 1746. New England, New York, New Jersey and Pensilvania [sic]. By H. Moll, Geographer.
 1 inch to ca. 40 miles. 15 x 19. Published. Shows only small parts of New York and Pennsylvania. Settlements and post route from Philadelphia to Piscataway, New Hampshire. Brief written description of route. Filed as Ref. Coll.: New England 1746.

155. A Map of the most Inhabited part of New England, containing the Provinces of Massachusetts Bay and New Hampshire, with the Colonies of Connecticut and Rhode Island, Divided into Counties and Townships: ... Published 12 May, 1794, by Laurie & Whittle.
 1 inch to 7 miles. 2 sections, each 42 x 19½. Published. English and Indian habitations, township meetinghouses, forts, and ponds. Inset plans of Boston and Boston Harbor. Filed as RG 77: US 54.

156. Connecticut, From Actual Survey, Made in 1811; By, and under the Direction of, Moses Warren and George Gillet; And by them Compiled. Published under the Authority of the General Assembly, by Hudson and Goodwin. Engraved by Abner Reed, East Windsor. To His Excellency Roger Griswold, Esq., and to the Honourable Legislature of the State of Connecticut, This Map is Respectfully Inscribed By the Publishers. Hartford, February 1812. Entered according to Act of Congress, the 29th day of May, 1813–By Hudson & Goodwin, of the State of Connecticut.
 1 inch to 2½ miles. 2 sections, each 22 x 37½. Published. Churches, courthouses, manufacturing establishments (woolens, cotton, guns, cutlery, clock, button, wire, distillery, glass, iron), mills (grist, saw, paper, powder), roads, townships, counties. County boundaries shown in color. List of Governors of Connecticut since the Charter of 1655, with dates of accession and termination of office. Filed as RG 77: US 20.

157. A Map of the New England States ... With the adjacent parts of New York & Lower Canada. Compiled and Published by Nathan Hale ... 1826. Engraved by J. V. N. Throop.
 1 inch to 8 miles. 2 sections, each 23 x 40½. Published. Counties (in color), settlements, civil townships, churches, and roads. Inset map "Northern & Eastern Part of Maine and Part of Lower Canada and New Brunswick." Filed as RG 77: US 58.

158. An Improved Reference Map of the Valley of the Connecticut and Western Section of New England. Published by Justin Pierce. Engraved by N. & S. S. Jocelyn, New Haven. Entered according to Act of Congress, Dec. 6th, 1828.
 1 inch to ca. 7 miles. 2 sections, each 25½ x 24. Annotated published. Towns, townships, counties, roads, turnpikes, churches. Counties shown in color. Includes Vermont, Massachusetts west of Worcester, and adjoining parts of New Hampshire and New York. Portion of Vermont is missing. Some roads are colored red without explanation. Table lists towns and their distances from Washington, D.C., and the State capital. Filed as RG 77: K 22.

159. [Map of] Connecticut [ca. 1840]
 1 inch to 8 miles. 14 x 18. Published. County names and boundaries, towns, names and boundaries of civil townships, roads, canals, and railroad lines. Filed as Ref. Coll.: Connecticut 1840.

160. Railroad Map of New England & Eastern New York, Compiled from the most authentic sources. By J. H. Goldthwait. 1849.
 Scale not indicated. 30 x 23. Published. Only southern tip of Maine appears. County names, names and boundaries of townships, railroad stations, and railroad lines completed and projected. Filed as Ref. Coll.: New England 1849.

161. Clark and Tackabury's New Topographical Map of the State of Connecticut. Compiled From New and accurate Surveys of each County, and the United States trigonometric Surveys of Long Island Sound by G. M. Hopkins, Jr., C. E. Published By Richard Clark and Robt. M. & Geo. N. Tackabury. 307 Wharton St., Philadelphia. 1860. Engraved By Friend & Aub.
 1 inch to 1½ miles. 4 sections, each 27 x 34. Published. Grist mills, sawmills, churches, schools, post offices, roads, railroads. Townships are shown in color. Table lists 1860 census population by township and county. Filed as Ref. Coll.: Connecticut 1860.

FLORIDA

162. Map of Connecticut Prepared by the U.S. Geological Survey in Co-operation with the State of Connecticut . . . Published . . . 1893.
1 inch to ca. 2 miles. 43 x 52. Published. Settlements, roads, and railroad lines. Drainage in blue; contours in brown. Wooded areas in green. Also a copy of this map reprinted in July 1912. Wooded areas are not shown. Filed as RG 57: Connecticut 1893, Pub.

See also entries 373, 390, and 557.

DELAWARE

163. Colton's Delaware and Maryland, Published by J. H. Colton . . . 1862.
1 inch to ca. 16 miles. 14 x 18. Published. Counties (in color), towns and cities, hundreds (in Delaware), roads, canals, and railroad lines. Relief is shown by hachures. Map includes parts of adjoining States and an inset map of the District of Columbia at a scale of 1 inch to 3 miles. Filed as Ref. Coll.: Delaware 1862.

164. [Map of Delaware compiled in the U.S. Geological Survey, 1912.]
1 inch to ca. 8 miles. 19 x 11. Published. County names and boundaries, towns and cities, steam and electric railroad lines, and drainage features. Noted: "Advance sheet. Subject to corrections." Filed as RG 57: Delaware 1912, Pub.

See also entries 379, 380, 383-387, 740-744, 809, and 810.

FLORIDA

165. Map of Florida. Compiled and Drawn from various Actual Surveys & Observations: By Charles Vignoles, Civil & Topographical Engineer. 1823. Engraved by H. S. Tanner & Assistants . . . Published by H. S. Tanner.
1 inch to 20 miles. 31½ x 26. Published. Boundaries of counties and private land claims are shown in color. Towns, Indian villages, Forbes Purchase, military posts, roads, trails, and physical features. (A similar map is filed as L 69 in RG 77.) Filed as Ref. Coll.: Florida 1823.

166. Map of Florida Constructed Principally from Authentic Documents in the Land Office at Tallahassee, By J. G. Searcy. Published by I. G. Searcy, Tallahassee, & F. Lucas, Jr., Baltimore . . . Entered according to Act of Congress the 24th day of September, 1829.
1 inch to ca. 14 miles. 2 sections, each 24 x 38. Counties (in color), towns, roads, extent of public land surveys, Indian boundary line, physical features, and private land grants. Annotated to show additional place names or changes in names. Also annotated to show extent of "Hackley's Grant" and an area in the Florida Keys and Tortugas reserved by the President in 1845, for "military purposes." Inset city plan of Tallahassee at a scale of 1 inch to 800 feet. Filed as Ref. Coll.: Florida 1829.

167. Map of Florida By J. Lee Williams, 1837. Lithographed by Greene & McGowran.
1 inch to 17 miles. 32½ x 29½. Counties, private land claims, towns, military posts, roads, trails, Indian villages, names of a few residents, and notes on vegetation. Filed as RG 77: General Staff Map Collection, Florida.

22   MAPS OF STATES AND TERRITORIES

168. A Plat Exhibiting the State of the Surveys in the Territory of Florida ... [Issued by] Surveyor General's Office, Tallahassee, Oct. 1839.
1 inch to 18 miles. 17 x 25. Published. Map includes explanation of colors and symbols used to indicate status of township surveys. Filed as RG 46: 26th Cong., 1st sess.

169. Map of the Seat of War in Florida compiled ... by order of Bvt. Brigr. Genl. Z. Taylor ... by Capt. John Mackay and Lieut. J. E. Blake, U.S. Topographical Engineers. ... 1839.
1 inch to 11 miles. 41 x 30½. Manuscript. Map shows Florida peninsula and area west to the Apalachicola River. Settlements, military posts, roads, sites and dates of battles, and remarks about vegetation. (A published copy of this map is filed as Army of the South 1 in RG 393.) Filed as RG 77: US 112.

170. Map of Florida Exhibiting the Post Offices, Post Roads, Canals, Rail Roads, &c. By David H. Burr (Late Topographer to the Post Office). ... Entered according to the Act of Congress, July 10th, 1839.
1 inch to 10 miles. 4 sections, 19 x 25½. Published. Also shows counties (in color), mileages between post offices, township and range numbers, military posts, physical features, and parts of adjoining States. Inset map of West Florida. RG 28: Burr Atlas, map 8.

171. A Plat Exhibiting the State of the Surveys in the Territory of Florida. [Issued by the Surveyor General's Office, Tallahassee, Oct., 1840.]
1 inch to 18 miles. 12 x 26. Published. Shows extent and status of public land surveys. Map includes an explanation of the colors and symbols used on the map to indicate the status of township surveys. A copy of this map is published in S. Doc. 61, 26th Cong., 2d sess., Serial 377. Filed as RG 46: 26th Cong., 2d sess.

172. A Plat Exhibiting the State of the Surveys in the Territory of Florida ... Surveyor General's Office, Tallahassee, Oct. 1841.
1 inch to 18 miles. 11½ x 23½. Published. Filed as RG 46: 27th Cong., 2d sess.

173. [Map of] Florida. Entered according to Act of Congress in the year 1842, by Sidney E. Morse and Samuel Breese in the Clerks Office of the Southern District of New York.
1 inch to ca. 32 miles. Published. 17½ x 14¼. Counties, township and range numbers, military posts, roads, railroads, and canals. State is shaded orange. Inset map of "West Part of Florida." Filed as Ref. Coll.: Florida 1842.

174. Map of the Seat of War in Florida, Compiled By Capt. J. McClellan and Lieut. A. A. Humphreys, U.S. Topographical Engineers ... Bureau of Topographical Engineers, 1843, With late corrections from Surveys under the direction of Brigadier General W. I. Worth.
1 inch to 8 miles. 2 sections, each 33½ x 48. Manuscript. Shows present State of Florida except area west of the Apalachicola River. Settlements, military posts, roads and trails, and topographical features. Inset maps of "Cedar Kays [sic] and the Mouths of the Suwanee River" and vicinity of Tampa Bay. Filed as RG 77: L 52 (a).

175. Map of the Peninsula of Florida Compiled by Capt. McClellan and Lieut. Humphreys, U.S.T.E. ... reduced from [the original] Map; in compliance [with] Resolu[tion] of the U.S. Senate of December 16th, 1845, By W. B. Franklin, Lieut., U.S.T.E. ... Drawn by J. G. Bruff.
1 inch to ca. 12 miles. 47 x 29. Manuscript. Shows present State of Florida except area west of the Apalachicola River. Shows settlements, military posts, roads and trails, and topographical features. Filed as RG 77: L 52 (b).

176. The State of Florida. Compiled in the Bureau of Topographical Engineers From the best authorities By J. Goldsborough Bruff. ... 1846.
1 inch to ca. 12 miles. 2 sections, each 23 x 41½. Published. Settlements, military posts, trails, and township and range numbers. Inset maps "Mouths of the Suwanee River and the Cedar Keys" and "General Map of part of Florida between Cedar Keys and St. John's River," both from Lieut. Blake's map. Also an inset map of "Key West as Surveyed February 1829, by Wm. A. Whitehead, Esqr." Filed as RG 77: 1846, Pub.

FLORIDA 23

177. Map of the State of Florida. . . . Published by Columbus Drew . . . Thos. S. Wagner, Lith. [ca. 1850].
1 inch to 18 miles. Three copies of map; 24½ x 24½, 27 x 26, 31 x 31½. Counties (in color), towns, military posts, township and range numbers, "Indian Hunting Ground," and physical features. Filed as Ref. Coll.: Florida 1850.

178. A Plat Exhibiting the State of the Surveys in the State of Florida . . . [Issued by Surveyor General's Office, St. Augustine, Oct. 31, 1854].
1 inch to 18 miles. 24 x 25. Published. Shows status of public land surveys. Filed as RG 46: S. Ex. Doc. 1, Pt. 3, 33d Cong., 2d sess.

179. Map of the State of Florida showing the Progress of the Surveys. [Map] accompanying Annual Report of the Surveyor General. . . . 1856.
1 inch to 12 miles. 28½ x 26½. Published. Filed as RG 46: S. Ex. Doc. 5, 34th Cong., 3d sess.

180. Map of the State of Florida compiled in the Bureau of Topogl. Engrs. from the most recent authorities, and prepared by order [of] the Honorable Jeff. Davis, Secretary of War . . . 1856.
1 inch to ca. 12 miles. 2 sections, 22½ x 46 and 21½ x 46. Published. Sometimes called the "Jeff Davis Map." County names, settlements, military posts, township and range numbers, roads, and railroad lines. (Other versions of this map are filed as L 84 in RG 77.) Filed as RG 77: 1856, Pub.

181. Map of the State of Florida, Showing the Progress of the Surveys. [Map] accompanying Annual Report of the Surveyor General. 1857.
1 inch to 18 miles. 31 x 28. Published. Shows status of public land surveys. Filed as RG 46: S. Ex. Doc. 11, 35th Cong., 1st sess.

182. Map of the State of Florida Showing the Progress of the Surveys. [Map] accompanying Annual Report of the Surveyor General. 1860.
1 inch to 18 miles. 24½ x 26½. Published. Shows status of public land surveys. Another copy of this map is colored to emphasize roads, railroad lines, and apparently swampy areas and water bodies. Filed as RG 46: S. Ex. Doc. 1, 36th Cong., 2d sess.

183. [Map of the] State of Florida. . . . 1876. Compiled from the official Records of the General Land Office.
1 inch to 20 miles. 26½ x 33½. Published. County boundaries, railroad land-grant limits, and private land claims are shown in color. Also shows public land surveys, towns, military posts, and physical features. Also a black and white base map for this date. 25 x 28. Filed as RG 49: Florida 1876, Pub.

184. [Map of the] State of Florida. . . . 1879. Compiled from the official Records of the General Land Office.
1 inch to 20 miles. 27 x 34. Published. County boundaries and private land claims shown in color. Also shows public land surveys, towns, military posts, railroad lines, railroad land-grant limits, and physical features. Filed as RG 49: Florida 1879, Pub.

185. [Map of the] State of Florida. . . . 1883. Compiled from the official Records of the General Land Office.
1 inch to 12 miles. 42½ x 42. Published. County boundaries, railroad land-grant limits, private land claims, and U.S. reservations (military and lighthouse) are shown in color. Also shows public land surveys, towns, railroad lines, and physical features. Filed as RG 49: Florida, 1883, Pub.

186. Post Route Map of the State of Florida with adjacent parts of Georgia and Alabama . . . showing post offices with the intermediate distances and mail routes in operation on the 1st of October, 1885. Published . . . under the direction of W. L. Nicholson, Topographer, P. O. Dept.
1 inch to 12 miles. 2 sections, each 26 x 44. Published. Annotated to show additional railroad lines. Frequency and types of service, mileages between post offices, discontinued post offices, counties, towns, railroads, and physical features. Post routes in color to show frequency of service. Inset "Map of the West India Islands with adjacent parts of Florida, Central and South America." 1 inch to ca. 100 miles. Shows steamship lines and telegraph cables. Filed as RG 28: series 1, folder XIII.

187. [Map of the] State of Florida. . . . 1886. Compiled from the official Records of the General Land Office . . . Drawn by G. P. Strum.
1 inch to 12 miles. 2 sections, each 26½ x 41½. Published. County boundaries, railroad

land-grant limits private land claims, and U.S. reservations (military and lighthouse) are shown in color. Also shows public land surveys, towns, railroad lines, and physical features. Also a black and white base map in 2 sections, each 20 x 39. Filed as RG 49: Florida 1886, Pub.

188. [Map of the] State of Florida. ... 1893. Compiled from the official Records of the General Land Office ... Drawn and Compiled by A. F. Dinsmore ... Traced and lettered by M. Hendges, I. P. Berthong, and F. E. Mahony.
   1 inch to 12 miles. 43 x 43½. Published. County and private land claim boundaries and U.S. reservations (military and lighthouse) are shown in color. Also shows public land surveys, towns, railroad lines, and physical features. Also a black and white base map, with drainage in blue. 40 x 40. Filed as RG 49: Florida 1893, Pub.

189. Geologic and Topographic Map of Florida, Prepared by the United States Geological Survey ... in cooperation with the Florida Geological Survey, 1909.
   1 inch to ca. 16 miles. 32 x 24½. Published. Towns and cities, township and range numbers, and railroad lines. Drainage features in blue. Inset map of "Westward Extension of Florida." 1 inch to ca. 16 miles. Filed as RG 57: Florida 1909, Pub.

190. [Map of the] State of Florida Compiled from the official Records of the General Land Office ... Compiled by A. F. Dinsmore ... Traced and lettered by Wm. Bauman, Jr.
   1 inch to 12 miles. 43 x 34. Published. County boundaries, national forests, Indian reservations, military and lighthouse reservations, and boundaries of bird reservations are shown in color. Also shows public land surveys, towns and cities, railroad lines, boundaries of private land claims, and physical features. Inset map of western Florida. Also black and white base map for this date. 42½ x 34. Filed as RG 49: Florida 1911, Pub.

191. Post Route Map of the State of Florida showing post offices with the intermediate distances on mail routes in operation on the 1st of March, 1911.
   1 inch to 10 miles. 49 x 34½. Published. Frequency and types of mail service, discontinued post offices, counties, towns, railroads, physical features, and parts of adjoining States. Inset map of western Florida. No scale indicated. Post routes in color. Filed as RG 28: Florida 1911.

GEORGIA

192. [Map of] Georgia, from the latest Authorities. Engraved for Carey's American Edition of Guthrie's Geography [ca. 1796].
   1 inch to ca. 52 miles. 12 x 19. Manuscript. Includes present States of Georgia, Alabama, and Mississippi. Shows towns, Indian villages, roads, and trails. Also shows general locations of Indian tribes. Filed as RG 75: map 1372.

193. Map of the State of Georgia. Prepared from actual Surveys and other Documents, for Eleazer Early, By Daniel Sturges. Published & Sold By Eleazer Early, Savannah, Georgia ... Engraved by Saml. Harrison, 1818.
   1 inch to 8 miles. 2 sections, each 46 x 28½. Towns, roads, military posts, Indian villages. Existing counties and Indian boundaries are shown in color. Tables list post offices, statistics relating to the individual counties, and geological information. (A similar map is filed in RG 77, as US 26.) Filed as Ref. Coll.: Georgia 1818

194. [Map of] Georgia. 1818 (Date added in pencil in lower margin).
   1 inch to 50 miles. 10½ x 8½. Published. Towns, Indian villages, roads, and physical features. "23" and "#4 S.D.C." appear in the upper right corner. Filed as Ref. Coll.: Georgia 1818.

195. Map of Georgia and Alabama By H. S. Tanner. 1827.
   1 inch to ca. 18 miles. 22½ x 28½. Annotated published. Towns, roads, township and range

numbers, and physical features. Annotated apparently to show land offices and land districts in Alabama. Part of Georgia along the boundary with Alabama is omitted. Filed as RG 49: Alabama 6.

196. Map of Georgia & Alabama Exhibiting the Post Offices, Post Roads, Canals, Rail Roads, &c. By David H. Burr (Late Topographer to the Post Office). . . . Entered according to the Act of Congress, July 10th, 1839.
1 inch to 10 miles. 4 sections, each 19¼ x 25½. Published. Also shows counties (in color), mileages between post offices, township and range numbers, forts, physical features, and parts of adjoining States. Filed as RG 28: Burr Atlas, map 7.

197. [Map of] Georgia. Entered according to act of Congress in the Year 1842, by Sidney E. Morse and Samuel Breese in the Clerks office of the Southern District of New York.
1 inch to ca. 25 miles. 17½ x 13½. Published. Towns, counties, canals, railroads, physical features. State is shaded green. Filed as Ref. Coll.: Georgia 1842.

198. [Map of] Georgia's Improvt[s]. Prepared by A. H. Brisbane, Engineer . . . for Hon. J. C. Spencer, Secretary of War. [1842]
1 inch to ca. 18 miles. 22½ x 29½. Manuscript. Includes Alabama. Sketch map showing some settlements, several railroad lines, and remarks on crops and land characteristics. Additional lines added in red. Also added are "points of supply," "circle of defence," and "Health circle of cantonment for south-eastern troops." Note added in red ink to title block states that the map accompanied "letter of A. H. Brisbane of April 8, 1842, in case in room 16." Filed as RG 77: US 374-55.

199. Map of the State of Georgia, Compiled Under the Direction of His Excellency George W. Crawford, By Wm. G. Bonner, Civil Engineer. Milledgeville. Published by Wm. G. Bonner. 1848.
1 inch to 7 miles. 4 sections, each 30½ x 27. Counties (color), towns, railroads, roads, colleges, and factories. Inset maps of the cities of Augusta, Columbus, Macon, and Savannah. Tables show population (1845) figures for all counties for whites and blacks, and a list of governors to 1847. Marginal illustrations show some public buildings and colleges. Filed as RG 77: US 140-2.

200. Map of the State of Georgia. Compiled By James R. Butts, Late Surveyor General. Macon, 1859. Printed, Colored, and Mounted By R. L. Barnes, Philadelphia.
1 inch to 7 miles. 4 sections, each 32½ x 27. Counties, roads, towns, railroads, factories, colleges. List of governors and dates of their terms of office to 1857. Illustrations in margins show various public buildings, educational institutions, and scenic points. Filed as RG 77: N 28.

201. Map of Georgia & Alabama Representing Railways, Post-Roads, Population, And Agricultural Productions. Prepared at the Census Office. Under direction of Jos. C. G. Kennedy . . . [Annotated ca. 1861 to show population and agricultural figures].
1 inch to 10 miles. 2 sections, each 39 x 26. Annotated published. Counties in Georgia and Alabama in color. Includes small portions of adjoining States. Population and agricultural production information is shown for each county. Population figures show number of "Whites, Free Colored, Slaves, [and] Military Males btwn 18 and 45 yrs of age." Agricultural figures show amount of production of grains, cotton, and livestock. This map appears to be a post route map annotated to show the above information. Filed as RG 77: US 266.

202. Post Route Map of Georgia and Outline Map of South Carolina with adjacent parts of North Carolina, Tennessee, Alabama, and Florida; Showing post offices with the intermediate distances and mail routes in operation on the 1st of April, 1894.
1 inch to 10 miles. 2 sections, each 43½ x 29. Published. Frequency and types of mail service, mileages between post offices, discontinued post offices, counties, towns, railroads, and physical features. Post routes in color to show frequency of service. Filed as RG 28: series 1, folder XXVII.

203. Post Route Map of the State of Georgia showing post offices with the intermediate distances on mail routes in operation on the 1st of January, 1917.
1 inch to 8 miles. 45 x 37. Published. Frequency and types of mail service, discontinued post offices, counties, towns, railroads, physical features, and parts of adjoining States. Inset map of "Atlanta and Vicinity." 1 inch to 3 miles. Filed as RG 28: Georgia 1917.

26   MAPS OF STATES AND TERRITORIES

204. [Map of Georgia issued by the U.S. Geological Survey in 1916 and reprinted in 1920.]
1 inch to ca. 16 miles. 23 x 19½. Published. County names and boundaries, towns and cities, steam and electric railroad lines, and drainage features. Filed as RG 57: Georgia 1920, Pub.

See also entry 4.

HAWAII

205. Lighthouse Chart of the Hawaiian Islands. [Oct., 1898.]
1 inch to 7 miles. 38 x 31. Blueprint. Shows locations and characteristics of lights and ranges of visibility. Date is written in corner of map in red crayon. Also shown on same sheet is "Lighthouse Chart of the West Indies between the Mona and Virgin Passages comprising Puerto Rico and Dependencies." Filed as RG 26: Hawaii 1898.

206. Map of the Territory of Hawaii ... 1901. [Compiled in the General Land Office.] Compiled and Lettered by I. P. Berthong.
1 inch to 12 miles. 25 x 36. Published. Settlements and names and boundaries of minor civil divisions. Relief shown by color. Inset map of "Hawaiian Archipelago." Also a black and white base map with drainage in blue for this date. Filed as RG 49: Hawaii 1901, Pub.

207. Map of the Territory of Hawaii ... 1909. [Compiled in the General Land Office.] Compiled and Lettered by I. P. Berthong.
1 inch to 12 miles. 24½ x 35½. Published. Settlements and names and boundaries of minor civil divisions. Relief shown by color. Inset map of "Hawaiian Archipelago" showing boundary of Hawaiian Islands Bird Reservation. Also a table of "Distances from Honolulu to the Principal Ports of the Pacific." Filed as RG 49: Hawaii 1909, Pub.

208. Map of the Territory of Hawaii ... 1913. [Compiled in the General Land Office.] Compiled and Lettered by I. P. Berthong.
1 inch to 12 miles. 25 x 35½. Published. Settlements and names and boundaries of minor civil divisions. Inset map of "Hawaiian Archipelago" showing boundary of Hawaiian Islands Bird Reservation. Also a table of "Distances from Honolulu to the Principal Ports of the Pacific." Filed as RG 49: Hawaii 1913, Pub.

209. Post Route Map of the Territory of Hawaii ... showing post offices with the intermediate distances on mail routes in operation on the 1st of April, 1914.
1 inch to ca. 9 miles. 29½ x 44. Published. Frequency and types of mail service, post offices, "villages and offices disc[ontinued]," railroad lines, and railroad stations. Frequency of service shown by colors. Inset maps of Guam, Samoan Islands, and Hawaiian Archipelago. Filed as RG 28: Hawaii 1914.

210. Map of the Territory of Hawaii ... 1914. [Compiled in the General Land Office.] Compiled and Lettered by I. P. Berthong.
1 inch to 12 miles. 24 x 34½. Published. Settlements and names and boundaries of minor civil divisions. Relief shown by color. Inset map of "Hawaiian Archipelago" showing boundary of Hawaiian Islands Bird Reservation. Also a table of "Distances from Honolulu to the Principal Ports of the Pacific." Filed as RG 49: Hawaii 1914, Pub.

211. Map of the Territory of Hawaii ... 1915. [Compiled in the General Land Office.] Compiled and Lettered by I. P. Berthong.
1 inch to 12 miles. 21 x 35½. Published. Settlements and names and boundaries of minor civil divisions. Relief is shown by color. Inset map of "Hawaiian Archipelago" showing boundary of Hawaiian Islands Bird Reservation. Also a table of "Distances from Honolulu to the Principal Ports of the Pacific." Filed as RG 49: Hawaii 1915, Pub.

212. Post Route Map of the Territory of Hawaii ... showing post offices with the intermediate distances on mail routes in operation on the 1st of January, 1917.
   1 inch to ca. 9 miles. 29 x 44. Published. Frequency and type of mail service, post offices, "villages and offices disc[ontinued]," railroad lines, and railroad stations. Inset maps of Guam, Samoan Islands, and Hawaiian Archipelago. Filed as RG 28: Hawaii 1917.

213. Hawaii Territory Survey ... The Hawaiian Islands ... Map by H. E. Newton, June 1919.
   1 inch to 60,000 feet. 28 x 40½. Published. Settlements, roads, trails, and national parks. Relief is shown by hachures. Inset maps showing "Hawaiian Archipelago with Reefs to the Westward," craters of Haleakala, Mokuaweoweo, and Kilauea, and distances from Hawaiian Islands to various Pacific Ocean ports. Filed as RG 126: Hawaii 1919.

IDAHO

214. Map of Idaho and Montana and of Portions of Other Territories. Compiled under the direction of Col. Geo. Thom, A.D.C. & Major of Engrs., For the use of Head Quarters of the Army, 1864.
   1 inch to ca. 32 miles. 24 x 32. Manuscript. "The large dotted blue lines indicate the travelled routes, and the small ones explored routes. The little red crosses indicate positions of worked gold mines." Also shows settlements, military posts, and drainage features. Filed as RG 77: W 125.

215. Map of Public Surveys in Idaho. [Map] to accompany Report to Commissioner of the General Land Office, 1869.
   1 inch to ca. 16 miles. 38½ x 28. Manuscript. County boundaries and locations of gold and silver mines are shown in color. Also shows status of public land surveys, towns, military reservations, Indian reservations, and land district boundaries. Relief is shown by hachures. Filed as RG 49: Idaho 1.

216. Map of Public Surveys in Idaho. [Map] to accompany Report to Commissioner of the General Land Office, 1870.
   1 inch to ca. 16 miles. 32½ x 22. Manuscript. County boundaries and what apparently are possible locations of gold and silver deposits are shown in color. Also shows status of public land surveys, towns, and Indian reservations. Relief is shown by hachures. Filed as RG 49: Idaho 2.

217. [Map of the] Territory of Idaho. ... 1876. Compiled from the official Records of the General Land Office.
   1 inch to 16 miles. 33½ x 24. Published. County and land district boundaries, Indian reservations, and railroad land-grant limits are shown in color. Also shows extent of public land surveys, towns, military posts, and locations of Indian agencies. Relief is shown by hachures. Also is a black and white base map for this date. 33 x 22. Filed as RG 49: Pub.

218. [Map of the] Territory of Idaho. ... 1879. Compiled from the official Records of the General Land Office.
   1 inch to 16 miles. 34 x 26. Published. County boundaries and Indian reservations are shown in color. Also shows extent of public land surveys, towns, military posts, locations of U.S. land offices, railroads, and railroad land-grant limits. Relief is shown by hachures. Filed as RG 49: Idaho 1879, Pub.

219. [Map of the] Territory of Idaho. ... 1879. Compiled from the official Records of the General Land Office.
   1 inch to 16 miles. 33½ x 26. Annotated published. Annotated apparently to show names of land districts and land district boundaries. Basic information same as that shown on entry 218. Filed as RG 49: Idaho 3.

220. [Map of the] Territory of Idaho. ... 1883. Compiled from the official Records of the General Land Office.
1 inch to 16 miles. 33½ x 26½. Published. County boundaries and Indian reservations are shown in color. Also shows extent of public land surveys, towns, military posts, locations of U.S. land offices, railroads, and railroad land-grant limits. Relief is shown by hachures. Also a black and white base map for this date. 37½ x 21. Filed as RG 49: Idaho 1883, Pub.

221. [Map of the] Territory of Idaho. ... 1888. Compiled from the official Records of the General Land Office ... Compiled and Drawn by Robert H. Morton.
1 inch to 15 miles. 38 x 25. Published. County boundaries and Indian reservations are shown in color. Also shows extent of public land surveys, towns, military reservations, locations of U.S. land offices, railroads, and railroad land-grant limits. Relief is shown by hachures. Also a black and white base map for this date. 40 x 26½. Filed as RG 49: Idaho 1888, Pub.

222. [Map of the] State of Idaho. ... 1891. Compiled from the official Records of the General Land Office ... Compiled and Drawn by Robert H. Morton.
1 inch to 13 miles. 42½ x 30. Published. County and Indian reservation boundaries are shown in color. Also shows extent of public land surveys, towns, military posts, a few roads, locations of U.S. land offices, railroad lines, and railroad land-grant limits. Relief is shown by color. Also a black and white base map with drainage shown in blue for this date. 42½ x 30. Filed as RG 49: Idaho 1891, Pub.

223. [Map of the] State of Idaho. Compiled from the official Records of the General Land Office ... 1899. ... Compiled by R. H. Morton ... Traced and Lettered by I. P. Berthong.
1 inch to 12 miles. 47 x 32. Published. County boundaries, Indian reservations, and national forests are shown in color. Also shows extent of public land surveys, towns, military reservations, locations of U.S. land offices, and railroad lines. Relief is shown by color. Also a black and white base map with drainage shown in blue. 46 x 32. Filed as RG 49: Idaho 1899, Pub.

224. [Map of the] State of Idaho. Compiled from the official Records of the General Land Office ... 1905. ... Revised by A. F. Dinsmore ... Traced and Lettered by I. P. Berthong and C. J. Helm.
1 inch to 12 miles. 45½ x 31. Published. County and land district boundaries, Indian reservations, and national forests are shown in color. Also shows public land surveys, towns and cities, military reservations, locations of U.S. land offices, and railroad lines. Relief is shown by color. Small inset maps of Pocatello, Wallace, Lewiston, and Boise, and vicinities. Also a black and white base map for this date. 44 x 29½. Filed as RG 49: Idaho 1905, Pub.

225. [Map of the] State of Idaho. Compiled from the official Records of the General Land Office ... 1907. ... Revised and drawn by Charles J. Helm.
1 inch to 12 miles. 46 x 31. Published. County and land district boundaries, Indian reservations, and national forests are shown in color. Also shows public land surveys, towns and cities, military reservations, locations of U.S. land offices, and railroad lines. Relief is shown in color. Small inset maps of Pocatello, Wallace, Lewiston, and Boise, and vicinities. Also a black and white base map for this date. 45 x 30 1/2. Filed as RG 49: Idaho 1907, Pub.

226. [Map of the] State of Idaho. Compiled from the official Records of the General Land Office ... 1907. ... Revised and drawn by Charles J. Helm.
1 inch to 12 miles. 46 x 31. Published. Annotated in the Surveyor General's Office, Boise City, Idaho, to show mining districts of which map bears typed list. Marked "(1909 compilation.)" Mining districts, names and boundaries of national forests, and county and land district boundaries are shown in color. See entry 225. Filed as RG 49: Idaho 15.

227. [Map of the] State of Idaho Compiled from the official Records of the General Land Office ... 1909. ... Revised and drawn by Charles J. Helm.
1 inch to 12 miles. 46½ x 31½. Published. County and land district boundaries, Indian reservations, national forests, reclamation projects, and lands set aside for irrigation under the Carey Act are shown in color. Also shows public land surveys, towns, military reservations, locations of U.S. land offices, and railroad lines. Relief shown in color. Also a black

ILLINOIS

and white base map for this date. Black and white map does not show reclamation projects or Carey Act lands. Filed as RG 49: Idaho 1909, Pub.

228. [Map of the] State of Idaho. Compiled from the official Records of the General Land Office . . . 1913. . . . Compiled and Drawn by Daniel O'Hare. . . . Traced and Lettered by Wm. Bauman–Geo. A. Daidy.

1 inch to 12 miles. 47 x 32. Published. County and land district boundaries, Indian reservations, national forests, national parks (also national monuments, and bird, fish, and game preserves), and reclamation projects are shown in color. Also shows public land surveys, towns and cities, military reservations, locations of U.S. land offices, and railroad lines. Relief is shown in color. Small inset maps of Wallace and Mullan Region, Boise, Coeur D'Alène, Twin Falls, American Falls, Pocatello, Moscow, and Lewiston. Also a black and white base map for this date. 47 x 32. Filed as RG 49: Idaho 1913, Pub.

229. [Map of the] State of Idaho, [showing] Lands designated by the Secretary of the Interior As subject to entry under the provisions of the Enlarged Homestead Act of June 17, 1910. Edition of November 1, 1910. [Issued by the Department of the Interior.]

1 inch to 24 miles. 24 x 16. Published. Areas designated are shaded red. Also shows public land surveys. Filed as RG 49: Idaho 4, Pub.

230. [Map of the] State of Idaho, [showing] Lands designated by the Secretary of the Interior Under the provisions of the Enlarged Homestead Acts. Edition of June 30, 1916. [Issued by the Department of the Interior.]

1 inch to 24 miles. 24½ x 17. Published. Areas designated under Sections 1-5 are shaded red; those designated under section 6 are in blue. Also shows public land surveys. Filed as RG 49: Idaho 5, Pub.

231. [Map of] State of Idaho, [showing] Lands designated as nonirrigable by the Secretary of the Interior under the provisions of the Enlarged Homestead Acts . . . Edition of June 30, 1920. [Issued by the Department of the Interior.]

1 inch to 24 miles. 24 x 17. Published. Areas designated under general provisions are shaded red and those under Section 6 are in blue. Also shows public land surveys. Filed as RG 49: Idaho 7, Pub.

See also entries 495, 496, 498-501, 512, 515, 697, 698, and 709.

ILLINOIS

232. Map of Illinois. Constructed from the Surveys in the General Land Office and other Documents, By John Melish. [Published by John Melish and Saml. Harrison, 1818.]

1 inch to 15 miles. 27 x 21. Annotated published. Settlements, military posts, township and range numbers, boundaries of Military Bounty Lands, Kaskaskia and Shawnee Districts, and roads. Filed as RG 77: US 31-1.

233. Map of Illinois. Constructed from the Surveys in the General Land Office and other Documents, By John Melish. [Published by John Melish. Improved to 1819.]

1 inch to 15 miles. 27 x 21. Annotated published. Counties (boundaries in color), settlements, military posts, township and range numbers, boundaries of Military Bounty Lands, and roads. Filed as RG 77: US 31-2.

234. New Sectional Map of the State of Illinois. Compiled from the United States Surveys. Also exhibiting the Internal Improvements; distances between Towns, Villages & Post Offices; the outlines of Prairies, Woodlands, Marshes &c. By J. M. Peck and John Messinger. Published by J. H. Colton & Co., New York, 1836. Engraved by S. Stiles & Co., New York.

1 inch to 10 miles. 43 x 31. Published. Counties (in color), township and section lines, towns, post offices, roads, canals, and projected railroads. Inset maps of the "Vicinity of Alton & St. Louis" and of

the "Vicinity of Galena, the Lead Region, and part of Wisconsin Territory." Both inset maps are on a scale of 1 inch to 4 miles. Filed as RG 77: US 104.

235. No. 2 (C) Diagram of the State of Illinois. (Accompanying report of 30th October 1837.)
1 inch to 18 miles. 27 x 16. Published. Shows status of public land surveys. Filed as RG 46: Doc. 11, No. 3, 25th Cong., 2d sess.

236. Diagram of the State of Illinois. [Issued by the Surveyor General's Office, St. Louis, Oct. 1, 1839.]
1 inch to 18 miles. 22 x 13. Published. Map includes explanation of colors and symbols used to indicate status of township surveys. "H (Referred to in Report of the 1st October)." Filed as RG 46: 26th Cong., 1st sess.

237. Map of Illinois & Missouri Exhibiting the Post Offices, Post Roads, Canals, Rail Roads, &c. By David H. Burr (Late Topographer to the Post Office) . . . Entered according to the act of Congress, July 10th, 1839.
1 inch to 10 miles. 4 sections, each 19¼ x 25½. Published. Also shows counties (in color), mileages between post offices, township and range numbers, military posts, and physical features. Filed as RG 28: Burr Atlas, map 12.

238. No. 3 [Map of] Illinois.
1 inch to ca. 38 miles. 13 x 9. Published. Shows land districts and locations of land offices in 1828 and 1841 and public land offered for sale, 1828-41. 1828 land district boundaries are shown in red. For further explanation of the map see S. Doc. 92, 26th Cong., 2d sess., Serial 377. (This map without the 1828 land districts shown is filed as Illinois 2, Published, in RG 49.) Filed as RG 46: 26th Cong., 2d sess.

239. H . . . Diagram of the State of Illinois. [Issued by the Surveyor General's Office, St. Louis, Oct. 1840.]
1 inch to 18 miles. 24 x 15. Published. Shows extent and status of public land surveys. Map includes an explanation of the colors and symbols used on the map to indicate the status of township surveys. A copy of this map is published in S. Doc. 61, 26th Cong., 2d sess., Serial 377. Filed as RG 46: 26th Cong., 2d sess.

240. Diagram of the State of Illinois [Issued by Surveyor's Office, St. Louis, Oct. 27, 1841].
1 inch to 18 miles. 22½ x 13½. Published. Shows status of public land surveys. "Referred to in Report of the 27th October 1841." Filed as RG 46: 27th Cong., 2d sess.

241. [Map of] Illinois . . . Entered according to Act of Congress in the year 1844, by Sidney E. Morse and Samuel Breese.
1 inch to ca. 28 miles. 18 x 14. Published. Shows county names and boundaries, towns, roads, canals, and railroad lines. Filed as Ref. Coll.: Illinois 1844.

242. G Diagram of the State of Illinois [Issued by Surveyor's Office, St. Louis, Oct. 20, 1848]
1 inch to 18 miles. 23 x 15½. Published. Show land districts and status of public land surveys Central Railroad and canal land-grant limits are shown in color. Filed as RG 49: Illinois 3, Pub.

243. G Diagram of the State of Illinois Accompanying report of the 30th October, 1852. [Issued by the Office of the Surveyor General fo Illinois and Missouri, Oct. 30, 1852.]
1 inch to 18 miles. 23½ x 16½. Published Shows status of public land surveys. Filed as RG 49 Illinois 4, Pub.

244. Map of the State of Illinois. [Issued by th General Land Office on Oct. 2, 1866.]
1 inch to 18 miles. 23 x 17. Published. Count boundaries and mineral regions are shown in color Also shows public surveys, county seats, railroa land-grant limits, and drainage; note on miner resources. Filed as RG 49: Illinois 5, Pub.

245. Colton's Sectional Map of the State of Illinois Compiled from the United States Surveys. Als exhibiting the Internal Improvements, distance between Towns, Villages, & Post Offices: the outlines of Prairies, Woodlands, Marshes, & the lands donated to the State by the Genl. Govt. for the purpose of Internal Improvements. By J. M. Peck John Messinger, and A. J. Mathewson. Published by G. W. and C. B. Colton & Co. . . . 1867.
1 inch to 10 miles. 42 x 28½. Published. Counties (in color), township and section lines, post offices, towns, roads, canals, and railroads. Inset map

of the cities of St. Louis and Chicago. Annotated apparently to show land survey base lines and principal meridians. Tables showing areas in square miles of individual counties and "Progressive Movement of Population." Filed as RG 77: US 104-2.

246. Illinois. Colton's Popular Series of Sectional Maps. Published By G. W. & C. B. Colton & Co. ... 1872.
1 inch to 12 miles. 34 x 23. Published. Counties (in color), township and section lines, towns, railroads, and outlines of private land claims. Filed as RG 77: P 166½.

247. Post Route Map of the States of Illinois, Iowa, and Missouri with adjacent parts of Indiana, Wisconsin, Minnesota, Nebraska, Kansas, and Arkansas ... up to date as of April 1, 1873.
1 inch to 10 miles. 4 sections, each 33 x 30. Published. Frequency and types of mail service, mileages between post offices, discontinued post offices, counties, towns, railroads, and physical features. Post routes shown in color to illustrate frequency of service. Section of map showing most of Missouri is missing. Filed as RG 28: series 1, folder II.

248. [Map of the] State of Illinois. ... 1878. Compiled from the official Records of the General Land Office.
1 inch to 14 miles. 34 x 21½. Published. County boundaries are shown in color. Also shows names of counties, public land surveys, towns, principal railroad stations, canals, railroad lines, railroad land-grant limits, and physical features. Filed as RG 49: Illinois 1878, Pub.

249. [Map of the] State of Illinois. ... 1885. Compiled from the official Records of the General Land Office.
1 inch to 14 miles. 34 x 27. Published. County boundaries and railroad land-grant limits are shown in color. Also shows county names, public land surveys, towns, principal railroad stations, canals, railroad lines, and physical features. Filed as RG 49: Illinois 1885, Pub.

250. Post Route Map of the States of Illinois, Iowa, and Missouri, with adjacent parts of Kansas and Arkansas, showing post offices with the intermediate distances and mail routes in operation on the 1st of October, 1885. Published ... under the direction of W. L. Nicholson, Topographer, P. O. Dept. ... Drawn by P. Goepel & A. Kilp.
1 inch to 10 miles. 4 sections, each 34½ x 29. Published. Frequency and types of mail service, mileages between post offices, discontinued post offices, counties, towns, railroads, and physical features. Post routes in color to show frequency of service. Filed as RG 28: series 1, folder VI.

251. Post Route Map of the State of Illinois showing post offices with the intermediate distances on mail routes in operation on the 1st of March, 1901.
1 inch to 8 miles. 46½ x 33. Published. Frequency and types of mail service, discontinued post offices, counties, towns, railroads, physical features, and parts of adjoining States. Post routes in colors to show frequency of service. Inset map "Environs of Chicago." 1 inch to ca. 4½ miles. Filed as RG 28: Illinois 1901.

252. [Map of the] State of Illinois ... Compiled in 1909 and 1910 in cooperation with the State of Illinois. [Issued by U.S. Geological Survey.]
1 inch to ca. 8 miles. 52 x 31. Published. County names and boundaries, township and range numbers, towns and cities, steam and electric railroad lines, and drainage features are shown. Filed as RG 57: Illinois 1910, Pub.

253. [Map of the] State of Illinois. Compiled from the official Records of the General Land Office ... 1911. ... Drawn by Charles J. Helm.
1 inch to 12 miles. 35 x 22. Published. County boundaries in color. Also shows names of counties, public land surveys, towns and cities, military reservations, electric railways, railroad lines, and city limits of Chicago. Also a black and white base map for this date. 35 x 22. Filed as RG 49: Illinois 1911, Pub.

254. [Map of Illinois issued by the U.S. Geological Survey, 1916.]
1 inch to ca. 16 miles. 26 x 17. Published. County names and boundaries, towns and cities, township and range numbers, steam and electric railroad lines, and drainage features. Filed as RG 57: Illinois 1916, Pub.

255. Post Route Map of the State of Illinois showing post offices with the intermediate distances on mail routes in operation on the 1st of January, 1917.
1 inch to 8 miles. 2 sections, each 25½ x 35. Published. Frequency and types of mail service, discontinued post offices, counties, towns, railroads, physical features, and parts of adjoining States. Inset "Chicago and Vicinity." 1 inch to 4 miles. Filed as RG 28: Illinois 1917.

See also entries 256, 459, 460, and 473.

INDIANA

256. Map of Indiana and Illinois Territories, compiled from the best authorities for Governor Edwards of the Illinois Territory by R. Paul, 1815. Copy by James Kearney.
Scale not indicated. 19 x 23½. Manuscript. Indian villages, rivers, military posts, towns, and General Scott and Governor Edwards traces. Filed as RG 77: US 33-2.

257. Map of Indiana Prepared by John Melish. The surveys furnished by Burr Bradley. Published in 1817 by John Melish. Improved to 1819.
1 inch to 18 miles. 28 x 20. Annotated published. County names and boundaries, extent of public surveys, Indian villages, towns, and military posts. Filed as RG 77: US 33-1.

258. [Map showing Indian land cessions in Indiana. 1809-1826.]
Scale not indicated. 14 x 13½. Manuscript. Filed as RG 75: map 139.

259. Map of the States of Indiana and Ohio with Part of Michigan Territory. Engraved & Printed by Fenner Sears & Co. [ca. 1830.]
1 inch to 25 miles. 11 x 17. Published. Shown are towns, rivers, county names and boundaries, military posts, and names of Indian tribes in northern part of Indiana. Small scale inset map of Cincinnati. Filed as Ref. Coll.: Indiana 1830.

260. No. 1 [Map of] Indiana.
1 inch to ca. 38 miles. 9½ x 7. Published. Shows land districts and locations of land offices in 1828 and 1841 and public land offered for sale, 1828-41. 1828 land district boundaries are shown in red. For further explanation of the map see S. Doc. 92, 26th Cong., 2d sess., Serial 377. (This map without the 1828 land districts shown is filed as Indiana 2, Published, in RG 49.) Filed as RG 46: 26th Cong., 2d sess.

261. [Map of] Indiana. Entered according to Act of Congress in the year 1843, by Sidney B. Morse and Samuel Breese.
1 inch to 20 miles. 18 x 14. Published. County names and boundaries, towns, canals, railroad lines, and drainage features are shown. Filed as Ref. Coll.: Indiana 1843.

262. Colton's Map of the State of Indiana. Compiled from the United States Surveys & other Authentic Sources, Exhibiting Sections, Fractional Sections, Railroads, Canals &c. Published by J. H. Colton ... 1863.
1 inch to ca. 7 miles. 39½ x 28. Annotated published. Also shows cities, towns, roads, and congressional districts. Annotated to show the route of the National (Cumberland) Road through Indiana. Filed as RG 77: P 105.

263. A Diagram of the State of Indiana. [Issued by the General Land Office on Oct. 2, 1866.]
1 inch to ca. 18 miles. 19 x 11½. Published. County boundaries are shown in color. Shows Public surveys, county seats, railroads, and drainage. Note on mineral resources. Filed as RG 49: Indiana 4, Pub.

264. Post Route Map of the States of Indiana and Ohio with Adjacent Parts of Pennsylvania, Michigan, Illinois, Kentucky, West Virginia. 1870.
1 inch to 8 miles. 39 x 56. Shows postal routes, railroads, towns and cities, counties, and frequency of mail delivery per week. Filed as RG 75: map 262.

INDIANA

265. [Map of] Indiana. Entered according to act of Congress in the year 1875, by O. W. Gray & Son in the Office of the Librarian of Congress at Washington.
1 inch to 12 miles. 27½ x 18½. Published. Shows county names and boundaries, township names, towns and cities, railroad lines completed and in progress, and canals. Filed as RG 77: US 373-58.

266. [Map of the] State of Indiana. ... 1878. Compiled from the official Records of the General Land Office.
1 inch to 10 miles. 33½ x 26¾. Published. County boundaries in color. Also shows names of counties, public land surveys, towns, principal railroad stations, canals, railroad lines, railroad land-grant limits, and physical features. Filed as RG 49: Indiana 1878, Pub.

267. Map of the State of Indiana Exhibiting the Lands ceded by the Indian Tribes to the United States. By C. C. Royce, Bureau of Ethnology, Smithsonian Institution. [ca. 1881.]
1 inch to 10 miles. 35 x 25½. Printed. Indian villages, towns, military posts, rivers and streams. Indian land cessions are numbered but not otherwise identified. Filed as RG 75: map 906.

268. [Map of the] State of Indiana. ... 1886. Compiled from the official Records of the General Land Office ... Drawn and Compiled by A. F. Dinsmore.
1 inch to 10 miles. 32½ x 26½. Published. County boundaries in color. Also shows county names, public land surveys, towns and cities, outlines of private land claims, boundaries of former Indian reservations, canals, proposed and completed railroad lines, railroad land-grant limits, and swamp and prairie lands. Filed as RG 49: Indiana 1886, Pub.

269. [Map of the] State of Indiana ... 1886. Compiled from the official Records of the General Land Office ... Drawn by M. Hendges.
1 inch to 12 miles. 28 x 21. Published. County boundaries in color. Also shows county names, public land surveys, towns and cities, outlines of private land claims, boundaries of former Indian reservations, canals, completed and proposed railroad lines, railroad land-grant limits, and swamp and prairie lands. Also a black and white base map for this date. Filed as RG 49: Indiana 1886, Pub.

270. Post Route Map of the State of Indiana showing post offices with the intermediate distances on mail routes in operation on the 1st of March, 1901.
1 inch to 8 miles. 43 x 26. Published. Frequency and types of mail service, discontinued post offices, counties, towns, railroads, physical features, and parts of adjoining States. Inset map of "Environs of Indianapolis." 1 inch to ca. 5 miles. Post routes in colors to show frequency of service. Filed as RG 28: Indiana 1901.

271. [Map of the] State of Indiana, Compiled from the official Records of the General Land Office ... 1916. ... Compiled and Drawn by A. F. Dinsmore ... Traced and Lettered by Thos. O. Wansleben.
1 inch to 12 miles. 26½ x 19. Published. County boundaries in color. Also shows county names, public land surveys, towns and cities, outlines of private land claims, boundaries of former Indian reservations, areas included in Vincennes and Clark's military grants, steam railroad lines, and electric railroad lines. Also a black and white base map for this date. 27 x 19½. Filed as RG 49: Indiana 1916, Pub.

272. Post Route Map of the State of Indiana, showing post offices with the intermediate distances on mail routes in operation on the 1st of January, 1917.
1 inch to 8 miles. 43 x 29. Published. Frequency and types of mail service, discontinued post offices, counties, towns, railroads, physical features, and parts of adjoining States. Filed as RG 28: Indiana 1917.

273. [Map of Indiana issued by the U.S. Geological Survey, 1917.]
1 inch to ca. 16 miles. 20 x 14. Published. County names and boundaries, towns and cities, township and range numbers, steam and electric railroad lines, and drainage features. Filed as RG 57: Indiana 1917, Pub.

274. [Map of Indiana Issued by the U.S. Geological Survey in 1919.]
1 inch to ca. 16 miles. 20 x 14. Published. County names and boundaries, towns and cities, township and range numbers, steam and electric railroad lines, and drainage features. Filed as RG 57: Indiana 1919, Pub.

IOWA

275. Sketch [map] of the Public Surveys in Iowa Territory. [n.d.]
1 inch to 18 miles. 12 x 9½. Published. Status of public land surveys. Includes explanation of colors and symbols used on map. Filed as RG 46: 26th Cong., 1st sess.

276. Sketch [map] of the Public Surveys in Iowa Territory. [n.d.]
1 inch to 18 miles. 12 x 9½. Published. Status of public land surveys. Explanation of colors and symbols used on map. Filed as RG 46: 26th Cong., 2d sess.

277. Iowa [Territory] and Wisconsin. Chiefly from the Map of J. N. Nicollet. Entered according to Act of Congress in the year 1844, by Sidney E. Morse and Samuel Breese in the Clerks Office of the Southern District of New York.
1 inch to ca. 50 miles. 14 x 18. Published. Indian trails, Indian villages, counties, towns, and physical features. Iowa Territory includes present State of Minnesota and parts of North and South Dakota. "Cession treaty July 15, 1830," is written in pencil in Sac and Fox area in Iowa Territory, but boundary lines of cession are not shown clearly. Filed as Ref. Coll.: Iowa 1844.

278. (B) [Sketch of] Public Surveys in Iowa 1850. [Issued by the Surveyor General's Office, Dubuque, Nov. 1, 1850.]
1 inch to 18 miles. 19 x 24. Published. Status of public land surveys. Filed as RG 49: Iowa 2, Pub.

279. A Township Map of The State of Iowa Compiled from the United States Surveys and personal reconnaissance showing the Streams, Roads, Towns, County Seats, Works of Internal Improvement, &c.&c. J. F. Abrahams, Publisher, Burlington, Iowa, And By R. L. Barnes, Philadelphia ... 1851. Friend & Aub, Lith., Phila.
1 inch to ca. 20 miles. 20 x 32½. Published. Counties (in color), towns, military posts, townships, railroads, roads, canals, and dams. Tables list population by county and of the principal cities for 1850. Part of northern Iowa is missing on map. Filed as RG 77: Q 27.

280. (No. 2.) Sketch of the Public Surveys in Iowa. [Issued by Surveyor General's Office, Dubuque, Oct. 21, 1853.]
1 inch to 18 miles. 19 x 23. Published. Status of public land surveys. Filed as RG 49: Iowa 4, Pub.

281. (No. 2) Sketch [map] of the Public Surveys in Iowa. [Issued by Surveyor General's Office, Dubuque, Oct. 21, 1854.]
1 inch to 18 miles. 19 x 23. Published. Shows status of public land surveys. Filed as RG 46: S. Ex. Doc. 1, Pt. 3, 33d Cong., 2d sess.

282. (No. 2.) Sketch [map] of the Public Surveys in Iowa ... Surveyor General's Office, Dubuque, October 21st, 1855.
1 inch to 18 miles. 19 x 22. Published. Shows status of public land surveys. Filed as RG 46: S. Ex. Doc. 11, 35th Cong., 1st sess.

283. (No. 2) Sketch [map] of the Public Surveys in Iowa. [Issued by Surveyor General's Office, Dubuque, Oct. 13, 1856.]
1 inch to 18 miles. 19½ x 21. Published. Shows status of public land surveys. Filed as RG 46: S. Ex. Doc. 5, 34th Cong., 3d sess.

284. A Sectional Map of Iowa, Compiled from the official Surveys of the United States and the Public Records of the State & Counties and from Personal Reconnoissance [sic]. By Henn, Williams & Co. of Fairfield, Iowa. 1857. Published by Keen & Lee, Chicago, Illinois. ... Engraved by Theodore Leonhardt from the direction of J. L. Hazzard.
1 inch to 6 miles. 4 sections, each 26½ x 33½. Annotated published. Counties (in color), towns, roads, railroad lines, public land surveys, and drainage features. Annotated to show additional drainage features. Filed as RG 77: M 331-26.

285. Henn, Williams & Co's. Sectional Map of the State of Iowa, Compiled from the Official Surveys of the United States and the Public Records of the State and Counties & from Personal Reconnaissance by Henn, Williams & Co., Fairfield, Iowa. Published by W. B. Keen., Chicago, Ill. 1858. ... Engraved & printed by Ferd. Mayer & Co., New York.
1 inch to ca. 25 miles. 28½ x 39. Published.

Counties (in color), towns, U.S. land offices, railroads, roads, and township and section lines. Filed in Ref. Coll.: Iowa 1858.

286. (No. 2.) Sketch [map] of the Public Surveys in Iowa and Dakota. [Issued by Surveyor General's Office, Dubuque, Oct. 10, 1860.]
1 inch to 18 miles. 19 x 22½. Published. Shows status of public land surveys. Only a very small area in the present State of South Dakota is shown. Filed as RG 46: S. Ex. Doc. 1, 36th Cong., 2d sess.

287. Diagram of the Public Surveys in Iowa. [Issued by the General Land Office on Oct. 2, 1866.]
1 inch to ca. 20 miles. 18 x 20. Published. County boundaries and mineral regions are shown in color. Also shows public surveys, county names, locations of land offices, land-grant railroads and their limits, towns, military posts, and drainage. Pieces of map are missing. Filed as RG 49: Iowa 6, Pub.

288. [Map of the] State of Iowa. . . . 1878. Compiled from the official Records of the General Land Office.
1 inch to 12 miles. 34 x 27. Published. County names and boundaries, towns, principal railroad stations, public land surveys, and railroad lines. Filed as RG 49: Iowa 1878, Pub.

289. [Map of the] State of Iowa. . . . 1885. Compiled from the official Records of the General Land Office.
1 inch to 12 miles. 26½ x 23½. Published. County boundaries in color. Also shows county names, public land surveys, towns, principal railroad stations, railroad lines, railroad land-grant limits, and physical features. Filed as RG 49: Iowa 1885, Pub.

290. Railroad and Sectional Map of Iowa. Published by Warner & Foote . . . Minneapolis, Minna. 1885.
1 inch to 15 miles. 16½ x 25½. Railroads, counties, towns, and township and section lines. Note in pencil in lower right margin states, "filed— July 27/85." Filed as RG 77: Q 531.

291. [Post route map of the State of Iowa showing post offices with the intermediate distances on mail routes in operation Sept. 1907.]
1 inch to 6 miles. 2 sections, each 41½ x 29. Annotated manuscript. Mail service, counties, towns, railroads, and physical features. Annotated to show additional post offices and post routes. Southeastern part of the State is incomplete. Map has no key. Date appears on reverse. Filed as RG 28: Iowa 1907.

292. [Map of the] State of Iowa. Compiled from the official Records of the General Land Office . . . 1917. . . . Compiled and Drawn by Daniel O'Hare . . . Traced and Lettered by George A. Daidy.
1 inch to 12 miles. 23 x 34½. Published. County boundaries in color. Also shows names of counties, public land surveys, towns and cities, military reservations, railroad lines, and physical features. Also a black and white base map for this date. 23 x 35. Filed as RG 49: Iowa 1917, Pub.

293. [Map of Iowa issued by the U.S. Geological Survey, 1917.]
1 inch to ca. 16 miles. 24 x 17. Published. County names and boundaries, towns and cities, township and range numbers, steam and electric railroad lines, and drainage features. Filed as RG 57: Iowa 1917, Pub.

294. Post Route Map of the State of Iowa showing post offices with the intermediate distances on mail routes in operation on the 1st of January, 1917.
1 inch to 7 miles. 35 x 51½. Published. Frequency and types of mail service, discontinued post offices, counties, towns, railroads, physical features, and parts of adjoining States. Filed as RG 28: Iowa 1917.

See also entries 247 and 851.

KANSAS

295. Map of the Kansas Ty., [sic] Enlarged from Map of the Corps of Topogl. Engs., published in 1850.
1 inch to 20 miles. 27½ x 49. Manuscript. Indian lands and reservations, military posts, roads, and physical features. Faint penciled annotations relate to Indian lands and reservations. Two large-scale insets: (1) "Eye Sketch of Fort Leavenworth Reserve Furnished by the Qur. Master Genl's Office." and (2) "Map of The U.S. Reserve [pertaining to Leavenworth], August 1837," with reductions made in 1840 and 1841 indicated in color. Filed as RG 49: Kansas 1.

296. [Map showing status of public land surveys in Kansas and Nebraska Territories. n.d.]
1 inch to 18 miles. 20½ x 13. Published. Filed as RG 46: S. Ex. Doc. 1, Pt. 3, 33d Cong., 2d sess.

297. Plan of the Public Surveys in Kansas and Nebraska [Issued by Surveyor General's Office, Wyandott, K.T., Oct. 20, 1856].
1 inch to 18 chains. 23 x 13. Published. Shows status of public land surveys. Filed as RG 46: S. Ex. Doc. 5, 34th Cong., 3d sess.

298. (3) Map Showing the progress of the Public Surveys in the Territories of Kansas and Nebraska. [Map] to accompany Annual Report of the Surveyor General, 1857.
1 inch to 18 miles. 26 x 19½. Published. Shows status of public land surveys and locations of Indian reservations. Filed as RG 46: S. Ex. Doc. 11, 35th Cong., 1st. sess.

299. Sectional Map of the Territory of Kansas, Compiled from the Field Notes in the Surveyor General's Office. Published by John Halsall . . . 1857.
1 inch to 8 miles. 28½ x 22. Annotated published. Map shows eastern half of Kansas. Public surveys, towns, counties (in color), Indian reservations and lands, military posts, roads including the "Santa Fee Road" and "Fort Laramie Road," and drainage. Annotated to show additional towns, and drainage. Filed as RG 77: Q 759.

300. MacLean & Lawrence's Sectional Map of Kansas Territory. Compiled from the U.S. Surveys by C. P. Wiggin. . . . 1857.
1 inch to 4 miles. 41 x 40. Annotated published. Shows approximately the eastern half of the present State; counties (boundaries in color), a few settlements, township and range numbers, Indian reservations, and roads. Filed as RG 75: map 239.

301. (4) Map Showing the progress of the Public Surveys in the Territories of Kansas and Nebraska. [Map] to accompany Annual Report of the Surveyor General, 1858.
1 inch to 18 miles. 26 x 21. Published. Shows status of public land surveys. Filed as RG 46: S. Ex. Doc. 1, 35th Cong., 2d sess.

302. (5) Map Showing the progress of the Public Surveys in the Territories of Kansas and Nebraska. [Map] to accompany Annual Report of the Surveyor General, 1859.
1 inch to 18 miles. 26½ x 19½. Annotated published. Indian lands and reserves, towns, military posts, and drainage features. Annotated apparently to show acreage in the Iowa and Sac and Fox Reserves. Filed as RG 49: Kansas 9.

303. (6) Map Showing the progress of the Public Surveys in the Territories of Kansas and Nebraska. [Map] to accompany Annual Report of the Surveyor General, 1860.
1 inch to 18 miles. 26½ x 21½. Manuscript. Indian lands and reserves, towns, military posts, and drainage features. See entry 304. Filed as RG 49: Kansas 10.

304. (6) Map Showing the progress of the Public Surveys in the Territories of Kansas and Nebraska. [Map] to accompany Annual Report of the Surveyor General, 1860.
1 inch to 18 miles. 26½ x 21. Published. Shows status of public land surveys and locations of Indian reservations. Filed as RG 46: S. Ex. Doc. 1, 36th Cong., 2d sess.

305. (7) Map Showing the progress of the Public Surveys in Kansas and Nebraska. [Map] to accompany Annual Report of the Surveyor General, 1861.
1 inch to 18 miles. 31 x 33. Manuscript. Indian lands and reserves, towns, military posts, and drainage features. See entry 306. Filed as RG 49: Kansas 11.

306. (7) Map Showing the progress of the Public Surveys in Kansas and Nebraska. [Map] to accompany Annual Report of the Surveyor General, 1861.
1 inch to 18 miles. 25 x 19. Published. Also shows locations of Indian reservations. Filed as RG 46: S. Ex. Doc. 1, 37th Cong., 2d sess.

307. Gunn & Mitchell's New Map of Kansas and the Gold Mines Embracing all the Public Surveys up to 1862. Compiled from the Original Field Notes by O. B. Gunn & D. T. Mitchell. . . . 1862.
1 inch to 9 miles. 28 x 29. Annotated published. Shows Kansas east from Saline, Ottawa, Shirley, and Republic Counties. Counties (boundaries in color), settlements, township and range numbers, military posts, Indian reservations, and roads. Inset map of "Routes from the Missouri River to the Kansas Gold Mines" (in the present State of Colorado). Table also is included showing population of Kansas by counties. Filed as RG 75: map 1234.

308. (11) Map Showing the progress of the Public Surveys in Kansas and Nebraska, 1865.
1 inch to 18 miles. 26 x 34½. Manuscript. Indian lands and reservations, towns, roads, military posts, and proposed railroad routes. Also shows drainage features. Filed as RG 49: Kansas 12.

309. Map Showing the progress of the Public surveys in Kansas and Nebraska, 1866. Surveyor General's Office, Leavenworth, Kansas, August 27th, 1866. [Issued by the General Land Office on Oct. 2, 1866.]
1 inch to ca. 18 miles. 23½ x 32. Published. County boundaries and mineral deposits are shown in color. Also shows county names, Indian villages, towns, locations of land offices, railroad land-grant limits, military posts, and physical features. Pieces of the map are missing. Filed as RG 49: Kansas 1, Pub.

310. A New Sectional Map of the State of Kansas Showing the Route of the Union Pacific Railway—E. D. to Denver City, Col., And complete system of projected Railroads . . . by W. J. Keeler, C. E., November 1866-67. Charles DuBois, Draughtsman. Joseph F. Gedney, Lithographer, Engraver, & Plate Printer . . . Washington, D.C.
1 inch to 4 miles. 2 sections, each 47 x 32. Eastern Kansas to western boundaries of Saline, Ottawa, Shirley, and Republic Counties. Counties (boundaries in color), towns, military posts, roads, and townships. Inset maps of "Proposed Extension of the Union Pacific Rail Road E. D. to Denver City, Colorado." Inset map also shows counties, military posts, Indian reservations, and mineral deposits. Filed as RG 77: Q 126.

311. Map Showing the extent of the Public surveys in Kansas, 1870.
1 inch to 12 miles. 23 x 36. Manuscript. County boundaries and drainage are shown in color. Public land surveys, locations of U.S. land offices, towns, and military reservations are shown. Filed as RG 49: Kansas 17.

312. Map showing the progress of the Public Surveys in Kansas. [Map] to accompany Annual Report of the Surveyor General, 1871.
1 inch to 12 miles. 25 x 38½. Manuscript. Shows county names and boundaries, towns, public land surveys, military reservations, and railroad lines. Also shows drainage features. Filed as RG 49: Kansas 18.

313. Map of Public Surveys in Kansas. [Map] to accompany annual report of Surveyor General, 1873.
1 inch to 18 miles. Corrected: 1 inch to 12 miles. 24½ x 37½. Manuscript. County and land district boundaries are shown in color. Public land surveys, towns, military reservations, and drainage features. Railroad lines are shown in red. Filed as RG 49: Kansas 19.

314. Map of the States of Kansas and Texas, and Indian Territory, with parts of the Territories of Colorado and New Mexico. From the most recent official surveys and explorations and other authentic information. Prepared . . . in the Office of the Chief of Engineers, U.S. Army, 1867. Second Edition, with corrections, issued in 1874.
1 inch to ca. 25 miles. 2 sections, each 25½ x 36½. Published. Towns, railroads, routes of military expeditions, military posts, Indian reservations and lands, roads including the "Santa Fe Road," trails including the "Grand Comanche War Trail" and "Comanche Trail," telegraph lines, and physical features. Relief is shown by hachures. (Annotated copies of several editions of this map are filed as US 318 in RG 77.) Filed as RG 77: 1874, Pub.

315. [Map of the] State of Kansas. . . . 1876. Compiled from the official Records of the General Land Office.
1 inch to 15 miles. 26 x 33½. Published. County boundaries, Indian reservations, and railroad land-grant limits are shown in color. Also shows status of public land surveys, military reservations, land district boundaries, locations of U.S. land offices, towns, railroad lines, and physical features. Also a black and white base map for this date. 23 x 31. Filed as RG 49: Kansas 1876, Pub.

316. [Map of the] State of Kansas. . . . 1879. Compiled from the official Records of the General Land Office.
1 inch to 15 miles. 26½ x 34. Published. County boundaries and military and Indian reservations are shown in color. Also shows public land surveys, towns, principal railroad stations, locations of U.S. land offices, railroad lines, railroad land-grant limits, and physical features. Filed as RG 49: Kansas 1879, Pub.

317. [Map of the] State of Kansas. . . . 1884. Compiled from the official Records of the General Land Office . . . Drawn by A. Pohlers.
1 inch to 15 miles. 21½ x 32. Published. County boundaries, military and Indian reservations, and boundaries of Indian trust lands are shown in color. Also shows public land surveys, towns, locations of U.S. land offices, railroad lines, railroad land-grant limits, and physical features. Also a black and white base map for this date. 26 x 33. Filed as RG 49: Kansas 1884, Pub.

318. Preliminary Post Route Map of the States of Kansas and Nebraska with adjacent parts of Missouri, Iowa, Dakota, Colorado, Texas, and Indian Territory, showing post offices with the intermediate distances and mail routes in operation on the 1st of October, 1885.
1 inch to 10 miles. 4 sections, each 29 x 34. Published. Shows frequency and types of mail service, mileages between post offices, discontinued post offices, counties, towns, railroads, military posts, Indian reservations, and physical features. Post routes in color to show frequency of service. Filed as RG 28: series 1, folder XI.

319. [Map of the] State of Kansas. . . . 1891. Compiled from the official Records of the General Land Office. . . . Compiled and drawn by I. P. Berthong. . . . Traced and lettered by I. P. Berthong.
1 inch to 11 miles. 29½ x 42. Shows county boundaries and names, public land surveys, towns, boundaries of military and Indian reservations, railroads, and physical features. Filed as RG 49: Kansas 1891, Pub.

320. [Map of the] State of Kansas. Compiled from the official Records of the General Land Office . . . 1898 . . . Compiled and drawn by I. P. Berthong. Revised and corrected to May 1898, by M. Hendges. Traced and lettered by I. P. Berthong.
1 inch to 12 miles. 26 x 38. Published. County boundaries, military and Indian reservations, and boundaries of Indian trust lands are shown in color. Also shows public land surveys, towns, locations of U.S. land offices, railroad lines proposed and completed, and physical features. Also a black and white base map with drainage in blue for this date. 26½ x 37½. Filed as RG 49: Kansas 1898, Pub.

321. Official Railroad Map of Kansas, 1904. Issued by the State Board of Railroad Commissioners. . . . Copyright . . . by The J. N. Matthews Co.
1 inch to 14 miles. 22 x 32. Annotated published. County names and boundaries, towns and cities, public land surveys, and drainage features. Railroad lines are shown in color and are keyed to a list on the map. Map is annotated to show boundaries of the Dodge City, Colby, and Wakeeney Districts (apparently land districts). Filed as RG 49: Kansas 25.

322. [Map of the] State of Kansas. Compiled from the official Records of the General Land Office . . . 1912. . . . Compiled and drawn by I. P. Berthong. Traced and lettered by I. P. Berthong.
1 inch to 12 miles. 26½ x 36½. Published. County and land district boundaries, military reservations, and national forests are shown in color. Also shows public land surveys, towns, locations of U.S. land offices, railroad lines, and physical features. Also a black and white base map with drainage in blue for this date. 27 x 38. Filed as RG 49: Kansas 1912, Pub.

323. Post Route Map of the State of Kansas showing post offices with the intermediate distances on mail routes in operation on the 1st of January, 1917.
1 inch to 10 miles. 2 sections, each 29 x 26. Published. Frequency and types of mail service, discontinued post offices, counties, towns, railroads, physical features, and parts of adjoining States. Filed as RG 28: Kansas 1917.

See also entry 516.

KENTUCKY

324. A Map of the State of Kentucky, from Actual Survey by Elihu Barker of Philadelphia. June 1st, 1795. Tracing by John H. Madert.
1 inch to 15 miles. 16 x 31½. Manuscript on tracing cloth. Settlements, military posts, roads and trails, physical features, and remarks about characteristics of the land. Filed as RG 75: CA 165.

325. Map of the States of Kentucky, And Tennessee. London, Published June 1, 1831, by I. T. Hinton and Simpkin & Marshall. Engraved & Printed by Fenner Sears & Co.
1 inch to 35 miles. 11½ x 15½. Annotated published. Counties, towns, roads, and physical features. Appearing in pencil, "1831 #23 SDC." Filed as Ref. Coll.: Kentucky 1831.

326. Kentucky. Reduced From Doct. Luke Munsell's Large Map of 1818. Improved to the present time from Authentic Documents by the Author. Published by Corey & Fairbank, Cincinnati, and Luke Munsell, Danville, Ky., 1835. Engraved by Doolittle & Munson, Cincinnati, assisted by Wm. Haviland.
1 inch to 8 miles. 2 sections, each 40½ x 26½. Published. Counties (in color), roads, towns, forts, iron works, and salt works. Inset maps of Louisville, Frankfort, Lexington, and Maysville. Also shown are drawings of the State capitol and profiles of the railroad from Lexington to Frankfort and the Louisville and Portland Canal locks. Statistical tables give population information. Filed as RG 77: T 13.

327. Map of Kentucky and Tennessee Exhibiting the Post Offices, Post Roads, Canals, Rail Roads, &c. By David H. Burr (Late topographer to the Post Office).... Entered according to the Act of Congress, July 10th, 1839.
1 inch to 10 miles. 4 sections, each 19¼ x 25½. Published. Also shows counties (in color), mileages between post offices, physical features, and parts of adjoining States. Filed as RG 28: Burr Atlas, map 11.

328. Kentucky and Tennessee.... Entered according to Act of Congress in the year 1845 by Sidney E. Morse and Samuel Breese in the Clerks Office of the Southern District of New York.
1 inch to ca. 28 miles. 14½ x 17½. Published. Both States shaded green. Counties, towns, roads, canals, railroads, and "slackwater navigation." Notes in pencil refer to Congressional documents relating to the Tennessee River and Cherokee Lands. Filed as Ref. Coll.: Kentucky 1845.

329. New Map of Kentucky Carefully Compiled From the Most Authentic Information By Edmund F. Lee, Civil Engineer. Engraved and Published by C. R. Milne ... 1852.
1 inch to ca. 20 miles. 18 x 29. Annotated published. Shows counties, towns, railroads, roads, caves, and springs. Annotated in color to show geological formations. No color key. Note in pencil in lower right margin gives date of "geological color" by Sidney S. Lyon, as Nov. 27, 1861. A similar map having a color key to the geological formations is filed as RG 77: T 17½-1. A note in the title block of T 17½-1 states that "geological color" is by Sidney S. Lyon, but no date is given. Other notations in pencil appear in the lower margin. This map filed as RG 77: T 17½-2.

330. New Map of Kentucky Carefully Compiled From The Most Authentic Original Maps, Documents, And Miscellaneous Information, By Edmund F. Lee, Civil Engineer. Published by J. H. Colton & Co.... 1856.
1 inch to 6 miles. 4 sections, each 23½ x 38.

Published. Counties (in color), towns, post offices, canals, roads, railroads, iron works, salt works, coal and lead mines, mills, and caves. Also shows portions of adjoining States. Table lists information such as population, value of farm machinery, land "in occupation," and number of schools and churches. (A copy of this map, annotated to show "Finished Railroads" in Kentucky and the adjacent part of Tennessee, is filed as T 17 in RG 77.) Filed as RG 77: T 15.

331. Military Map of the States of Kentucky and Tennessee within eleven [m]iles of the 35th Parallel of Latitude or Southern Boundary of Tennessee . . . Commenced under the Authority of Major General Don Carlos Buell, Commanding the Department of the Ohio, by Capt. N. Michler, Corps Topogl. Engrs., U.S.A. . . . July 1863. Drawn by Charles E. Swann.

1 inch to 5.524 miles. 3 sections, each 51 x 28¼. Manuscript. Kentucky, Tennessee, and adjoining States in color. Towns, post offices, "common" roads, turnpike and stage roads, iron works and forges, salt works, mills, and physical features. Annotated to show "Illinois Coal Field" and railroad lines. "Memoranda" lists sources used in preparation of map. (A published copy of this map is filed as Dept. of the Ohio 3 in RG 393.) RG 77: T 68.

332. Lloyd's Official Map of the State of Kentucky. Compiled from Actual Surveys and Official Documents . . . 1863. . . . New York, J. T. Lloyd, Publisher.

1 inch to 8 miles. 31 x 44. Published. Counties (in color), portions of adjoining States, towns, roads, physical features, railroads, canals, mills, caves, salt works, coal and iron mines. Filed as Ref. Coll.: Kentucky 1863.

333. Kentucky Geological Survey, 1875. Preliminary Map Compiled From Various Surveys. N. S. Shaler, Director. By L. Trouvelot, Artist of Survey. J. Mayer & Co., Lith., Boston.

1 inch to ca. 50 miles. 18 x 36. Annotated published. Counties, towns, roads, and physical features. Note added in title block states "Proof Sheet N. S. S." Filed as RG 77: T 217.

334. Gray's New Map of Kentucky and Tennessee, By Frank A. Gray. Philadelphia: O. W. Gray & Son. [1876.]

1 inch to ca. 18 miles. 18½ x 30½. Published. Counties (in color), towns, railroads, canals, physical features, and sites of "important" battles. Inset maps of the two States showing railroad systems, density of population, and a hysometric sketch (elevations above sea level). Tables show comparative increases in population, 1790-1870. Note on reverse states "Atlas of the United States.-Specimen & advance sheets of an- . . . ." Filed as RG 77: US 373-52.

335. Kentucky Geological Survey, John R. Procter, Director. Preliminary County Map of Kentucky By J. B. Hoeing, Topographer. 1887. . . . Copyrighted, 1887, by John R. Procter, Director, Ky. Geol. Survey. Julius Bien & Co., Lith.

1 inch to 20 miles. 16¼ x 27. Published. Counties (in color), towns, roads, and physical features. Filed as RG 77: T 172.

336. Kentucky Geological Survey, John R. Procter, Director. Preliminary Map of Kentucky By J. B. Hoeing, Topographer. 1887. . . . Copyrighted 1887, by John R. Procter, Director, Ky. Geol. Survey. Julius Bien & Co. Lith.

1 inch to 20 miles. 16½ x 27. Published. Geological formations shown in color. Counties, towns, and roads. Filed as RG 77: T 171.

337. Post Route Map of the States of Kentucky and Tennessee with parts of adjacent States showing post offices with the intermediate distances and mail routes in operation on the 1st of February, 1887.

1 inch to 8 miles. 4 sections, each approximately 31 x 34. Published. Shows frequency and types of mail service, mileages between post offices, discontinued post offices, counties, towns, railroads, and physical features. Post routes are in color to show frequency of service. Filed as RG 28: series 1, folder XXII.

338. Post Route Map of the States of Kentucky and Tennessee showing post offices with the intermediate distances on mail routes in operation on the 1st of September, 1912.

1 inch to 8 miles. 2 sections, each 47 x 35. Annotated published. Shows frequency and types of mail service, discontinued post offices, counties, towns, railroads, physical features, and parts of adjoining States. Post routes are in color to show frequency of service. Annotated to show locations of coal mines. Filed as RG 28: Kentucky 1912.

LOUISIANA

339. Post Route Map of the States of Kentucky and Tennessee showing post offices with the intermediate distances on mail routes in operation on the 1st of April, 1915.
1 inch to 8 miles. 2 sections, each 47 x 35. Annotated published. Shows frequency and types of mail service, discontinued post offices, counties, towns, railroads, physical features, and parts of adjoining States. Post routes are in color to show frequency of service. Parts of State are marked off without explanation. Filed as RG 28: Kentucky 1915.

340. [Map of Kentucky issued by the U.S. Geological Survey, 1916.]
1 inch to ca. 16 miles. 15 x 30. Published. Shows county names and boundaries, towns and cities, steam and electric railroad lines, and drainage features. A copy of this edition was reprinted in 1918. Filed as RG 57: Kentucky 1916, Pub.

LOUISIANA

341. A Map of the State of Louisiana With Part of the Mississippi Territory, From Actual Survey By Wm. Darby ... Philadelphia. Published May the 1st, 1816, By John Melish.
1 inch to ca. 10 miles. 33 x 45. Parishes (boundaries in color), towns, roads, drainage, military posts, and depth soundings of coastal waters. Filed as RG 77: General Staff Map Collection, Louisiana.

342. No. 7 [Map of] Louisiana.
1 inch to ca. 40 miles. 9½ x 10. Published. Shows land districts and locations of land offices in 1828 and 1841 and public land offered for sale, 1828-41. 1828 land district boundaries are shown in red. For further explanation of the map see S. Doc. 92, 26th Cong., 2d sess., Serial 377. (This map without the 1828 land districts shown is filed as Louisiana 1, Published, in RG 49.) Filed as RG 46: 26th Cong., 2d sess.

343. [Map of] Louisiana. Entered according to Act of Congress in the year 1842, By Sidney E. Morse and Samuel Breese in the Clerks Office of the Southern District of New York.
1 inch to ca. 28 miles. 12 x 15. Published. Parishes, towns, railroads, roads, canals, and townships. Filed as Ref. Coll.: Louisiana 1842.

344. Map of Louisiana. Subdivided into Townships, in each township of which is placed the number of acres of Estimated Swamp Lands as stated in the Surveyor General's Report of Oct. 20th 1847, To the Commissioner of the General Land Office. Prepared the 19th December, 1849 ... R. W. Boyd, Surveyor General, La. Published By Dr. Hunter ... Litho. of X. Magny.
1 inch to 24 miles. 17½ x 18. Published. Also shows towns, drainage, and Claim of the Baron de Bastrop. Filed as Ref. Coll.: Louisiana 1849.

345. (I) Map of Louisiana Representing the Several Land Districts. [Map] Prepared to accompany the Surveyor General's annual Report. [Issued by the Surveyor General's Office, Donaldsville, La., October 1, 1853.]
1 inch to 18 miles. 17½ x 17½. Published. Shows extent and status of public land surveys and the assumed extent of the swamp and overflowed lands. Filed as RG 49: Louisiana 4, Pub.

346. New and Improved Map of Louisiana Compiled ... by G. W. R. Bayley, Civil Engineer. 1853.
1 inch to ca. 10 miles. 32 x 39. Annotated published. Parishes (boundaries in color), settlements, township and range numbers, and roads. Annotated in color to show railroad lines completed and projected, "Boundaries of the uplands, or diluvial formation," and "Alluvium generally." Map includes tables of 1850 population, senatorial districts, and representatives, by parish. Filed as RG 77: Z 262.

347. La Tourrette's Reference Map of the State of Louisiana from the Original Surveys of the United States Which Show the Townships, Sections or Mile Squares, Spanish Grants, Settlement Rights &c. Also the Plantations With

the owners' names Engraved thereon. Compiled and Published By John La Tourrette, New Orleans, La., A. D. 1853.

1 inch to 6 miles. 4 sections, each 26 x 28½. Land grants and boundaries of parishes are shown in color. Table gives 1840 census figures. Inset maps of the city of New Orleans and Louisiana showing land districts. Filed as RG 77: M 95.

348. (H) Map of Louisiana, Representing the Several Land Districts. [Map] Prepared to accompany the Surveyor General's annual Report. [Issued by the Surveyor General's Office, Donaldsonville, La., Oct. 1, 1854.]

1 inch to 18 miles. 17½ x 17½. Published. Shows extent and status of public land surveys and the "assumed extent of the Swamp and Overflowed Lands . . . ." A copy of this map also is filed as RG 46: S. Ex. Doc. 1, Pt. 3, 33d Cong., 2d sess. Filed as RG 49: Louisiana 5, Pub.

349. (H) Map of Louisiana. . . . Prepared to accompany the Surveyor General's annual Report. [Issued by Surveyor General's Office, Donaldsonville, La., Oct. 1, 1856.]

1 inch to 18 miles. 17½ x 17. Published. Shows status of public land surveys, and "assumed extent of the Swamp and Overflowed Lands . . . ." Filed as RG 46: S. Ex. Doc. 5, 34th Cong., 3d sess.

350. No. 8 (H) Map of Louisiana. . . . Prepared to accompany the Surveyor General's annual Report. [Issued by Surveyor General's Office, Donaldsonville, La., Oct. 1, 1857.]

1 inch to ca. 20 miles. 17 x 18½. Published. Shows status of public land surveys and "assumed extent of the Swamp and Overflowed Lands . . . ." Filed as RG 46: S. Ex. Doc. 11, 35th Cong., 1st sess.

351. No. 8 (H) Map of Louisiana . . . Prepared to accompany the Surveyor General's annual report. [Issued by Surveyor General's Office, Donaldsonville, La.. Oct. 1, 1859.]

1 inch to ca. 20 miles. 17 x 17½. Published. Shows status of public land surveys and "assumed extent of the Swamp and Overflowed Lands . . . ." Filed as RG 46: S. Ex. Doc. 2, 36th Cong., 1st sess.

352. No. 8 (H) Map of Louisiana . . . Prepared to accompany the Surveyor General's annual Report. [Issued by Surveyor General's Office, Donaldsonville, La.,Oct. 1, 1860.]

1 inch to ca. 20 miles. 17 x 18. Published. Shows status of public land surveys and "assumed extent of the Swamp and Overflowed Lands . . . ." Filed as RG 46: S. Ex. Doc. 1, 36th Cong., 2d sess.

353. [Map of] Louisiana . . . Photographed under the direction of the Engineer Department. [ca. 1861-65]

Scale not indicated. 23 x 25. Photoprocessed. Population figures (white, slave, and freed) and type and amount of agricultural produce shown by county. Railroad lines also shown. Filed as RG 77: M 448.

354. Department of the Gulf. Map No. 13, State of Louisiana. Showing Theatre of Operations of the Forces under command of Maj. Gen. Banks during the months of March, April, May, June, and July, and ending with the Reduction of Port Hudson, July 8th, 1863. [Prepared August 1863.]

1 inch to ca. 10 miles. 30 x 33. Published. Settlements, roads, and railroad lines. Filed as RG 393: Dept. of the Gulf 11.

355. Map of Louisiana. [Issued by the General Land Office on Oct. 2, 1866.]

1 inch to ca. 18 miles. 15½ x 16. Published. Parish boundaries are shown in color. Shows public surveys, land districts, locations of land offices, railroad land-grant limits, military posts, towns, and physical features. Filed as RG 49: Louisiana 6, Pub.

356. The Louisiana State University Topographical Map of Louisiana, Showing the Characteristic Features of the Surface of the State in Symbols and Colors. Compiled from the Latest and most Authentic Sources . . . By S. H. Lockett, Professor of Engineering, Assisted in the draughting by D. M. Bosnan of the class of 1872. Entered according to Act of Congress in the year 1873 . . . Engraved, Printed, and Manufactured By G. W. & G. B. Colton & Co.

1 inch to 10 miles. 31½ x 35. Published. Colored to show soil and drainage features. Names and boundaries of parishes, towns, roads, railroads, and township and section lines. Filed as RG 77: M 164.

357. [Map of the] State of Louisiana. . . . 1876. Compiled from the official Records of the General Land Office.

1 inch to 14 miles. 33½ x 26½. Published.

LOUISIANA

Parish and land district boundaries and railroad land-grant limits are shown in color. Also shows status of public land surveys, towns and cities, military posts, locations of U.S. land offices, railroad lines, and physical features. Also a black and white base map for this date. 31 x 24. Filed as RG 49: Louisiana 1876, Pub.

358. Gray's New Map of Louisiana By Frank A. Gray.... Copyright, 1878, by O. W. Gray & Son.
    1 inch to 18.93 miles. 18 x 27. Parishes (in color), towns, physical features, railroads, and townships. Insets of the "City of New Orleans," scale: 1 inch to almost ¾ mile, showing ward and district numbers. Also a map of "The Passes of the Mississippi River" at a scale of 1 inch to ca. 4 miles. Filed as RG 77: US 373-60.

359. [Map of the] State of Louisiana.... 1879. Compiled from the official Records of the General Land Office.
    1 inch to 14 miles. 33½ x 26½. Published. County (parish) boundaries and private land claims are shown in color. Also shows status of public land surveys, towns and cities, military reservations, locations of U.S. land offices, railroad lines, railroad land-grant limits, and physical features. Filed as RG 49: Louisiana 1879, Pub.

360. Post Route Map of the State of Louisiana with adjacent parts of Mississippi, Arkansas, and Texas showing post offices with the intermediate distances and mail routes in operation on the 1st of October, 1885. Published ... under the direction of W. L. Nicholson, Topographer, P. O. Dept.
    1 inch to 8 5/8 miles. 2 sections, each 41 x 28½. Published. Frequency and types of mail service, mileages between post offices, discontinued post offices, counties, towns, railroads, military posts, and physical features. Post routes in color to show frequency of service. Filed as RG 28: series 1, folder VII.

361. Post Route Map of the State of Louisiana with adjacent parts of Mississippi, Arkansas, and Texas showing post offices with the intermediate distances and mail routes in operation on the 1st of December, 1885. Published ... under the direction of W. L. Nicholson, Topographer, P. O. Dept.
    1 inch to 8 5/8 miles. 2 sections, each 41½ x 28½. Published. Frequency and types of mail service, mileages between post offices, discontinued post offices, counties, towns, railroads, and physical features. Post routes in color to show frequency of service. Filed as RG 28: series 1, folder VIII.

362. [Map of the] State of Louisiana.... 1886. Compiled from the official Records of the General Land Office ... Compiled by A. F. Dinsmore.... Drawn by G. P. Strum.
    1 inch to 14 miles. 32 x 26½. Published. Parish boundaries, railroad land-grant limits, military reservations, names of land districts, and boundaries of "old" land districts are shown in color. Status of public land surveys, towns and cities, canals, locations of U.S. land offices, railroad lines, and physical features are also shown. Also a black and white base map for this date, 31 x 26½, which does not show boundaries of previous land districts. Filed as RG 49: Louisiana 1886, Pub.

363. Post Route Map of the State of Louisiana with adjacent parts of Mississippi, Arkansas, and Texas showing post offices with the intermediate distances and mail routes in operation on the 1st of February, 1887. Published ... under the direction of W. L. Nicholson, Topographer, P. O. Dept.
    1 inch to 8 5/8 miles. 2 sections, each 41½ x 28½. Published. Frequency and types of mail service, mileages between post offices, discontinued post offices, counties, towns, railroads, and physical features. Post routes in color to show frequency of service. Filed as RG 28: series 1, folder XIX.

364. [Map of the] State of Louisiana.... 1887. Compiled from the official Records of the General Land Office.... Compiled by A. F. Dinsmore.... Drawn by G. P. Strum.
    1 inch to 14 miles. 30 x 28. Published. Parish boundaries, railroad land-grant limits, military reservations, names of land districts, and boundaries of "old" land districts are shown in color. Status of public land surveys, towns and cities, canals, locations of U.S. land offices, railroad lines, and physical features are also shown. Also a black and white base map for this date, 31 x 26½, which does not show boundaries of previous land districts. Filed as RG 49: Louisiana 1887, Pub.

44 MAPS OF STATES AND TERRITORIES

365. Post Route Map of the State of Louisiana showing post offices with the intermediate distances on mail routes in operation on the 1st of March, 1895.

1 inch to ca. 10 miles. 30½ x 35. Published. Frequency and types of mail service, discontinued post offices, counties, towns, railroads, physical features, and parts of adjoining States. Post routes in color to show frequency of service. Filed as RG 28: Louisiana 1895.

366. [Map of the] State of Louisiana. Compiled from the official Records of the General Land Office ... 1896. ... Revised and Drawn by Daniel O'Hare.

1 inch to 12 miles. 33 x 32½. Published. Parish boundaries and military reservations are shown in color. Drainage in blue. Also shows public land surveys, towns and cities, lighthouses and vessels, locations of U.S. land offices, and railroad lines. Also a black and white base map for this date. Drainage in blue. 32 x 32. Filed as RG 49: Louisiana 1896, Pub.

367. [Map of the] State of Louisiana Compiled from the official Records of the General Land Office ... 1916. ... Compiled by A. F. Dinsmore. ... Traced and lettered by Wm. Bauman, Jr.

1 inch to 12 miles. 30 x 31. Published. Parish boundaries, military reservations, and boundaries of bird reservations are shown in color. Also shows public land surveys, towns and cities, railroad lines, and lighthouses. Lines indicate Mississippi River as shown on public survey plats and by 1907 survey by Mississippi River Commission. Small inset map of New Orleans. Also a black and white base map for this date. 30 x 31. Filed as RG 49: Louisiana 1916, Pub.

See also entries 443 and 450.

MAINE

368. A Map of the District of Maine. Drawn from the latest surveys and other best Authorities, by Osgood Carleton. ... Engraved for Judge Sullivan's History of the District of Maine, Published by Thomas & Anderson, Boston, 1795.

1 inch to 18 miles. 29 x 17½. Published. Boundaries of counties, township and plantation boundaries, "County Towns, or Towns where Courts are held," land grants, and physical features. Attached to the map is the title page from Sullivan's *The History of the District of Maine*. Filed as RG 76: series 8, map 36.

369. Map of the District of Maine, Massachusetts. Compiled from Actual Surveys made by Order of the General Court, and under the inspection of Agents of their appointment. By Osgood Carleton ... Boston: Published by B. & J. Loring, 1802.

1 inch to 6 miles. 2 sections, each 26½ x 37½. Published. Schools, meetinghouses, courthouses, grist and saw mills, iron works, iron deposits, roads, bridges, and physical features. Also shows county and township boundary lines and distances to Boston and the county seat from each town. Filed as Ref. Coll.: Maine 1802.

370. Map of the District of Maine From the Latest and Best Authorities, By Moses Greenleaf, Esq., 1815. ... Published by Cummings & Hilliard ... Boston. Engraved by W. B. Annin, Boston.

1 inch to 9 miles. 42 x 27. Counties, townships, towns, and physical features. County boundary lines shown in color. Also engraved on the map: "To the Honourable The Legislature of The State of Massachusetts, This Map Is Respectfully Inscribed By the Author." Filed as Ref. Coll.: Maine 1815.

371. Map of the State of Maine from the latest and best authorities, By Moses Greenleaf, Esqr., 1822. Engraved by W. B. Annin, Boston.

1 inch to 8 miles. 42 x 27. Published. Names of counties, township names and boundaries, land grants, and physical features. Filed as RG 76: series 8, map 38.

MAINE

372. Map of Maine, New Hampshire, and Vermont. London. Published April 15, 1832, by I. T. Hinton & Simpkin & Marshall. Engraved & Printed by Fenner Sears & Co.
1 inch to ca. 35 miles. 16½ x 11½. Published. Names of counties, settlements, and roads. Also shows adjoining areas in Canada. Filed as Ref. Coll.: Maine 1832.

373. Map of Maine, New Hampshire, Vermont, Massachusetts, Rhode Island, and Connecticut. Exhibiting the Post Offices, Post Roads, Canals, Rail Roads, &c. By David H. Burr (Late Topographer to the Post Office). . . . Entered according to the Act of Congress, July 10th, 1839.
1 inch to 10 miles. 4 sections, each 19 x 25½. Published. Also shows counties (in color), mileages between post offices, townships, physical features, and parts of adjoining States and Canada. Names of counties are not shown. Filed as RG 28: Burr Atlas, map 2.

374. [Map of] Maine. [ca. 1840]
1 inch to ca. 22 miles. 16 x 13. Published. Shows boundaries of counties and minor civil divisions, villages, railroads, and canals. Filed as Ref. Coll.: Maine 1840.

375. Post Route Map of the State of Maine and of the adjacent parts of New Hampshire and the Dominion of Canada . . . by W. L. Nicholson, Topographer of P. O. Dep't. 1869. . . . Engraved by D. McClelland . . . Paul Goepel, Draughtsman . . . [Revised] to date of August 1, 1873.
1 inch to 8½ miles. 40 x 31½. State boundaries in color. Frequency and types of mail service, mileages between post offices, counties, towns, and railroads. Post routes shown in color to illustrate frequency of service. Table lists distances between principal eastern cities. Inset "Map of the State of Maine showing the connection with the surrounding States and Provinces." Scale 1 inch to 45 miles. Filed as RG 28: series 1, folder II.

376. Post Route Map of the State of Maine [and parts of New Hampshire and Canada] showing post offices with the intermediate distances and mail routes in operation on the 1st of February, 1886. Published . . . under the direction of W. L. Nicholson, Topographer, P. O. Dept.
1 inch to 8½ miles. 40 x 30. Published. Frequency and types of mail service, mileages between post offices, discontinued post offices, counties, towns, railroads, and physical features. Post routes in color to show frequency of service. Inset "Map of the State of Maine showing the connections with the surrounding States and Provinces." Scale 1 inch to 45 miles. Filed as RG 28: series 1, folder XVI.

377. Post Route Map of the State of Maine showing post offices with the intermediate distances on mail routes in operation on the 1st of September, 1896.
1 inch to 8 miles. 40 x 30½. Published. Frequency and types of mail service, discontinued post offices, counties, towns, railroads, physical features, and parts of adjoining States and Canada. Post routes in color to show frequency of service. Small pieces of map are missing. Inset map of "Environs of Portland." Scale 1 inch to ca. 4 miles. Filed as RG 28: Maine 1896.

378. The Official Map of Maine, Compiled from United States Government Surveys, Official State Surveys, and Original Sources. Published by the National Survey Co. . . . L. V. Crocker, Topographer. Copyright, 1918.
1 inch to ca. 7 miles. 48 x 36. Published. Shows boundaries of counties and minor civil divisions, highways, trails, railroad lines, drainage features, and villages. Symbols used on map are identified in "Explanation of Signs." Map also includes table of population statistics from the 1910 census. Filed as Ref. Coll.: Maine 1918.

See also entries 157 and 160.

MAPS OF STATES AND TERRITORIES
MARYLAND

379. Map of the State of Maryland Laid down from an actual Survey of all the principal Waters, public Roads, and Division of Counties therein; describing the Situation of the Cities, Towns, Villages, Houses of Worship and other public Buildings, Furnaces, Forges, Mills, and other remarkable Places; and of the Federal Territory as also a Sketch of the State of Delaware; shewing the probable connexion of the Chesapeake and Delaware Bays, By Dennis Griffith. June 20th, 1794. Engraved by J. Thackara & J. Vallance, Philadelphia. Published June 6th, 1795, by J. Vallance, Engraver.

1 inch to 5 miles. 2 sections, each 31 x 27. Published. Also shows physical features. Inset map of Washington, D.C., at a scale of 1 inch to 3,300 feet. Filed as RG 77: US 103.

380. [Map of] Maryland and Delaware. [ca. 1840.]
1 inch to ca. 18 miles. 12 x 15. Published. Counties, cities and towns, railroads, canals, and physical features. State shaded green. Profiles of Baltimore and Ohio Railroad from Harpers Ferry to Baltimore and the Chesapeake and Ohio Canal from Pittsburgh to Washington, D.C. Inset map of Washington, D.C., at a scale of 1 inch to 3 miles. Filed as Ref. Coll.: Maryland 1840.

381. A Map of the State of Maryland [and parts of adjoining States]. Constructed from the best authorities By Fielding Lucas Jr., Baltimore. Engraved by John Warr, Philadelphia. Published by F. Lucas Jr. [1841.]

1 inch to 6 miles. 2 sections, each 35½ x 26. Published. Counties (in color), towns, roads, railroads, and physical features. Table lists 1840 census figures for individual counties and Baltimore, Frederick, and Annapolis. (This map in black and white is filed as drawer 135, sheet 3, in RG 77.) Filed as RG 77: US 39.

382. Herrick's Map of Maryland and District of Columbia, From Original, The U.S. Coast, and Other Reliable Surveys, By S. W. Herrick, Civil Engineer. Published By Jennings, Herrick, & Dearborn, Baltimore, 1859.

1 inch to ca. 6 miles. 32½ x 47. Published. Counties (in color), towns, roads, railroads, and canals. Inset map of Washington, D.C., at a scale of 1 inch to ca. 1¼ miles and Baltimore at a scale of 1 inch to ca. 1 mile. Several paragraphs contain historical and statistical information about Maryland. Filed as RG 77: F 56.

383. McJilton's Outline Map of Maryland and Delaware, 1866. Lithographed & Published by A. Hoen & Co., Baltimore.

Large scale. 4 sections, each 23 x 37. Annotated published. Counties are shown in color but are not identified. "Geological Signs" indicate rock types and other geological information. Routes of railroads, canals, and National Road are shown. Towns are represented by dots, but names are not shown. Filed as RG 75: map 533.

384. Maryland, Delaware, and the District of Columbia, By Frank A. Gray. . . . Copyright, 1875, by O. W. Gray.

1 inch to 10 miles. 18 x 31. Published. Counties, cities, and towns, districts (Md.), hundreds (Del.), sites and dates of important battles, physical features, and canals. Inset maps of Dover and Wilmington, Delaware, and Annapolis and Annapolis Harbor, Maryland. Blank space in lower left portion of map apparently intended for inset map of Washington, D.C. Filed as RG 77: US 373-57.

385. Post Route Map of the States of Maryland and Delaware and of the District of Columbia, showing post offices with the intermediate distances on mail routes in operation on the 1st of December, 1908.

1 inch to 5 miles. 2 sections, each 34 x 25½. Published. Frequency and types of mail service, discontinued post offices, counties, towns, railroads, physical features, and adjoining States. Post routes in color to show frequency of service. Inset maps of "District of Columbia and Vicinity" and "Baltimore City and Vicinity" at a scale of 1 inch to ca. 1¾ miles. Filed as RG 28: Maryland 1908.

386. Post Route Map of the States of Maryland and Delaware and of the District of Columbia, showing post offices with the intermediate distances on mail routes in operation on the 1st of June, 1910.

1 inch to 5 miles. 2 sections, each 34½ x 25½. Published. Frequency and types of mail service, discontinued post offices, counties, towns, railroads, physical features, and parts of adjoining States. Post

routes in color to show frequency of service. Inset maps of District of Columbia and Baltimore and vicinity at a scale of 1 inch to ca. 1¾ miles. Filed as RG 28: Maryland 1910.

387. [Map of Maryland and Delaware issued by the U.S. Geological Survey in 1916 and reprinted in 1920.]

1 inch to ca. 16 miles. 12 x 19. Published. County names and boundaries, towns and cities, steam and electric railroad lines, and drainage features. Filed as RG 57: Maryland 1920, Pub.

See also entries 741-745 and 809-811.

MASSACHUSETTS

388. Map of Massachusetts Proper. Compiled from Actual Surveys made by Order of the General Court, and under the inspection of Agents of their appointment, By Osgood Carleton. Revised, Corrected, and Republished By Amos Lay ... Albany, 1822 ... Engraved by Joseph Callender and Samuel Hill, Boston.

1 inch to 4 miles. 32 x 47½. Published. Counties (boundaries in color), towns, townships, academies, meetinghouses, courthouses, bridges, and iron ore deposits. Filed as RG 77: US 97.

389. [Map of] Massachusetts and Rhode Island. [ca. 1840.]

1 inch to ca. 14 miles. 14 x 18. Published. Counties, townships, villages, canals, and railroad lines. Filed as Ref. Coll.: Massachusetts 1840.

390. [Map of] Massachusetts, Rhode Island, and Connecticut, By Frank A. Gray. Entered according to act of Congress in the year 1875 by O. W. Gray & Son.

1 inch to 9 miles. 18½ x 28. Published. Counties, townships, villages, canals, railroad lines, and topographical features. Inset map of "Environs of Boston." Filed as RG 77: US 373-59.

391. [Topographic Map of Massachusetts issued by the U.S. Geological Survey in 1889.]

1 inch to ca. 4 miles. 4 sections, each 17½ x 27½. Published. Settlements, county boundaries and names, and railroad lines. Drainage in blue; contours in brown. Filed as RG 57: Massachusetts 1889, Pub.

392. Topographic Map of Massachusetts and Rhode Island ... Surveyed in 1884-1888 [Issued by U.S. Geological Survey in 1915].

1 inch to ca. 4 miles. 34 x 52. Published. Settlements, county boundaries and names, and railroad lines. Drainage in blue; contours in brown. Filed as RG 57: Massachusetts 1915, Pub.

See also entries 157, 158, 161, and 373.

MICHIGAN

393. An Improved Map of the Surveyed Part of the Territory of Michigan. . . . By John Farmer, 1830. V. Balch and S. Stiles, Engravers, Utica.

1 inch to 8 miles. 21 x 33. Published. Counties (in color), extent of public land surveys, towns, Indian villages, Indian trails, Indian reservations, roads, mills, and inns. Also shows what apparently are outlines of French land grants. Inset maps of the Straits of Michillimackinac, Pte. Ste. Ignace, part of the lead mine district near the Mississippi River, private land claims at Green Bay [Wisconsin], and Michillimackinac Island. Filed as Ref. Coll.: Michigan 1830.

394. Map of the Territories of Michigan and Ouisconsin [sic] . . . By John Farmer of Detroit, 1830. Engraved by Rawdon Clark & Co., Albany, N.Y.

1 inch to 50 miles. 21 x 35. Published. Counties (in color), roads, trading posts, Indian villages, residences of Indian agents, townships, and routes of Major Long and Henry Schoolcraft. Also parts of adjoining States and Canada. Inset map of Ste. Marie River, at a scale of 1 inch to 8 miles. Filed as Ref. Coll.: Michigan 1830.

395. Map of the Surveyed Part of Michigan, By John Farmer. Published by J. H. Colton & Co., New York. 1837. Engraved by S. Stiles & Co., New York.

1 inch to ca. 8 miles. 23¼ x 33½. Published. Counties (in color), roads, towns, railroads, townships, Indian reservations, and mills. Inset maps of the unsurveyed part of Michigan and the Straits of Mackinaw. Filed as RG 77: O 117.

396. Map of Michigan & Part of Wisconsin Territory, Exhibiting the Post Offices, Post Roads, Canals, Rail Roads, &c. By David H. Burr (Late Topographer to the Post Office). . . . Entered according to the Act of Congress, July 10th, 1839.

1 inch to 10 miles. 4 sections, each 19¼ x 25½. Published. Also shows counties (in color), mileages between post offices, township and range numbers, military posts, Indian reservations, physical features, and adjoining portions of Canada. Filed as RG 28: Burr Atlas, map 13.

397. Sketch [map] of the Public Surveys in the North Part of Michigan. [n.d.]

1 inch to 18 miles. 22 x 13. Published. "Notes" of explanation concerning the status of township surveys as indicated by colors and symbols are given on the map. Filed as RG 46: 26th Cong., 1st sess.

398. C. Sketch [map] of the Public Surveys in the North Part of Michigan. [n.d.]

1 inch to 18 miles. 20½ x 16½. Published. All of the present State of Michigan is shown except the extreme southeastern portion. Shows extent and status of public land surveys. Map includes an explanation of the colors and symbols used on the map to indicate the status of township surveys. A copy of this map is published in S. Doc. 61, 26th Cong., 2d sess., Serial 377. Filed as RG 46: 26th Cong., 2d sess.

399. No. 2 [Map of] Michigan.

1 inch to ca. 38 miles. 12½ x 10½. Published. Shows land districts and locations of land offices in 1828 and 1841, and public lands offered for sale, 1828-41. 1828 land district boundaries are shown in red. For further explanation of the map see S. Doc. 92, 26th Cong., 2d sess., Serial 377. (This map without the 1828 land districts shown is filed as Michigan 5, Published, in RG 49.) Filed as RG 46: 26th Cong., 2d sess.

400. Sketch [Map] of the Public Surveys in the North Part of Michigan. [n.d.]

1 inch to 18 miles. 19½ x 16. Published. Shows status of public land surveys. Filed as RG 46: 27th Cong., 2d sess.

401. [Map of] Michigan . . . Entered according to Act of Congress in the year 1844 by Sidney E. Morse and Samuel Breese in the Clerks Office of the Southern District of New York.

1 inch to ca. 35 miles. 14½ x 18. Published. Counties, towns, roads, railroads, canals, and townships. Also portions of adjoining States. Filed as Ref. Coll.: Michigan 1844.

402. Map of the State of Michigan And the Surrounding Country Exhibiting the Sections and the latest surveys. Compiled from Authentic Sources By John Farmer, Detroit. 23rd Edition. . . . Engraved by John Farmer [1849].

1 inch to 12 miles. 32 x 23. Published. County (in color), towns, Indian villages, townships, mills, canals, railroads, and Indian reservations. Inset map of the "Copper District." Entered according to Act of Congress ... 1849. Filed as Ref. Coll.: Michigan 1849.

403. G Sketch [map] of the Public Surveys in Michigan [Issued by Surveyor General's Office, Detroit, Oct. 28, 1853].
1 inch to 18 miles. 23 x 22½. Published. Filed as RG 49: Michigan 7, Pub.

404. G Sketch [map] of the Public Surveys in Michigan [Issued by Surveyor General's Office, Detroit, Nov. 8, 1854].
1 inch to 18 miles. 23 x 22. Published. Filed as RG 49: Michigan 8, Pub.

405. G Sketch [map] of the Public Surveys in Michigan [Issued by Surveyor General's Office, Detroit, Oct. 23, 1856].
1 inch to 18 miles. 23 x 21. Published. Shows status of public land surveys. Filed as RG 46: S. Ex. Doc. 5, 34th Cong., 3d sess.

406. G Sketch (map) of the Public Surveys in Michigan [Issued by Surveyor General's Office, St. Paul, Oct. 26, 1857].
1 inch to 18 miles. 22 x 22. Published. Shows status of public land surveys. Filed as RG 46: S. Ex. Doc. 11, 35th Cong., 1st sess.

407. G Sketch of the Public Surveys in Michigan ... To accompany the annual Report of the Commissioner, Genl. Land Office. [Issued by the General Land Office on Oct. 2, 1866.]
1 inch to 18 miles. 22½ x 22. Published. County boundaries and mineral regions are shown in color. Also shows public surveys, county names, county seats, locations of land offices, wagon roads, railroads, land-grant railroads and their limits, and physical features. Inset map of Isle Royale [sic] and vicinity. No scale indicated. Filed as RG 49: Michigan 9, Pub.

408. Post Route Map of the States of Michigan and Wisconsin with adjacent parts of Ohio, Indiana, Illinois, Iowa, and Minnesota. ... by W. L. Nicholson, Topographer of P. O. Dept., 1871. ... Engraved by D. McClelland. ... Drawn by C. H. Poole ... [Revised] up to date of June 1, 1873.

1 inch to 10 miles. 2 sections, each 43½ x 29½. Frequency and types of mail service, mileages between post offices, counties, towns, and railroads. Post routes shown in color to illustrate frequency of service. Table lists distances between major cities. Filed as RG 28: Series 1, folder II.

409. [Map of the] State of Michigan. ... 1878. Compiled from the official Records of the General Land Office.
1 inch to 16 miles. 32½ x 26½. Published. County boundaries and Indian reservations are shown in color. Also shows public land surveys, towns and cities, principal railroad stations, locations of U.S. land offices, railroad lines, railroad land-grant limits, and physical features. Filed as RG 49: Michigan 1878, Pub.

410. [Map of the] State of Michigan. ... 1888. Compiled from the official Records of the General Land Office. ... Compiled and Drawn by A. F. Dinsmore.
1 inch to 16 miles. 35 x 29½. Published. County boundaries, Indian reservations, and private land claims are shown in color. Also shows public land surveys, towns and cities, locations of U.S. land offices, proposed and completed railroad lines, railroad land-grant limits, and physical features. Filed as RG 49: Michigan 1888, Pub.

411. Post Route Map of the States of Michigan and Wisconsin showing post offices with the intermediate distances on mail routes in operation on the 1st of March, 1901.
1 inch to 10 miles. 2 sections, each 47½ x 32¼. Published. Frequency and types of mail service, discontinued post offices, counties, towns, railroads, physical features, and parts of adjoining States. Post routes in color to show frequency of service. Inset map of Isle Royal. No scale indicated. Filed as RG 28: Michigan, 1901.

412. [Map of the] State of Michigan. Compiled from the official Records of the General Land Office. ... 1904. Revised and drawn by Charles J. Helm.
1 inch to 16 miles. 32 x 27. Published. County boundaries and Indian and military reservations are shown in color. Also shows towns and cities, public land surveys, and private land grants. Filed as RG 49: Michigan 1904, Pub.

MAPS OF STATES AND TERRITORIES

413. [Map of Michigan issued by the U.S. Geological Survey, 1916.]
1 inch to ca. 16 miles. 33 x 27½. Published. County names and boundaries, township and range numbers, towns and cities, steam and electric railroad lines, and drainage features. Filed as RG 57: Michigan 1916, Pub.

414. Post Route Map of the States of Michigan and Wisconsin showing post offices with the intermediate distances on mail routes in operation on the 1st of January, 1917.
1 inch to 9 miles. 4 sections, each 24 x 32. Published. Frequency and types of mail service, discontinued post offices, counties, towns, railroads, physical features, and parts of adjoining States. Inset map of Isle Royal. No scale indicated. Inset map of "Grand Rapids and Vicinity." Scale 1 inch to ca. 3 miles. Filed as RG 28: Michigan 1917.

MINNESOTA

415. Sectional Map of the Territory of Minnesota, Exhibiting the official Surveys, With a General Topographical Description. Compiled by J. Knauer, Civil Enginr. Published by J. H. Colton ... 1853.
1 inch to 6 miles. 26½ x 28½. Annotated published. Annotated to show additional roads and place names. Settlements including Indian villages, military posts, public land surveys, roads, and trails. Map accompanied by book *Minnesota Territory: An account of Its Geography, Resources, and Settlement; Together with the Census of 1850.* 17 pp. 6 x 4. Filed as RG 77: Q 58.

416. (H) Sketch [map] of the Public Surveys in the Territory of Minnesota. [Issued by Surveyor General's Office, St. Paul, "October 26th, 1856."]
1 inch to 18 miles. 23 x 21. Published. Shows status of public land surveys. Filed as RG 46: S. Ex. Doc. 11, 35th Cong., 1st sess.

417. (H) Sketch [map] of the Public Surveys in the Territory of Minnesota. [Dated Oct. 26, 1856, Surveyor General's Office, St. Paul, Minnesota Territory.]
1 inch to 18 miles. 22 x 20½. Annotated published. Annotated to show land district boundaries and locations of land offices. Also shows military posts and a few towns. See entry 416. Filed as RG 49: Minnesota 3.

418. Sectional Map of the Surveyed Portion of Minnesota and the North Western Part of Wisconsin ... C. A. Swett, Engraver, Boston, Mass. Entered according to Act of Congress in the year 1857, by J. S. Sewall.
1 inch to 12 miles. 33 x 25. Published. Counties (in color), towns, roads, Indian reservations, townships, and physical features. Also shows part of Wisconsin. Filed as Ref. Coll.: Minnesota, 1857.

419. (F) Sketch [map] of the Public Surveys in the State of Minnesota. [Dated Oct. 10, 1859, Surveyor General's Office, St. Paul, Minn.]
1 inch to 18 miles. 24 x 21. Annotated published. Annotated apparently with information relating to land districts and land offices in 1860. Also shows towns and cities, military posts, and Indian reserves. See entry 420. Filed as RG 49: Minnesota 5.

420. (F) Sketch [map] of the Public Surveys in State of Minnesota [Issued by Surveyor General's Office, St. Paul, Oct. 10, 1859].
1 inch to 18 miles. 24 x 22½. Published. Shows status of public land surveys. Filed as RG 46: S. Ex. Doc. 2, 36th Cong., 1st sess.

421. Map Exhibiting the location of the U.S. Military Roads in Minnesota And also in the N.W. Portions of Iowa & Wisconsin. Surveyed & constructed between the years 1851 and 1859 Under the direction of Captains J. H. Simpson, Geo. Thom, and Howard Stansbury, Corps Topl. Engrs.
1 inch to ca. 16 miles. 31½ x 22. Manuscript. Shows status and types of roads, towns, and military reservations. Map is dated January 10th, 1859, in the "Office of U.S. Gov't. roads" in St. Paul, Minn. Filed as RG 77: Rds. 156.

MINNESOTA

422. (F) Sketch [map] of the Public Surveys in the State of Minnesota [Issued by Surveyor General's Office, St. Paul, Oct. 10, 1860].

    1 inch to 18 miles. 23 x 20½. Published. Shows status of public land surveys. Filed as RG 46: S. Ex. Doc. 1, 36th Cong., 2d sess.

423. Sketch of the Public Surveys in the State of Minnesota. [Issued by the General Land Office on Oct. 2, 1866.]

    1 inch to 18 miles. 23 x 20. Annotated published. Annotated and colored to show Chippewa land cessions of 1854, 1855, and 1863, and reservations established by various treaties. Includes note on the removal of the Chippewas to the White Earth Reservation as provided by act of Congress approved May 29, 1872. County boundaries, railroad land-grant limits, and mining areas also are shown in color. Map also shows locations of land offices, completed and proposed railroad lines, military posts, and a few towns. Filed as RG 49: Minnesota 7.

424. Chapman's Sectional Map of the Surveyed part of Minnesota, Published By Silas Chapman, Milwaukee, Wis., 1870. Lith. by Doniat & Zastrow, Milwaukee, Wis.

    1 inch to ca. 10 miles. 32 x 29½. Published. Counties (in color), parts of adjoining States, towns, physical features, townships and sections, and railroads. Shows all of Minnesota except northern and extreme northeastern portion. Filed as Ref. Coll.: Minnesota 1870.

425. Map of Minnesota Showing the extent of the Public Surveys and other detail. Compiled under the direction of C. T. Brown, Surveyor General ... 1871.

    1 inch to 12 miles. 36 x 33. Manuscript. County and land district boundaries are shown in color. Also shows locations of U.S. land offices, completed and proposed railroad lines, towns and villages, and mines and mineral ranges. Filed as RG 49: Minnesota 8.

426. Post Route Map of the State of Minnesota with adjacent parts of Iowa, Nebraska, Dakota, Wisconsin, and of the British Possessions. . . . 1876.

    1 inch to 10 miles. 57½ x 42½. Published. Counties, settlements, railroad lines, post offices, and distances between post offices. Post routes shown in color to illustrate frequency of service. Filed as RG 75: map 277.

427. [Map of the] State of Minnesota. . . . 1876. Compiled from the official Records of the General Land Office.

    1 inch to 15 miles. 31 x 24½. Published. County names and boundaries, status of public land surveys, towns and cities, Indian reservations and lands, railroad lines, and railroad land-grant limits. Filed as RG 49: Minnesota 1876, Pub.

428. [Map of the] State of Minnesota. . . . 1879. Compiled from the official Records of the General Land Office.

    1 inch to 15 miles. 33½ x 27. Annotated published. County and land district boundaries are shown in color. Also shows status of public land surveys, locations of U.S. land offices, towns and cities, principal railroad stations, military posts, railroad lines and land-grant limits, and Indian lands and reservations. Annotated in upper margin apparently with information relating to the land-grant limits of the Northern Pacific Railroad. Filed as RG 49: Minnesota 14.

429. Post Route Map of the State of Minnesota with Adjacent parts of Iowa, Nebraska, Dakota, Wisconsin, and of the British Possessions, showing post offices, with the intermediate distances between them and mail routes in operation on 1st December, 1883 ... under direction of C. Roeser, Jr., Topographer of P. O. Dept., 1883. ... Engraved by D. McClelland.

    1 inch to 10 miles. 2 sections, each 30½ x 43. Frequency and types of mail service, mileages between post offices, counties, towns, military posts, and railroads. Post routes shown in color to illustrate frequency of service. Table lists distances between major cities in the United States. Filed as RG 28: series 1, folder V.

430. [Map of the] State of Minnesota. . . . 1884. Compiled from the official Records of the General Land Office.

    1 inch to 15 miles. 26½ x 29½. Published. County boundaries and Indian reservations are shown in color. Also shows status of public land surveys, towns and cities, principal railroad stations, locations of U.S. land offices, railroad lines, railroad land-grant limits, and physical features. Filed as RG 49: Minnesota 1884, Pub.

431. Post Route Map of the State of Minnesota with adjacent parts of Iowa, Nebraska, Dakota,

Wisconsin, and of the British Possessions; Showing post offices with the intermediate distances and mail routes in operation on the 1st of October, 1885. Published ... under the direction of W. L. Nicholson, Topographer, P. O. Dept. ... Engraved by D. McClelland.

1 inch to 10 miles. 2 sections, each 29½ x 44. Published. Frequency and types of mail service, mileages between post offices, discontinued post offices, counties, towns, railroads, and physical features. Post routes in color to show frequency of service. Filed as RG 28: series 1, folder XIII.

432. [Map of the] State of Minnesota.... 1887. Compiled from the official Records of the General Land Office ... Compiled and drawn by A. F. Dinsmore.

1 inch to 15 miles. 34 x 27. Published. County boundaries and Indian reservations are shown in color. Also shows status of public land surveys, towns and cities, locations of U.S. land offices, railroad lines and land-grant limits, and physical features. Also a black and white base map for this date. 26½ x 33½. Filed as RG 49: Minnesota 1887, Pub.

433. [Map of the] State of Minnesota.... 1887. Compiled from the official Records of the General Land Office ... Compiled and drawn by A. F. Dinsmore.

1 inch to 15 miles. 32 x 26½. Annotated published. Annotated to show township and range numbers and land districts. Basic information is the same as that shown on entry 432. Filed as RG 49: Minnesota 15.

434. [Map of the] State of Minnesota.... 1894. Compiled from the official Records of the General Land Office ... Corrected to date by R. H. Morton. Traced and Lettered by I. P. Berthong.

1 inch to 12 miles. 38 x 33. Published. County names and boundaries, towns and cities, public land surveys, Indian reservations, and railroad lines. Drainage is shown in blue. Filed as RG 49: Minnesota 1894, Pub.

435. [Map of the] State of Minnesota.... 1894. Compiled from the official Records of the General Land Office ... Corrected to date by R. H. Morton. Traced and Lettered by I. P. Berthong.

1 inch to 12 miles. 38½ x 33½. Annotated published. Annotated to show land district boundaries and locations of land offices. Basic information is the same as that shown on entry 434. Filed as RG 49: Minnesota 22.

436. Post Route Map of the State of Minnesota, showing the post offices with the intermediate distances on mail routes in operation on the 1st of March, 1901.

1 inch to 10 miles. 42 x 35½. Published. Frequency and types of mail service, discontinued post offices, counties, towns, railroads, physical features, and parts of adjoining States and Canada. Post routes in color to show frequency of service. Inset map of "Environs of Saint Paul and Minneapolis." Scale 1 inch to ca. 5 miles. Filed as RG 28: Minnesota 1901.

437. [Map of the] State of Minnesota. Compiled from the official Records of the General Land Office ... 1905. ... Revised by A. F. Dinsmore ... Drawn by Charles J. Helm.

1 inch to 12 miles. 38 x 33. Published. County boundaries and Indian and military reservations are shown in color. Also shows public land surveys, towns and cities, locations of U.S. land offices, and railroad lines. Inset plan of Minneapolis-St. Paul and vicinity. Also a black and white base map for this date. 38½ x 33. Filed as RG 49: Minnesota 1905, Pub.

438. Post Route Map of the State of Minnesota showing post offices with the intermediate distances on mail routes in operation on the 1st of January, 1917.

1 inch to 10 miles. 45½ x 36½. Published. Frequency and types of mail service, discontinued post offices, counties, towns, railroads, physical features, and parts of adjoining States. Inset map of postal service in Cook County. No scale indicated. Also inset map of "Environs of Saint Paul and Minneapolis." Scale 1 inch to ca. 5 miles. Filed as RG 28: Minnesota 1917.

439. [Map of Minnesota issued by the U.S. Geological Survey, 1917.]

1 inch to ca. 16 miles. 33 x 23. Published. County names and boundaries, towns and cities, township and range numbers, steam and electric railroad lines, and drainage features. Filed as RG 57: Minnesota 1917, Pub.

See also entries 851-853.

MISSISSIPPI

440. Map of Mississippi Constructed from the Surveys in the General Land Office and other Documents, by John Melish. . . . Published by John Melish, 1819

1 inch to 15 miles. 24½ x 16½. Annotated published. County and Indian boundaries in color. Counties, township and range numbers, military posts, Indian lands, settlements, Indian villages, physical features, "G1. Gaines Road," "Gel. Jacksons Road from New Orleans to the Muscle Shoals," and "Road Made by Order of Government from Pierre River to Nashville 383 Miles." Map is annotated to show unexplained marks placed at intervals on the road from Pierre River to Nashville. Map also shows parts of adjoining States. Filed as RG 77: US 118.

441. Map of Mississippi Constructed from the Surveys in the General Land Office and other Documents, by John Melish. . . . Published by John Melish, 1819. Improved to 1820.

1 inch to 15 miles. 25½ x 18. Annotated published. County and Indian boundaries in color. Counties, public land surveys, military posts, settlements, Indian lands, Indian villages, roads and trails. Annotated to show a few additional townships, apparently locations of land offices, and Choctaw Boundary Line according to cession of 1820. Map is extremely discolored. Filed as RG 49: Mississippi 5.

442. [Map of] Mississippi From the Surveys in the General Land Office, By E. Gilman, Draughtsman . . . [1837].

1 inch to 12 miles. 34 x 24. Published. Shows public land surveys, Indian boundaries, and drainage features. Filed as RG 49: Mississippi 1, Pub.

443. Map of Mississippi, Louisiana, & Arkansas Exhibiting the Post Offices, Post Roads, Canals, Rail Roads, &c. By David H. Burr (Late Topographer to the Post Office). . . . Entered according to the Act of Congress, July 10th, 1839.

1 inch to 10 miles. 4 sections, 19¼ x 25½. Published. Also shows counties and parishes (in color), mileages between post offices, township and range numbers, forts, and physical features. Filed as RG 28: Burr Atlas, map 9.

444. Diagram of the Surveying District South of Tennessee. [Issued by the Surveyor's Office, Jackson, Miss., Oct. 1, 1840.]

1 inch to 18 miles. 16½ x 14. Published. Map shows State of Mississippi except area in northeastern portion. Shows extent and status of public land surveys. Map includes an explanation of the colors and symbols used to indicate the status of township surveys. A copy of this map is published in S. Doc. 61, 26th Cong., 2d sess., Serial 377. Filed as RG 46: 26th Cong., 2d sess.

445. Diagram of the Surveying District South of Tennessee. [Issued by the Surveyor's Office, Jackson, Miss., Oct. 1, 1840.]

1 inch to 18 miles. 17 x 14. Published. Map shows Mississippi except the extreme northeastern portion. Shows status of public land surveys, Indian boundaries, and names and boundaries of land districts. (A copy of this map is published in S. Doc. 61, 26th Cong., 2d sess.) Filed as RG 49: Mississippi 3, Pub.

446. Diagram of the Surveying District South of Tennessee. [n.d.]

1 inch to 18 miles. 17 x 14. Published. Map shows State of Mississippi except area in northeastern portion. Map includes an explanation of the colors and symbols used to indicate the status of township surveys. Filed as RG 46: 26th Cong., 1st sess.

447. Diagram of the Surveying District South of Tennessee. [Issued by Surveyor's Office, Jackson, Miss., Oct. 1, 1841.]

1 inch to 18 miles. 18½ x 19. Published. Shows status of public land surveys. Filed as RG 46: 27th Cong., 2d sess.

448. No. 8 [Map of] Mississippi.

1 inch to ca. 38 miles. 9½ x 8. Published. Shows land districts and locations of land offices in 1828 and 1841 and public land offered for sale, 1828-41. 1828 land district boundaries are shown in red. For further explanation of the map see S. Doc. 92, 26th Cong., 2d sess, Serial 377. (This map without the 1828 land districts shown is filed as Mississippi 2, Published, in RG 49.) Filed as RG 46: 26th Cong., 2d sess.

449. E Diagram of the Surveying District South of Tennessee. [Issued by the Surveyor's Office, Jackson, Miss., Oct. 15, 1847.]

1 inch to 18 miles. 18½ x 12. Published. Map

shows Mississippi except the extreme northeastern portion. Shows status of public land surveys, Indian boundaries, and names and boundaries of land districts. Filed as RG 49: Mississippi 4, Pub.

450. [Published post route map of Mississippi, Louisiana, and Arkansas annotated to show population by race, agricultural production, and kinds and number of livestock. ca. 1861-65.]
1 inch to 10 miles. 68 x 44. Annotated published. Population figures (white, free colored, and slave) shown by county or parish. This map is believed to have been compiled by the Census Office for the use of the Army during the Civil War. Filed as RG 57: Geological Survey Library.

451. Sketch of the Public Surveys in the State of Mississippi. [Issued by the General Land Office on Oct. 2, 1866.]
1 inch to 18 miles. 20 x 13. Published. County boundaries are shown in color. Public surveys, county names, towns, locations of land offices, railroad land-grant limits, land districts, Choctaw boundary lines, and drainage. Filed as RG 49: Mississippi 5, Pub.

452. Hardee's Geographical, Historical, and Statistical Official Map of Mississippi, Embracing Portions of Arkansas, Louisiana, and Tennessee, From Recent Surveys and Investigations and Officially Compiled Under Authority From the State Legislature by T. S. Hardee, State Engineer, A. D. 1872. [Approved July 12, 1872, by Governor R. C. Powers.]
1 inch to 12 miles. 41x29½. Annotated published. County names and boundaries, land districts (in color), public land surveys, roads, and railroad lines. Annotated to show names of land districts. Small inset map "Railroad and Geological Map of Mississippi." Various statistical tables. Filed as RG 49: Mississippi 12.

453. [Map of the] State of Mississippi.... 1878. Compiled from the official Records of the General Land Office.
1 inch to 12 miles. 33½ x 22½. Published. County boundaries in color. Public land surveys, towns, railroad lines, principal rail stations, and railroad land-grant limits. Drainage features. Filed as RG 49: Mississippi 1878, Pub.

454. Gray's New Map of Mississippi By Frank A. Gray. ... Copyright, 1878, by O. W. Gray & Son.
1 inch to ca. 15 miles. 31 x 18½. Published. Counties (in color), parts of adjoining States, railroads, canals, towns, townships, lighthouses, and lightships. Filed as RG 77: US 373-54.

455. [Map of the] State of Mississippi.... 1885. Compiled from the official Records of the General Land Office ... Drawn by G. P. Strum.
1 inch to 12 miles. 33 x 21½. Published. County boundaries, military and naval reservations, and railroad land-grant limits are shown in color. Also shows public land surveys, towns, principal railroad stations, railroad lines, and physical features. Also a black and white base map for this date. 32½ x 22½. Filed as RG 49: Mississippi 1885, Pub.

456. Post Route Map of the State of Mississippi showing post offices with the intermediate distances on mail routes in operation on the 1st of March, 1911.
1 inch to ca. 8 miles. 47 x 32. Published. Frequency and types of mail service, discontinued post offices, counties, towns, railroads, physical features, and parts of adjoining States. Post routes in color to show frequency of service. Filed as RG 28: Mississippi 1911.

457. [Map of the] State of Mississippi, Compiled from the official Records of the General Land Office ... 1915.... Compiled and Drawn by A. F. Dinsmore.... Traced and Lettered by George A. Daidy.
1 inch to 12 miles. 35 x 22½. Published. County and bird reservation boundaries, military and naval reservations, and surveying districts governed by Chickasaw, Huntsville, Choctaw, Washington, and St. Stephens meridians. Also shows township and range numbers, towns and cities, and railroad lines. Relief is shown in color. Also a black and white base map for this date. Does not show surveying districts. 36 x 23. Filed as RG 49: Mississippi 1915, Pub.

458. [Map of Mississippi issued by the U.S. Geological Survey, 1916.]
1 inch to ca. 16 miles. 24 x 16½. Published. County names and boundaries, township and range numbers, towns and cities, railroad lines, and drainage features. Also a copy of this map reprinted in 1918. Filed as RG 57: Mississippi 1916, Pub.

MISSOURI

459. Map of the States of Missouri & Illinois and Territory of Arkansas, taken from recent surveys in the Office of the Surveyor General at St. Louis by E. Browne and E. Barcroft. Engd. by John Warr. [Printed in 1827.]
 1 inch to 12 miles. 2 sections, each 30 x 41. Published. Counties (in color), township and range numbers, settlements, roads, forts, canals, Indian villages, lead mines, iron works, and information about characteristics of the land. Also includes descriptions of Military Bounty Lands. On reverse, "Col. McKinney, Off. Ind. Affairs, Washington City, 1827." Filed as RG 75: map 263.

460. Map of the States of Missouri and Illinois. 1831 [Added in pencil]. London. Published April 15, 1832, by I. T. Hinton & Simpkin & Marshall. Engraved & Printed by Fenner Sears & Co.
 1 inch to ca. 30 miles. 11½ x 16½. Published. Existing counties, towns, physical features, forts, and Indian lands. Filed as Ref. Coll.: Missouri 1832.

461. Diagram of the State of Missouri ... No. 3. (A). Accompanying Report of 29th Nov., 1838.
 1 inch to ca. 19 miles. 19 x 26. Published. "Notes" of explanation concerning the status of township surveys as indicated by colors and symbols given on the map. Filed as RG 46: S. Doc. 17, No. 11, 25th Cong., 3d sess.

462. Diagram of the State of Missouri. [Issued by the Surveyor General's Office, St. Louis, Mo., Oct. 1, 1839.]
 1 inch to ca. 20 miles. 19 x 24. Published. Shows extent of public land surveys. Map includes an explanation of the colors and symbols used to indicate the status of township surveys. "I. (Referred to in Report of the 1st of October, 1839.)" Filed as RG 46: 26th Cong., 1st sess.

463. Diagram of the State of Missouri. [Issued by the Surveyor General's Office, St. Louis, Oct. 1, 1840.]
 1 inch to ca. 18 miles. 19 x 23. Published. Shows extent and status of public land surveys. Map includes an explanation of the colors and symbols used on the map to indicate the status of township surveys. A copy of this map is published in S. Doc. 61, 26th Cong., 2d sess., Serial 377. Filed as RG 46: 26th Cong., 2d sess.

464. No. 5 [Map of] Missouri.
 1 inch to ca. 40 miles. 10 x 11. Published. Shows land districts and locations of land offices in 1828 and 1841 and public land offered for sale, 1828-41. 1828 land district boundaries are shown in red. For further explanation of the map see S. Doc. 92, 26th Cong., 2d sess., Serial 377. (This map without the 1828 land districts shown is filed as Missouri 2, Published, in RG 49.) Filed as RG 46: 26th Cong., 2d sess.

465. [Map of] Missouri ... Entered according to Act of Congress in the year 1844 by Sidney E. Morse and Samuel Breese in the Clerks Office of the Southern District of New York.
 1 inch to ca. 25 miles. 14 x 18. Published. Counties, towns, roads, railroads, canals, townships, and physical features. Also parts of adjoining States. Missouri is shaded orange. Filed as Ref. Coll.: Missouri 1844.

466. Sectional Map of the State of Missouri Compiled from the United States Surveys and other sources by the Publisher Edward Hutawa. . . . Engd. on Stone by Julius Hutawa. Entered in the Clerks Office of the U.S. District Court of Missouri on the 4th March, 1844.
 1 inch to 9 miles. 2 sections, each 43½ x 24½. Published. Counties (in color), towns, townships, roads, lead and coal mines, furnaces, navigable rivers, mills, forts, prairies, U.S. land districts, and parts of Indian reservations in adjoining Indian territory. Tables list area and population by county, land districts, and astronometrical observations. Inset sketch shows "Landings and Distances" along the Mississippi and Illinois rivers. Filed as RG 77: US 133.

467. H Diagram of the State of Missouri. [Issued by Surveyor General's Office, St. Louis, Nov. 1, 1844.]
 1 inch to ca. 20 miles. 19 x 24. Published. Shows extent and status of public land surveys. Filed as RG 49: Missouri 3, Pub.

468. A New Map of Missouri With Its Roads & Distances. H. S. Tanner. Published by C. S. Williams ... Philadelphia, 1846.
 1 inch to 30 miles. 14½ x 12. Published. Counties (in color), towns, canals, railroads, and physical

features. Table lists steamboat routes. Filed as Ref. Coll.: Missouri 1846.

469. B Diagram of the State of Missouri. [Issued by Surveyor General's Office, St. Louis, Nov. 17, 1851.]

1 inch to 18 miles. 19 x 24. Published. Shows extent and status of public land surveys. Filed as RG 49: Missouri 4, Pub.

470. E and F (combined) Diagram of the State of Missouri accompanying report of the 30th October, 1852. [Issued by the Surveyor General's Office, St. Louis, Oct. 30, 1852.]

1 inch to 18 miles. 20 x 25. Published. Shows status of public land surveys and progress of office work in connection with reclamation of swamp lands. Filed as RG 49: Missouri 5, Pub.

471. New Map of the State of Missouri, Compiled and constructed from United States Surveys and other authentic Sources by John T. Fiala, Civil Engineer. Published & sold by Chas. Robyn & Co., Lithographers ... St. Louis, Mo. [ca. 1860].

1 inch to 18 miles. 21¼ x 25. Annotated published. Counties (outlined in brown), towns, townships, railroads, roads, U.S. land districts, and parts of adjoining States and Territories. Annotated to show parts of several rivers colored red without explanation. Date on map from comparison with other maps. Filed as RG 77: Q 141.

472. Township Map of the State of Missouri, Showing the Location of Cities, Villages, Post Offices, Railways & Stations, Turnpikes, Common Roads &c. Published by E. Mendenhall ... 1860. ... Middleton Stroridge & Co., Lith., Cincinnati, O.

1 inch to 24 miles. 15½ x 18½. Published. Counties (in color), towns, roads, railroads, forts, and physical features. Small pieces of map are missing. Filed as Ref. Coll.: Missouri 1860.

473. [Published post route map of Missouri and Illinois annotated to show population by race in Missouri, ca. 1861-65.]

1 inch to 10 miles. 2 sections, each 34 x 44. Annotated published. Population of white, free colored, and slave, by county. Population figures are not shown for every county. Map is believed to have been compiled by the Census Office for the use of the Army during the Civil War. Filed as RG 57: Geological Survey Library.

474. Lloyd's Official Map of Missouri. 1861. Drawn and Engraved from actual Surveys for the ꞁ and Office Department. ... J. T. Lloyd, Publisher.

1 inch to 12 miles. 26¼ x 30. Published. Counties (in color), towns, townships, railroads, roads, and parts of adjoining States and Territories. Also advertisements for two other maps published by Lloyd. Filed as Ref. Coll.: Missouri 1861.

475. Fiala and Haren's New Sectional Map of the State of Missouri. Published by Gray & Crawford ... 1861. Lith. by Chas. Robyn & Co.

1 inch to ca. 12 miles. 29½ x 35. Published. Counties (in color), towns, roads, railroads, townships, U.S. land districts, furnaces, copper and lead mines, mineral deposits, and caves. Also parts of adjoining States. Filed as Ref. Coll.: Missouri 1861.

476. Colton's New Sectional Map of the State of Missouri, Compiled from the United States Surveys & Other Authentic Sources Exhibiting the Sections, Fractional Sections, Counties, Cities, Towns, Villages, Post Offices, Rail Roads & other Internal Improvements. Published by J. H. Colton ... 1861.

1 inch to 10 miles. 2 sections, each 38 x 21. Published. Counties shown in color. Filed as RG 77: Q 82.

477. (Map of the) State of Missouri. [Issued by the General Land Office on Oct. 2, 1866.]

1 inch to ca. 18 miles. 19½ x 22. Published. County boundaries, railroad land-grant limits, and mineral deposits are shown in color. Also shows public surveys, locations of land offices, county names, county seats, and physical features. Filed as RG 49: Missouri 6, Pub.

478. [Map of the] State of Missouri. ... 1878. Compiled from the official Records of the General Land Office.

1 inch to 14 miles. 27 x 34. Published. County boundaries (in color), public land surveys, towns and cities, principal railroad stations, railroad lines, and railroad land-grant limits. Drainage features. Filed as RG 49: Missouri 1878, Pub.

479. [Map of the] State of Missouri. ... 1886. Compiled from the official Records of the General Land Office.

1 inch to 14 miles. 27 x 29½. Published. County boundaries and railroad land-grant limits are shown in color. Also shows public land surveys, towns and cities, principal railroad stations, locations of U.S. land offices, railroad lines, and drainage features. Also a black and white base map for this date. 26 x 30. Filed as RG 49: Missouri 1886, Pub.

480. [Map of the] State of Missouri.... 1891. Compiled from the official Records of the General Land Office ... Compiled, drawn and lettered by M. Hendges.
1 inch to 12 miles. 31 x 35. Published. Counties (boundaries in color), public land surveys, towns and cities, locations of U.S. land offices, railroad lines, and drainage features. Also a black and white base map for this date. Drainage in blue. 29 x 33. Filed as RG 49: Missouri 1891, Pub.

481. [Map of the] State of Missouri. Compiled from the official Records of the General Land Office ... 1911. ... Compiled by M. Hendges.... Traced and Lettered by Thos. O. Wansleben.
1 inch to 12 miles. 31 x 35. Published. Counties (boundaries in color), public land surveys, towns and cities, railroad lines, and drainage features. Also a black and white base map for this date. 31 x 35. Filed as RG 49: Missouri 1911, Pub.

482. [Map of Missouri issued by the U.S. Geological Survey, 1917.]
1 inch to ca. 16 miles. 22½ x 26. Published. County names and boundaries, township and range numbers, towns and cities, steam and electric railroad lines, and drainage features. Filed as RG 57: Missouri 1917, Pub.

See also entries 237 and 247.

MONTANA

483. Map of the Territory of Montana with Portions of the Adjoining Territories. Showing the Gulch or Placer Diggings actually worked, and Districts where Quartz (Gold & Silver) Lodes have been discovered to January 1st, 1865. ... Drawn by W. W. de Lacy, for the use of The First Legislature of Montana. A. E. Smith, Lith. [1865]
1 inch to ca. 24 miles. 24½ x 33½. Annotated published. Counties, gulch diggings, and quartz lodes in color. Also towns, physical features, roads, and military posts. Inset map "... showing the Routes from the Missouri River to Fort Laramie, where they connect with the large Map." Filed as Ref. Coll.: Montana 1865.

484. Map of the Territory of Montana to Accompany the Report of the Surveyor General. [Dated 1869, but the "9" is corrected in pencil to "8".]
1 inch to 15 miles. 32 x 42½. Manuscript. Extent of public land surveys, towns, roads, and military posts. County boundaries and mining areas are added in color. Noted in GLO as "Map accompanying the Commissioner's Annual Report for 1868." Relief is shown by hachures. Filed as RG 49: Montana 2.

485. Map of the Public Land Surveys in Montana Territory, to accompany the Annual Report of the Commissioner of the General Land Office. 1869.
1 inch to 15 miles. 32 x 44. Manuscript. Extent of public land surveys, towns, trails, and military posts. County boundaries, Indian reservation boundaries, and mining areas are added in color. Relief is shown by hachures. Filed as RG 49: Montana 3.

486. Map of the Territory of Montana, to Accompany the Report of the Surveyor General ... 1870.
1 inch to 15 miles. 32 x 43. Manuscript. Extent of public land surveys, towns, trails, and military posts. County boundaries, Indian reservation boundaries, and mining areas are added in color. Relief is shown by hachures. Filed as RG 49: Montana 4.

487. Map of the Territory of Montana, to Accompany the Report of the Surveyor General.... 1871.

1 inch to 15 miles. 32 x 42½. Manuscript. Extent of public land surveys, towns, roads, and military posts. County and Indian reservation boundaries and mining areas are added in color. Relief is shown by hachures. Filed as RG 49: Montana 5.

488. Map of the Territory of Montana, to Accompany the Report of the Surveyor General. 1874.

1 inch to 12 miles. 2 sections, each 37 x 27. Manuscript. Extent of public land surveys, towns, roads, military reservations, and proposed railroads. County and Indian reservation boundaries and mining areas are added in color. Filed as RG 49: Montana 6.

489. [Map of the] Territory of Montana.... 1876. Compiled from the official Records of the General Land Office.

1 inch to 20 miles. 26½ x 33½. Published. County and land district boundaries, railroad land-grant limits, and Indian reservations are shown in color. Also shows status of public land surveys, towns, locations of U.S. land offices, and military reservations. Relief is shown by hachures. Also a black and white base map for this date. 24 x 33. Filed as RG 49: Montana 1876, Pub.

490. Map of the Territory of Montana, with Portions of the Adjoining Territories, Compiled and drawn by W. W. DeLacy, Civil Engineer & Surveyor, Helena, M. T., 1878. Second Edition, corrected & improved. Engraved, Printed and Published by G. W. & C. B. Colton & Co.

1 inch to 20 miles. 29½ x 43. Published. Counties, military reserves, and mineral deposits shown in color. Also towns, military posts, townships, physical features, Indian reservations, roads, and railroads. Inset map of "The Northwestern Portion of the United States" showing States as far east as Wisconsin and Illinois. Filed as RG 77: Q 324.

491. [Map of] Montana Territory, 1879. Compiled from the official Records of the General Land Office.

1 inch to 20 miles. 27 x 34. Published. County boundaries, and military and Indian reservations are shown in color. Also shows status of public land surveys, towns, locations of U.S. land offices, railroad lines, and railroad land-grant limits. Relief is shown by hachures. Filed as RG 49: Montana 1879, Pub.

492. [Map of] Montana Territory, 1879. Compiled from the official Records of the General Land Office.

1 inch to 20 miles. 26½ x 33½. Annotated published. Annotated to show land districts. Basic information same as that shown on entry 491. Filed as RG 49: Montana 7.

493. [Map of] Montana Territory ... 4th Edition, 1881. Compiled under direction of Lieut. Edward Maguire, Corps of Engrs., by Prvt. Julius J. Durage, Topogl. Asst.

1 inch to ca. 12 miles. 2 sections, 36 x 28 and 30 x 28. Published. Settlements, military posts, wagon roads, Indian reservations, and routes of exploration. Relief is shown by hachures. Portion of map showing extreme southwestern Montana is missing. Filed as RG 77: 1881, Pub.

494. [Map of] Montana Territory. ... 1883. Compiled from the official Records of the General Land Office.

1 inch to 18 miles. 26½ x 33½. Published. County boundaries and military and Indian reservations are shown in color. Also shows status of public land surveys, towns, locations of U.S. land offices, and railroad lines and land-grant limits. Relief is shown by hachures. Also a black and white base map for this date. 25 x 34½. Filed as RG 49: Montana 1883, Pub.

495. Post Route Map of the Territories of Montana, Idaho, and Wyoming with parts of adjacent States and Territories showing post offices, with the intermediate distances between them and mail routes in operation on 1st December, 1883 ... under direction of C. Roeser Jr., Topographer of P. O. Dept., 1883.

1 inch to 15 miles. 2 sections, each 43 x 30. Frequency and types of mail service, mileages between post offices, counties, discontinued post offices, towns, military posts, and railroads. Post routes shown in color to illustrate frequency of service. Filed as RG 28: series 1, folder V.

496. Post Route Map of the Territories of Montana, Idaho, and Wyoming, with parts of Adjacent States and Territories, showing post offices with the intermediate distances and mail routes in operation on the 1st of October, 1885. Published ... under the direction of W. L. Nicholson, Topographer, P. O. Dept.

1 inch to 15 miles. 2 sections, each 44 x 29.

Published. Frequency and types of mail service, mileages between post offices, discontinued post offices, counties, towns, railroads, military posts, and physical features. Post routes in color to show frequency of service. Filed as RG 28: series 1, folder IX.

497. Official Map of the Territory of Montana. Drawn for the use of the Territorial Schools By William P. Snow, 1886. George E. Boos & Co., Helena, Montana. Engraved and Manufactured by G. W. & C. B. Colton & Co.

1 inch to 15 miles. 32 x 42. Published. County boundaries and Indian reservations in color. Also towns, railroads, military reservations, military posts, and townships. Map is signed by Governor of Montana, President of the Council, and Supt. of Public Instruction. Filed as RG 77: Q 538.

498. Post Route Map of the Territories of Montana, Idaho, and Wyoming with parts of adjacent States and Territories, showing post offices with the intermediate distances and mail routes in operation on the 1st of December, 1886. Published . . . under the direction of W. L. Nicholson, Topographer, P. O. Dept.

1 inch to 15 miles. 2 sections, each 44 x 29½. Published. Frequency and types of mail service, mileages between post offices, discontinued post offices, counties, towns, railroads, military posts, and physical features. Post routes in color to show frequency of service. Filed as RG 28: series 1, folder XVI.

499. Post Route Map of the Territories of Montana, Idaho, and Wyoming with parts of adjacent States and Territories, showing post offices with the intermediate distances and mail routes in operation on the 1st of February, 1887. Published . . . under the direction of W. L. Nicholson, Topographer, P. O. Dept.

1 inch to 15 miles. 2 sections, each 44 x 27½. Published. Frequency and types of mail service, mileages between post offices, discontinued post offices, counties, towns, railroads, and physical features. Post routes in color to show frequency of service. Filed as RG 28: series 1, folder XXII.

500. Post Route Map of the States of Montana, Idaho, and Wyoming with parts of adjacent States and Territories, showing post offices with the intermediate distances and mail routes in operation on the 1st of April 1891. Published . . . under the direction of C. Roeser Jr., Topographer, P. O. Dept. [Corrected to May 1, 1891.]

1 inch to 12 miles. 2 sections, each 44 x 27½. Published. Frequency and types of mail service, mileages between post offices, discontinued post offices, counties, towns, railroads, military posts, and physical features. Post routes in color to show frequency of service. Filed as RG 28: series 1, folder XXV.

501. Post Route Map of the States of Montana, Idaho, and Wyoming with parts of adjacent States and Territories, showing post offices with the intermediate distances and mail routes in operation on the 1st of June, 1891. Published . . . under the direction of C. Roeser Jr., Topographer, P. O. Dept.

1 inch to 12 miles. 2 sections, each 43½ x 27½. Published. Frequency and types of service, mileages between post offices, discontinued post offices, counties, towns, railroads, and physical features. Post routes in color to show frequency of service. Filed as RG 28: series 1, folder XXVI.

502. [Map of the] State of Montana. . . . 1892. Compiled from the official Records of the General Land Office. . . . Traced and Lettered by I. P. Berthong.

1 inch to 15 miles. 30 x 40. Published. County boundaries and military and Indian reservations are shown in color. Also shows status of public land surveys, towns and cities, locations of U.S. land offices, boundaries of Yellowstone National Park, and proposed and completed railroad lines. Relief is shown in color. Also a black and white base map for this date. Drainage shown in blue. 27½ x 40. Filed as RG 49: Montana 1892, Pub.

503. [Map of the] State of Montana. . . . 1894. Compiled from the official Records of the General Land Office.

1 inch to 12 miles. 35 x 50. Published. County boundaries and military and Indian reservations are shown in color. Also shows status of public land surveys, towns and cities, locations of U.S. land offices, boundaries of Yellowstone National Park, and railroad lines. Relief is shown in color. Also a black and white base map for this date. 33 x 50. Relief in brown. Filed as RG 49: Montana 1894, Pub.

504. Map of the State of Montana. Compiled from the official Records of the General Land Office ... 1897. ... Compiled by R. H. Morton. ... Revised and Lettered by I. P. Berthong.

1 inch to 12 miles. 32½ x 49. Published. County boundaries and military and Indian reservations are shown in color. Also shows status of public land surveys, towns and cities, locations of U.S. land offices, boundaries of Yellowstone National Park, and railroad lines. Relief is shown in color. Also a black and white base map for this date, with drainage shown in blue. 32½ x 48½. Filed as RG 49: Montana 1897, Pub.

505. Map of the State of Montana. Compiled from the official Records of the General Land Office ... 1897. ... Compiled by R. H. Morton. ... Revised and Lettered by I. P. Berthong.

1 inch to 12 miles. 34 x 50½. Annotated published. Annotated to show land district boundaries and locations of land offices. Basic information same as that shown in entry 504. Filed as RG 49: Montana 25.

506. [Map of the] State of Montana. Compiled from the official Records of the General Land Office ... 1907. [Compiled, drawn, and lettered by Daniel O'Hare.]

1 inch to 12 miles. 33 x 51½. Published. County boundaries and names, status of public land surveys, locations of U.S. land offices, Indian and military reservations, boundaries of Yellowstone National Park, names of national forests, railroad lines, and drainage features. Small inset plans of Missoula, Butte, Helena, and Great Falls. Filed as RG 49: Montana 1907, Pub.

507. [Map of the] State of Montana. [Showing] Lands designated by the Secretary of the Interior, April 27, 1909, under the Enlarged Homestead Act of Feb. 19, 1909. [Issued by the Department of the Interior.]

1 inch to 24 miles. 19 x 26½. Published. Areas designated are shaded red. Also shows public land surveys. Filed as RG 49: Montana 6, Pub.

508. [Map of the] State of Montana. Compiled from the official Records of the General Land Office ... 1911. ... Compiled and Drawn by Daniel O'Hare.

1 inch to 12 miles. 33¾ x 51. Published. County and land district boundaries, national forests, national parks and monuments, boundaries of Indian and military reservations, boundaries of State parks and game preserves, and reclamation projects are shown in color. Also shows status of public land surveys, towns and cities, locations of U.S. land offices, and railroad lines. Relief is shown in color. Small inset plans of Missoula, Butte, Helena, and Great Falls. Also a black and white base map for this date. 36½ x 51. Filed as RG 49: Montana 1911, Pub.

509. [Map of] State of Montana. Compiled from the official Records of the General Land Office ... 1911. ... Compiled and Drawn by Daniel O'Hare.

1 inch to 12 miles. 35 x 52. Annotated published. Annotated to show new county boundaries and land district boundaries. Basic information same as that shown on entry 508. Filed as RG 49: Montana 45.

510. [Map of the] State of Montana. [Showing] Lands designated by the Secretary of the Interior Under the provisions of the Enlarged Homestead Acts. Edition of July 1, 1916. [Issued by the Department of the Interior.]

1 inch to 24 miles. 19 x 26. Published. Areas designated are shaded red. Also shows public land surveys. Filed as RG 49: Montana 12, Pub.

511. [Map of the] State of Montana. Compiled from the official Records of the General Land Office ... 1917. ... Compiled by A. F. Dinsmore. ... Traced and lettered by Wm. Bauman, Jr.

1 inch to 12 miles. 34 x 50½. Published. County and land district boundaries, national forests, national parks and monuments, boundaries of military and Indian reservations, and reclamation projects. Also shows status of public land surveys, towns and cities, locations of U.S. land offices, and railroad lines. Small inset plans of Missoula, Butte, Helena, Great Falls, and Billings. Also a black and white base map for this date. 33 x 51½. Filed as RG 49: Montana 1917, Pub.

512. Post Route Map of the States of Montana, Idaho, and Wyoming, showing post offices with the intermediate distances on mail routes in operation on the 1st of January, 1917.

1 inch to ca. 12 miles. 2 sections, each 49½ x 32½. Published. Frequency and types of mail service, discontinued post offices, counties, towns, railroads, physical features, and parts of adjoining States. Filed as RG 28: Montana 1917.

NEBRASKA

513. [Map of the] State of Montana. [Showing] Lands designated by the Secretary of the Interior Under the provisions of the Enlarged Homestead Acts. Edition of June 30, 1918. [Issued by the Department of the Interior.]
1 inch to 24 miles. 18 x 26. Published. Areas designated are shaded red. Shows public land surveys. Filed as RG 49: Montana 14, Pub.

514. [Map of the] State of Montana. [Showing] Lands designated as non-irrigable by the Secretary of the Interior under the provisions of the Enlarged Homestead Acts ... Edition of June 30, 1920. [Issued by the Department of the Interior.]
1 inch to 24 miles. 17½ x 26½. Published. Areas designated are shaded red. Shows public land surveys. Filed as RG 49: Montana 15, Pub.

515. [Map of part of the United States showing Montana and Idaho. n.d.]
Small scale. 14½ x 18. Annotated published. Annotated to show in color the boundaries of Montana and Idaho and Indian reservations and ceded land therein. Notations concerning appropriations of 1864 and 1866 and treaties and acts pertaining to Indian lands from 1867 to 1870. Filed as RG 49: Montana 1.

See also entry 214.

NEBRASKA

516. Map of Nebraska and Kansas Territories. Showing the Locations of the Indian Reserves, according to the Treaties of 1854. Compiled by S. Eastman, Captain, U.S.A., 1854.... Published by Lippincott, Grambo & Co.
1 inch to 20 miles. 25 x 36½. Annotated published. Map includes parts of the present States of Wyoming, Colorado, and Oklahoma. Territorial and Indian reservation boundaries shown in color. Also shows general locations of Indian tribes not assigned to reservations, military posts, physical features, acres (some approximate) in Indian reservations, and the route of the Santa Fe Trail. List of "Notes from Indian Treaties Made in 1854" briefly describing Indian land cessions. Note in lower left corner of map signed by Commissioner of Indian Affairs states: "I have examined this map in regard to the Indian Reserves and find the same correct." Filed as RG 77: IR 69.

517. Map of Nebraska From Explorations of Lt. G. K. Warren, Topl. Engrs., in 1855, 56, & 57, and other authorities.
1 inch to ca. 100 miles. 12 x 12½. Published. Includes present States of Nebraska and North and South Dakota as well as parts of other neighboring States. Settlements, military posts, and physical features. Note states "Heavy dotted lines show Routes probably practicable." (Two other versions of this map, together with a letter by Lt. Warren dated January 29, 1858, concerning his explorations in Nebraska Territory are filed as RG 77: Q 238.) Filed as RG 77: 1857, Pub.

518. Military Map of Nebraska and Dakota By Lieut. G. K. Warren, Topl. Engrs. From the Explorations made by him in 1855, 56, and in 1857.
1 inch to ca. 20 miles. 45 x 33. Published. Settlements, military posts, Indian reservations, and routes of expeditions including those of earlier explorers. Note signed by Warren states "March 4th, 1860, Engraving carefully revised." Filed as RG 46: 35th Cong., 1st sess.

519. Territory of Nebraska Embracing the public Surveys up to the summer of 1857. Compiled & drawn in the Surveyor General's Office from original notes, by Quin, Smith, & Van Zandt ... Leopold Gast & Brother, Lith.
1 inch to 5 miles. 36 x 24. Annotated published. Map shows Nebraska east of the sixth principal meridian and south of the seventh standard parallel. Public surveys, counties, towns, Indian reservations, Indian villages, roads including small segment of the "Mormon Road to Utah," and physical features. County boundaries are in color. "Lieut. Warren" is written in upper right margin. Filed as RG 77: Q 758.

520. Sectional Map of Nebraska Territory, Compiled from the Field Notes in the Surveyor General's Office, by Robert L. Ream. Showing the Counties, Townships Sections, Topography, Cities, Villages, and Internal Improvements &c. Published by E. Mendenhall . . . 1857. Middleton Wallace & Co., Lithographers.

1 inch to 8 miles. 27 x 20. Area from the Missouri River to about 98° longitude. Counties (in color), towns, Indian reservations, extent of public land surveys, and physical features. Three red lines have been drawn on the map but no explanation is given. Map bears stamp "Office Expl[oratio]ns. & Surveys War Dept." Filed as RG 77: Q 761.

521. (11) Map Showing the Progress of the Public Surveys in . . . Nebraska, 1865.

Scale not indicated. 12½ x 33. Annotated published. Shows a few towns, military posts, and Indian reserves. Annotated with information pertaining to the appropriations and cost of surveys for 1866-68. Two sheets previously attached have been detached and laminated separately. Part of the map showing Kansas has been cut off. Filed as RG 49: Nebraska 5.

522. Map Showing the progress of the Public surveys in Nebraska. 1868.

1 inch to 12 miles. 21½ x 44. Manuscript. County boundaries, railroad land-grant limits, locations of land offices, and coal and salt lands are shown in color. Also shows towns, military and Indian reservations, and railroad lines. Noted on map, "Map accompanying the Commissioners Annual Report for 1868." Filed as RG 49: Nebraska 6.

523. (A) Diagram of Nebraska Exhibiting character of the Soil and Timber, and Projected and completed Railroads. [Dated Aug. 21, 1869, Surveyor General's Office, Plattsmouth, Neb.]

1 inch to 24 miles. 19½ x 23½. Manuscript. Timber and coal lands, sandhills, swamplands, clay and marl bluffs, salt springs, and projected railroad lines are shown in color. No towns or place names are shown. Filed as RG 49: Nebraska 7.

524. Map showing the Progress of the Public Surveys in Nebraska, 1870.

1 inch to 12 miles. 31 x 39½. Manuscript. County and land district boundaries, railroad land-grant limits, and coal and salt lands are shown in color. Parts of this map are missing. Map also shows towns, military posts, and Indian reserves. Filed as RG 49: Nebraska 8.

525. Map showing the state and progress of public Surveys in Nebraska, 1871, made under the direction of E. E. Cunningham, Surveyor General for Nebraska and Iowa.

1 inch to 12 miles. 32 x 40½. Manuscript. Map bears description of land district boundaries, and shows locations of land offices, county boundaries, railroad land-grant limits, and coal and salt lands in color. Also shows towns and military and Indian reservations. Filed as RG 49: Nebraska 9.

526. Map of Military Department of the Platte, Nebraska. Sheet No. 2. Compiled under the direction of Captain W. A. Jones, Corps of Engineers, Omaha, Nebraska, 1872.

1 inch to 18.94 miles. 22½ x 30. Published. Map includes Nebraska and parts of adjacent States and Territories. Shows settlements, Indian reservations, roads, railroads, military posts, and drainage features. Filed as RG 77: 1872, Pub.

527. [Map of the] State of Nebraska. . . . 1876. Compiled from the official Records of the General Land Office.

1 inch to 15 miles. 21 x 32½. Published. County names and boundaries, names of land districts, status of public land surveys, towns, locations of U.S. land offices, military and Indian reservations, railroad lines and land-grant limits, and drainage features. Filed as RG 49: Nebraska 1876, Pub.

528. [Map of the] State of Nebraska. . . . 1879. Compiled from the official Records of the General Land Office.

1 inch to 15 miles. 22½ x 32½. Published. County boundaries and military and Indian reservations are shown in color. Also shows status of public land surveys, towns, locations of U.S. land offices, railroad lines and land-grant limits, and drainage features. Filed as RG 49: Nebraska 1879, Pub.

529. Map of Nebraska compiled and drawn under direction of Capt. W. S. Stanton, Corps of Engineers, by Mathew Hendges, Draughtsman, and Corp'l. Ernst Wagner, 9th Infy., 1881.

1 inch to 7.89 miles. 2 sections, each 30 x 34. Published. Map includes Nebraska and parts of adjoining States and Territories. Shows settlements, military posts, Indian reservations, roads, railroads, drainage features, and remarks about the characteristics of the land. Filed as RG 77: Q 430.

530. [Map of the] State of Nebraska. ... 1884. Compiled from the official Records of the General Land Office ... Compiled and Drawn by M. Hendges.

1 inch to 15 miles. 23 x 32½. Published. County boundaries, military and Indian reservations, and railroad land-grant limits are shown in color. Also shows status of public land surveys, towns and cities, locations of U.S. land offices, railroad lines, and physical features. Relief is shown by hachures. Also a black and white base map for this date. 23½ x 32. Filed as RG 49: Nebraska 1884, Pub.

531. [Map of] Nebraska ... 1884.

1 inch to 12 miles. 29 x 42. Manuscript. Public land surveys, towns and cities, county names and boundaries, military reservations, and railroad lines. Filed as RG 49: Nebraska 13.

532. [Map of] State of Nebraska. ... 1890. Compiled from the official Records of the General Land Office ... Compiled and drawn by M. Hendges.

1 inch to 14 miles. 26½ x 37. Published. County names and boundaries, public land surveys, towns and cities, locations of U.S. land offices, railroad lines, and drainage features. Filed as RG 49: Nebraska 1890, Pub.

533. Official Railway Map of Nebraska, 1907. Map of Nebraska issued by the Nebraska State Railway Commission ... Copyright 1907, by The J. N. Matthews Co.

1 inch to 12 miles. 22 x 40. Published. County boundaries and railroads in color. Also towns, townships, canals, and electric railways. Table lists "Shipment of Live Stock and Farm Products." Inset maps show production of corn, wheat, and swine in Nebraska. Graphs show population information. Filed as Ref. Coll.: Nebraska 1907.

534. [Map of the] State of Nebraska Compiled from the official Records of the General Land Office ... 1908. ... Compiled by A. F. Dinsmore. ... Traced and lettered by Wm. Bauman, Jr.

1 inch to 12 miles. 29 x 41. Published. County and land district boundaries, military reservations, and national forests are shown in color. Also shows public land surveys, towns and cities, locations of U.S. land offices, railroad lines, and drainage features. Relief is shown in color. Inset plan of Omaha. Also a black and white base map for this date. 29 x 41. Filed as RG 49: Nebraska 1908, Pub.

535. Post Route Map of the State of Nebraska showing post offices with the intermediate distances on mail routes in operation on the 1st of January, 1917.

1 inch to 10 miles. 2 sections, each 29½ x 26. Published. Frequency and types of mail service, discontinued post offices, counties, towns, railroads, physical features, and parts of adjoining States. Filed as RG 28: Nebraska 1917.

See also entries 296-298, 300-308, 318, and 632.

NEVADA

536. Degroot's Map of Nevada Territory, Exhibiting a Portion of Southern Oregon & Eastern California ... Published by Warren Holt ... 1863.

1 inch to 12¼ miles. 39 x 32. Annotated published. Counties (in color), mining districts, mining and Indian camps, wagon roads, proposed railroad routes, trails, and tule lands. Annotated to show several Indian reservations. Filed as RG 75: map 302.

537. Map of the State of Nevada, Published by Warren Holt ... 1866.

1 inch to 12 miles. 35 x 29½. Annotated published. Counties (in color), settlements, mining districts, trails, and roads. Annotated in red ink to show "The names and population of the different Indian tribes—The boundary lines of the districts over which they roam; and of the 'Walker,' 'Pyramid,' and 'Timber' Reserves ...." Filed as RG 75: map 178.

538. Map of the State of Nevada to accompany the Annual Report of the Commr., Genl. Land Office, 1866. [Issued by the General Land Office on Oct. 2, 1866.]
1 inch to 18 miles. 27 x 19½. Published. County boundaries, mining districts, and mineral deposits are shown in color. Also shows public surveys, names of counties, names of mining districts, settlements, roads, military posts, Indian reservations, proposed route of the Central Pacific Railroad, and physical features. Filed as RG 49: Nevada 1, Pub.

539. Map of the Public Surveys in Nevada to accompany the Annual Report of the Commr., Genl Land Office, 1870.
1 inch to 14 miles. 41 x 28½. Manuscript. Status of public land surveys, towns, locations of U.S. land offices, military posts, railroad lines, and 20-mile limits of the Central Pacific Railroad. Relief is shown by hachures. Filed as RG 49: Nevada 6.

540. Map of the Public Surveys in the State of Nevada to accompany the Annual Report of the Commr., Genl Land Office, 1871.
1 inch to 14 miles. 39½ x 27½. Manuscript. Status of public land surveys, towns, locations of U.S. land offices, military posts, railroad lines, and land-grant limits of the Central Pacific Railroad. Relief is shown by hachures. Filed as RG 49: Nevada 7.

541. [Map of the] State of Nevada.... 1876. Compiled from the official Records of the General Land Office.
1 inch to 16 miles. 33 x 26½. Published. County boundaries and Indian reservations are shown in color. Also shows status of public land surveys, towns, locations of U.S. land offices, boundaries of land districts, and military reservations. Relief is shown by hachures. Filed as RG 49: Nevada 1876, Pub. (Atlas).

542. [Map of the] State of Nevada.... 1879. Compiled from the official Records of the General Land Office.
1 inch to 16 miles. 34 x 25. Published. County boundaries and military and Indian reservations are shown in color. Also shows status of public land surveys, towns, locations of U.S. land offices, railroad lines, and railroad land-grant limits. Relief is shown by hachures. (A copy of this map, annotated to show land districts, is filed as Nevada 10 in RG 49.) Filed as RG 49: Nevada 1879, Pub.

543. [Map of the] State of Nevada.... 1886. Compiled from the official Records of the General Land Office... Compiled by A. F. Dinsmore.... Drawn by M. Hendges.
1 inch to 12 miles. 44 x 32½. Published. County boundaries, military and Indian reservations, and railroad land-grant limits are shown in color. Also shows status of public land surveys, towns, locations of U.S. land offices, and proposed and completed railroad lines. Relief is shown by hachures. Filed as RG 49: Nevada 1886, Pub.

544. [Map of the] State of Nevada, Compiled from the official Records of the General Land Office... 1894.... Drawn by M. Hendges.
1 inch to 12 miles. 44 x 32½. Published. County boundaries and Indian reservations are shown in color. Also shows status of public land surveys, towns, locations of U.S. land offices, proposed and completed railroad lines, and railroad land-grant limits. Relief is shown by hachures. Also a black and white base map for this date. 44 x 32½. Filed as RG 49: Nevada 1894, Pub.

545. [Map of the] State of Nevada, Compiled from the official Records of the General Land Office... 1903.... Compiled and drawn by Daniel O'Hare.... Lettered by Chas. J. Helm.
1 inch to 12 miles. 42 x 30½. Published. County names and boundaries, towns, status of public land surveys, Indian reservations, railroad lines, and drainage features. Filed as RG 49: Nevada, 1903, Pub.

546. [Map of the] State of Nevada, Compiled from the official Records of the General Land Office... 1908.... Compiled and drawn by Daniel O'Hare.... Lettered by Chas. J. Helm.
1 inch to 12 miles. 45 x 30. Published. County boundaries, national forests, and Indian reservations are shown in color. Also shows status of public land surveys, towns and cities, and railroad lines. Relief is shown in color. Small inset plans of Reno, Goldfield, and North Goldfield. Also a black and white base map for this date. 45 x 30½. (A copy of map, annotated to show mining districts and mineral or location monuments, is filed as Nevada 18 in RG 49.) Filed as RG 49: Nevada 1908, Pub.

547. [Map of the] State of Nevada [showing] Lands designated by the Secretary of the Interior, April 27, 1909, under the Enlarged Homestead

Act of Feb. 19, 1909. [Issued by the Department of the Interior.]
1 inch to 24 miles. 23 x 17. Published. Areas designated are shaded red. Shows public land surveys. Filed as RG 49: Nevada 2, Pub.

548. [Map of the] State of Nevada, Compiled from the official Records of the General Land Office ... 1914.... Lettered by Chas. J. Helm.
1 inch to 12 miles. 45 x 32½. Published. County boundaries, national forests, Indian and bird reservations, land district boundaries, and reclamation projects are shown in color. Also shows status of public land surveys, towns and cities, and railroad lines. Relief is shown in color. Small inset plans of Reno, Winnemucca, Elko, Ely, Goldfield and Columbia, Tonopah, and Carson City. Also a black and white base map for this date. 45 x 32. Filed as RG 49: Nevada 1914, Pub.

549. [Map of the] State of Nevada [showing] Lands designated by the Secretary of the Interior Under the provisions of the Enlarged Homestead Act. Edition of June 30, 1916. [Issued by the Department of the Interior.]
1 inch to 24 miles. 23½ x 17. Published. Areas designated are shaded red. Shows public land surveys. Filed as RG 49: Nevada 3, Pub.

550. [Map of the] State of Nevada [showing] Lands designated by the Secretary of the Interior Under the provisions of the Enlarged Homestead Act. Edition of June 30, 1918. [Issued by the Department of the Interior.]
1 inch to 24 miles. 24 x 18. Published. Areas designated are shaded red. Shows public land surveys. Filed as RG 49: Nevada 4, Pub.

551. [Map of the] State of Nevada [showing] Lands designated as nonirrigable by the Secretary of the Interior under the provisions of the Enlarged Homestead Acts ... Edition of June 30, 1920. [Issued by the Department of the Interior.]
1 inch to 24 miles. 23½ x 17½. Published. Areas designated are shaded red. Also shows public land surveys. Filed as RG 49: Nevada 5, Pub.

552. [Map of Nevada and portions of adjoining States and Territories. n.d.]
1 inch to 12 miles. 36½ x 27½. Manuscript on tracing cloth. Settlements, military posts, trails, Overland Mail Route, and many place names some of which apparently are Indian names. Relief shown by hachures. Filed as RG 77: US 324-83.

553. [Map of Nevada and portions of adjoining States and Territories.] U.S. Engineer's Office, San Francisco, Calif., John D. Hoffmann, Chf. Draughtsman. [n.d.]
1 inch to 12 miles. 35 x 29. Manuscript on tracing cloth. Settlements, military posts, trails, and place names. Relief shown by hachures. Similar to entry 552, above. Filed as RG 77: US 324-105

See also entries 95, 99, 100, 104, 105, 109, 114, and 123.

NEW HAMPSHIRE

554. A Topographical Map of the Province of New Hampshire, surveyed agreeably to the Orders and Instructions of the Right Honourable the Lords Commissioners for Trade and Plantations unto Samuel Holland, Esqr., His Majesty's Surveyor General of Lands for the Northern District of North America; By the following Gentlemen His Deputies.... London: Printed for William Faden, Geographer to the King... March 1st, 1784.
1 inch to 4 miles. 2 sections, each 25 x 34½. Published. Townships, "patents," towns, roads, mills, and physical features. Filed as RG 77: US 9.

555. New-Hampshire, From Late Survey; To The Citizens of which this Map is most respectfully Dedicated by their obedient Servant, Edward Ruggles ... O. T. Eddy, sc. [1819].
1 inch to ca. 7 miles. 32 x 19½. Counties (boundaries in color), townships, physical features.

roads, and parts of adjoining States and Canada. . . . There are symbols for buildings, but no explanation is given concerning these symbols. Inset illustration of "View of Bellows Falls and Mansion House Hotel." Filed as RG 77: US 106.

556. New Hampshire, by Recent Survey, Made under the Supreme Authority and Published according to Law by Philip Carrigain, Counsellor at Law and late Secretary of the State . . . 1818 . . . W. Harrison Sc[ulptor] . J. J. Barralet, del.

  1 inch to 3 miles. 62 x 48. Annotated published. Includes parts of adjoining States. Counties, townships, roads, ferries, bridges, county seats, post towns, churches, academies, universities and colleges, iron foundries, cotton factories, mills, and 1810 population figures for individual townships. Map annotated to show ". . . John Clinton's (U.S. Engineer) surveys & reconnesances [sic] in Vermont and New Hampshire in 1825." Table lists population statistics for States and several cities in 1810. Map is dedicated to the Governor and the State Legislature. Inset illustrations of scenic views. Inset map of the United States to the Mississippi River including Louisiana, showing towns, roads, and military posts. Scale is 1 inch to 75 miles. Also an inset map of "The States of the Union East of the Hudson With the adjacent British Colonies [in Canada]," showing towns and roads. Scale is 1 inch to 30 miles. Filed as RG 77: US 28.

557. Post Route Map of the States of New Hampshire, Vermont, Massachusetts, Rhode Island, Connecticut, and Parts of New York and Maine . . . by W. L. Nicholson, Topographer of P. O. Dep't., 1866. . . . Eng. by D. McClelland . . . Lithd. by P. S. David . . . brought up to date of Oct. 1, 1867.

  1 inch to 6 miles. 2 sections, each 31 x 41½. Published. State boundaries in color. Frequency and types of mail service, mileages between post offices, counties, towns, and railroads. Post routes shown in color to illustrate number of deliveries per week (once, twice, three times, six times). Tables list statistical information such as distances between principal eastern cities, and population and areas of States shown on map. Filed as RG 28: series 1, folder I.

558. Post Route Map of the States of New Hampshire, Vermont, Massachusetts, Rhode Island, Connecticut, and parts of New York and Maine. Showing post offices with the intermediate distances and mail routes in operation on the 1st of June, 1894. Published . . . under the direction of A. von Haake, Topographer, P. O. Dept.

  1 inch to 6 miles. 2 sections, each 32½ x 41. Published. Frequency and types of mail service, mileages between post offices, discontinued post offices, counties, towns, railroads, and physical features. Post routes in color to show frequency of service. Most of Rhode Island portion is missing. Inset map of "Environs of Boston" shows carrier stations of the Boston post office and railroad lines. Scale 1 inch to 3 miles. Filed as RG 28: series 1, folder XXVII.

559. [Map of the States of New Hampshire and Vermont compiled in the U.S. Geological Survey, 1911-14.]

  1 inch to ca. 8 miles. 30 x 22. Published. County names and boundaries, villages and cities, steam and electric railroad lines, and drainage features. Noted: "Advance sheet. Subject to corrections." Also a copy of this map reprinted in 1918. Filed as RG 57: New Hampshire 1911-14, Pub.

See also entries 156, 158, 161, 372, and 373.

NEW JERSEY

560. [Map of] The Province of New Jersey Divided into East and West, commonly called The Jerseys. Second Edition with considerable improvements. Engraved & Published by Wm. Faden, Charing Cross, December 1st, 1778.
1 inch to ca. 7 miles. 33 x 26. Published. Counties, towns, roads, mills, forts, line dividing "the Jerseys" established in 1743, Keith's Line of 1687, and names of some residents. Also shows parts of present States of New York, Pennsylvania, Delaware, and Maryland. Filed as Ref. Coll.: New Jersey 1778.

561. A Map of the State of New Jersey [1812].
1 inch to 4 miles. 41 x 29. Published. Counties (boundaries in color), towns, roads, mills, forges, civil divisions within counties, and names of some residents. Statement "To His Excellency Joseph Bloomfield, Governor, the Council and Assembly of the State of New Jersey, this Map is respectfully inscribed by William Watson, Gloucester County, September 25, 1812." Filed as RG 77: US 18.

562. Map of New Jersey and Pennsylvania Exhibiting the Post Offices, Post Roads, Canals, Rail Roads, &c. By David H. Burr (Late Topographer to the Post Office)... [1839].
1 inch to 10 miles. 4 sections, each 19 x 25½. Published. Also shows county boundaries (but not names), mileages between post offices, and parts of adjoining States. Filed as RG 28: Burr Atlas, map 4.

563. [Map of] New Jersey... Entered according to Act of Congress in the year 1841, by T. Gordon, in the Clerks Office of the District Court of New Jersey. Reduced from T. Gordon's Map.
1 inch to ca. 12 miles. 18 x 14. Published. Counties, towns, roads, railroads, and canals. State is shaded orange. Filed as Ref. Coll.: New Jersey 1841.

564. [Map of New Jersey issued by the U.S. Geological Survey in 1913 and reprinted in 1915.]
1 inch to ca. 8 miles. 25½ x 21. Published. County names and boundaries, towns and cities, steam and electric railroad lines, and drainage features. Noted: "Advance sheet. Subject to corrections." Filed as RG 57: New Jersey 1915, Pub.

565. Post Route Map of the State of New Jersey showing post offices with the intermediate distances on mail routes in operation on the 1st of April, 1915.
1 inch to ca. 4 miles. 46¼ x 33. Published. Frequency and types of mail service, discontinued post offices, counties, towns, railroads, physical features, and parts of adjoining States. Post routes in color to show frequency of service. Filed as RG 28: New Jersey 1915.

See also entries 601, 738, and 741-745.

NEW MEXICO

566. Map of the Territory of New Mexico, made by order of Brig. Gen S. W. Kearny... by Lieuts. J. W. Abert and W. G. Peck, U.S.T.E., 1846-'7.
1 inch to ca. 10 miles. 28 x 23. Published. Settlements, "ruins," ranchos, and roads. Relief is shown by hachures. Filed as RG 77: 1846-7, Pub.

567. Map of the Territory of New Mexico. Compiled by Bvt. 2nd Lt. Jno. G. Parke, U.S.T.E., Assisted by Mr. Richd H. Kern... Drawn by Richd H. Kern. Santa Fe, N. M., 1851.
1 inch to 10 miles. 2 sections, each 31 x 85. Manuscript. Map includes present state of Arizona and portions of other adjoining States. Shows Indian pueblos, wagon roads, mule trails, routes of explorations, military posts, general locations of Indian tribes, and notes on the characteristics of the land. Relief is shown by hachures. Part of international boundary is shown in red. For published map, see next entry. Filed as RG 77: W 4.

568. Map of the Territory of New Mexico. Compiled by Bvt. 2nd Lt. Jno. G. Parke, U.S.T.E., assisted by Mr. Richard H. Kern... drawn by

R. H. Kern. Santa Fe, N. M., 1851.... Lith. of J & D Major... N.Y.
1 inch to ca. 25 miles. 27 x 37. Published. Map includes the present State of Arizona and portions of other adjoining States. Shows Indian pueblos, wagon roads, mule trails, routes of exploration, military posts, general locations of Indian tribes, and notes on the characteristics of the land. Relief is shown by hachures. Filed as RG 77: 1851, Pub.

569. T Sketch [map] of Public Surveys in New Mexico to accompany Report of Surveyor General, 1856.
1 inch to 24 miles. 25 x 32½. Published. Includes Arizona. Filed as RG 46: S. Ex. Doc. 5, 34th Cong., 3d sess.

570. Map of the Department of New Mexico and adjacent territory. Compiled and drawn... under orders of Colonel B. L E. Bonneville, Third Infy.... By Alexander Heberlein... 1857.
1 inch to ca. 20 miles. 2 sections, each 43 x 27. Manuscript. Reserves of Pueblo Indians, Navajos, and various Apache tribes are shown in color. Note states that Indian reserves are not yet confirmed. Also shows Indian agencies, settlements and pueblos ("Indian villages"), placers ("mineral districts"), wagon roads, and Indian trails. Filed as RG 77: W 607.

571. Sketch [map] of Public Surveys in New Mexico, to accompany Report of Surveyor General, 1858.
1 inch to 24 miles. 23½ x 29. Published. Shows status of public land surveys. Filed as RG 46: S. Ex. Doc. 1, 35th Cong., 2d sess.

572. Sketch of Public Surveys in New Mexico [Territory], 1859. [Compiled from maps on file in the Surveyor General's Office, Santa Fe, N. Mex.]
1 inch to 24 miles. 23 x 32½. Annotated published. Map is marked "(Copy)." Annotated in color to show private and pueblo claims surveyed and townships subdivided. Later annotations refer to contracts of 1861 for the survey of private land claims and to letters of December 24, 1861, and February 15, 1862, to the Indian Office and the Surveyor General apparently relating to Indian reservations in New Mexico and the area that later became Arizona. Map also shows locations of Indian tribes, Indian villages, and wagon roads. Filed as RG 49: New Mexico 2.

573. [Map of the] Territory and Military Department of New Mexico, compiled in the Bureau of Topogl. Engrs. of the War Dept., Chiefly for military purposes, under the authority of The Secretary of War, 1859.
1 inch to ca. 25 miles. 25 x 35½. Annotated published. Map includes present States of New Mexico and Arizona. Date of publication is not given; latest date included in list of authorities is 1865. Map is annotated to show approximate locations of Indian tribes. Also shows settlements, military posts, roads and trails, and routes of explorations. See also entry 577. Filed as RG 49: New Mexico 1.

574. Sketch of Public Surveys in New Mexico [Territory] To Accompany The Annual Report of The Surveyor General for 1862.
1 inch to ca. 28 miles. 21 x 28. Annotated published. Annotated to show the boundary of New Mexico Territory and information pertaining to private land claims, military and Indian reservations, and appropriations and costs of surveys of certain townships, to 1868. Also shows mining regions, towns, military posts, and wagon roads in both New Mexico and Arizona Territories. Filed as RG 49: New Mexico 5.

575. Map of the Military Department of New Mexico. Drawn under the direction of Brig. General James H. Carleton, By Captain Allen L. Anderson, U.S. 5th Infantry, Acting Engineer Officer. 1864.
1 inch to ca. 24 miles 26½ x 36. Annotated photoprocessed. Shows settlements, wagon roads, trails and routes of reconnoitering parties, and military posts both occupied and abandoned. Map includes the present State of Arizona. Annotated to show additional military posts. Note "The *New Mexico Posts in Red* are located from a Map loaned to the Bureau from Gen'l Grant's HdQuarters. January 16th, 1866. D.C." Filed as RG 77: W 83-2.

576. Map of New Mexico... expressly prepared for Maj. Genl. M. C. Meigs, Q. Mast: Genl., U.S.A., in the Engineers Office at Hd. Qus. 5th Military Distt., Bvt. Captain Wm Hoelcke, U.S.A., in charge. H. Holtz, Del. [ca. 1864-65.]
1 inch to 10 miles. 4 sections, each 29 x 44½. Manuscript. Map includes present States of Arizona and New Mexico. Settlements, military posts, "principal... [and] secondary travelled Routes," routes of exploration, and drainage features. Title preceded

by "Office of the Chief Engineer, Fifth Military District." Relief shown by color. Filed as RG 77: W 603.

577. Sketch of Public Surveys in New Mexico and Arizona [Territories] To Accompany the Annual Report of the Commissioner of the General Land Office for 1866. [Issued by the General Land Office on October 2, 1866.]
1 inch to ca. 28 miles. 21 x 28. Annotated published. Annotated with information concerning private land claims, Indian and military reservations, and (on the reverse) appropriations and costs of surveys. Some annotations refer to Executive orders as late as 1873 and 1874. Map also shows extent of public land surveys, towns, trails, wagon roads, military posts, locations of mineral deposits (in color), and boundaries and names of mining districts. Filed as RG 49: New Mexico 6.

578. [Map of] Old Territory and Military Department of New Mexico, compiled in the Bureau of Topogl. Engrs. of the War Dept., Chiefly for military purposes, under the authority of The Secretary of War, 1859. Partially revised and corrected to 1867.
1 inch to ca. 25 miles. 25 x 35½. Published. Map includes present States of New Mexico and Arizona. Settlements, military posts, roads and trails, and routes of explorations. Relief is shown by shading. W 55-1 in RG 77 apparently is the manuscript version of this map. See also entry 573. Filed as RG 77: 1867, Pub.

579. [Map of New Mexico] 1873. Sheet 4. Department of the Missouri. Lieut. E. H. Ruffner, Chief Engineer. Drawn by Ado Hunnius.
1 inch to ca. 15 miles. 33½ x 26. Published. Includes adjoining area in Texas. Settlements, military posts, and roads. Relief shown by hachures. Filed as RG 393: Dept. of Missouri 8.

580. [Map of the] District of New Mexico. 1875. Lieut. C. C. Morrison, 6th Cav., Acting Engineer Officer. Drawn by Anton Karl. Copied by C. A. Lichtenberg, Sergt., Engrs.
1 inch to ca. 16 miles. 32½ x 28. Manuscript. Map shows the present State of New Mexico and portions of adjoining States. Settlements, military posts, and roads. Relief is shown by hachures. See entry 581. Filed as RG 77: W 197-1.

581. [Map of the] District of New Mexico. Showing Rail-Roads and Stations. 1875. Lieut. C. C. Morrison, 6th Cav., Acting Engineer Officer. Drawn by Anton Karl. Copies by C. A. Lichtenberg, Sergt., Engrs.
1 inch to ca. 20 miles. 28½ x 23. Manuscript. Annotated to show railroad lines, projected railroad lines, and railroad stations. "Showing Rail-Roads and Stations" added to title in pencil. Note in pencil in margin states, "Received from Lieut. Thomas N. Bailey with his letter of May 23rd, 1881." See entry 580. Filed as RG 77: W 197-3.

582. [Map of the] Territory of New Mexico. . . . 1876. Compiled from the official Records of the General Land Office.
1 inch to 16 miles. 33 x 26½. Published. County boundaries, military and Indian reservations, and private land claims are shown in color. Also shows status of public land surveys, towns and cities, and railroad land-grant limits. Relief is shown by hachures. Filed as RG 49: New Mexico 1876, Pub. (Atlas).

583. [Map of the] Territory of New Mexico. . . . 1876. Compiled from the official Records of the General Land Office.
1 inch to 16 miles. 33 x 26½. Annotated published. Annotated to show new boundaries of Indian reservations. Basic information is the same as that shown on entry 582. Filed as RG 49: New Mexico 8.

584. [Map of] Territories of New Mexico & Arizona. Prepared in the Office of the Chief of Engineers, U.S.A., 1879.
1 inch to ca. 25 miles. 27 x 33½. Published. Map includes Arizona, New Mexico, parts of adjoining States and Territories, and adjacent areas in Mexico. Towns, roads, railroads, military posts, Indian reservations and lands, and physical features. Relief is shown by hachures. Filed as RG 77: 1879, Pub.

585. [Map of the] Territory of New Mexico. . . . 1879. Compiled from the official Records of the General Land Office.
1 inch to 16 miles. 34½ x 27. Published. County boundaries, military and Indian reservations, and private land claims are shown in color. Also shows status of public land surveys, towns and cities,

railroad lines, and railroad land-grant limits. Relief is shown by hachures. Also a black and white base map for this date. 34 x 27. Filed as RG 49: N. Mex. 1879, Pub.

586. [Map of the] Territory of New Mexico.... 1882. Compiled from the official Records of the General Land Office.
1 inch to 16 miles. 31 x 27. Published. County boundaries, military and Indian reservations, private land claims confirmed, and boundaries of unconfirmed private land grants are shown in color. Also shows status of public land surveys, cities and towns, railroad lines, and railroad land-grant limits. Also a black and white base map for this date. 30½ x 25½. Filed as RG 49: New Mexico 1882, Pub.

587. Post Route Map of the Territories of New Mexico and Arizona with parts of Adjacent States and Territories showing post offices with the intermediate distances and mail routes in operation on the 1st of October, 1885. Published ... under the direction of W. L. Nicholson, Topographer, P. O. Dept.
1 inch to ca. 12 miles. 2 sections, each 38½ x 29½. Published. Frequency and types of mail service, mileages between post offices, discontinued post offices, counties, towns, military reservations and posts, Indian reservations, railroads, and physical features. Post routes in color to show frequency of service. Filed as RG 28: series 1, folder VIII.

588. [Map of the] Territory of New Mexico.... 1886. Compiled from the official Records of the General Land Office.... Compiled and Drawn by Robert H. Morton.
1 inch to 16 miles. 33½ x 26½. Published. County boundaries, military and Indian reservations, private land claims confirmed, and boundaries of uncomfirmed private land claims are shown in color. Also shows status of public land surveys, towns and cities, proposed and completed railroad lines, and railroad land-grant limits. Relief is shown by hachures. Filed as RG 49: New Mexico 1886, Pub.

589. [Map of the] Territory of New Mexico.... 1894. Compiled from the official Records of the General Land Office .... Compiled and Drawn by Robert H. Morton. Traced and Lettered by Wm. Naylor and I. P. Berthong.
1 inch to 12 miles. 44 x 34. Published. County names and boundaries, towns and cities, names of military and Indian reservations, names of private land claims, status of public land surveys, and railroad lines. Relief is shown by hachures. Filed as RG 49: New Mexico 1894, Pub.

590. [Map of the] Territory of New Mexico.... 1896. Compiled from the official Records of the General Land Office .... Compiled and Drawn by Robert H. Morton. Traced and Lettered by Wm. Naylor and I. P. Berthong.
1 inch to 12 miles. 39 x 32. Published. County boundaries, military and Indian reservations, national forests, confirmed private land claims, boundaries of uncomfirmed private land claims, confirmed claims needing new boundary lines, and U.S. reservoirs are shown in color. Also shows status of public land surveys, towns and cities, and railroad lines. Relief is shown by hachures. Also a black and white base map for this date. 43 x 33. Filed as RG 49: New Mexico 1896, Pub.

591. Post Route Map of the Territory of New Mexico showing post offices with the intermediate distances on mail routes in operation on the 1st of June, 1902. Also railways under construction June 30th, 1902, and the several mining districts of the Territory.
1 inch to ca. 20 miles. 24 x 19. Published. Frequency and types of mail service, discontinued post offices, counties, towns, physical features, and parts of adjoining States. Also shows forest reserves (in green) existing October 7, 1902. Post routes in color to show frequency of service. Mining districts are numbered and listed in upper left corner, and corresponding numbers appear in red on map. Filed as RG 28: New Mexico 1902.

592. [Map of the] Territory of New Mexico. Compiled from the official Records of the General Land Office ... 1903. ... Revised and drawn by Charles J. Helm.
1 inch to 12 miles. 41¼ x 33. Published. County and land district boundaries, military and Indian reservations, and national forests are shown in color. Also shows status of public land surveys, towns and cities, private land claims, and railroad lines. Relief is shown in color. Also a black and white base map for this date. 41 x 33. Filed as RG 49: New Mexico 1903, Pub.

593. [Map of the] Territory of New Mexico. Compiled from the official Records of the General Land Office . . . 1908. . . . Compiled by A. F. Dinsmore. . . .Traced and Lettered by Wm. Bauman.

1 inch to 12 miles. 39½ x 33. Published. County boundaries, military and Indian reservations, and national forests are shown in color. Also shows status of public land surveys, towns and cities, boundaries of private land claims and land districts, and railroad lines. Relief is shown in color. Also a black and white base map for this date. 39½ x 34. Filed as RG 49: New Mexico 1908, Pub.

594. [Map of the] Territory of New Mexico. Compiled from the official Records of the General Land Office . . . 1908. . . . Compiled by A. F. Dinsmore. . . . Traced and Lettered by Wm. Bauman.

1 inch to 20 miles. 27 x 13. Published. County boundaries, military and Indian reservations, and national forests are shown in color. Also shows status of public land surveys, towns and cities, boundaries of private land claims and land districts, and railroad lines. Relief is shown in color. Filed as RG 49: New Mexico 1908, Pub.

595. [Map of the] Territory of New Mexico [showing] Lands designated by the Secretary of the Interior, April 27, 1909, under the Enlarged Homestead Act of Feb. 19, 1909. [Issued by the Department of the Interior.]

1 inch to 24 miles. 20 x 17½. Published. Areas designated are shaded red. Also shows public land surveys. Filed as RG 49: New Mexico 5, Pub.

596. [Map of the] Territory of New Mexico. Compiled from the official Records of the General Land Office . . . 1911. . . . Compiled by A. F. Dinsmore. Traced and Lettered by Wm. Bauman.

1 inch to 20 miles. 21 x 18. Published. County and land district boundaries, military and Indian reservations, and forest reserves are shown in color. Also shows status of public land surveys, towns and cities, boundaries of private land claims, and railroad lines. Relief is shown in color. Filed as RG 49: New Mexico 1911, Pub.

597. [Map of the] State of New Mexico. Compiled from the official Records of the General Land Office . . . 1912. . . . Compiled by A. F. Dinsmore. . . . Traced and Lettered by Wm. Bauman.

1 inch to 12 miles. 38½ x 34. Published. County and land district boundaries, military and Indian reservations, national forests, and boundaries of national monuments are shown in color. Also shows status of public land surveys, towns and cities, boundaries of private land claims, railroad lines, and reclamation projects. Relief is shown in color. Also a black and white base map for this date. 39 x 34. Filed as RG 49: New Mexico 1912, Pub.

598. [Map of the] State of New Mexico [showing] Lands designated by the Secretary of the Interior Under the provisions of the Enlarged Homestead Acts. [Issued by the Department of the Interior.] Edition of June 30, 1916.

1 inch to 24 miles. 20½ x 18. Published. Areas designated are shaded red. Also shows public land surveys. Filed as RG 49: New Mexico 6, Pub.

599. Post Route Map of the State of New Mexico showing post offices with the intermediate distances on mail routes in operation on the 1st of January, 1917.

1 inch to 12 miles. 39½ x 33. Published. Frequency and types of mail service, discontinued post offices, counties, towns, railroads, physical features, and parts of adjoining States. Filed as RG 28: New Mexico 1917.

600. [Map of the] State of New Mexico [showing] Lands designated as non-irrigable by the Secretary of the Interior, under the provisions of the Enlarged Homestead Acts. Includes Patented and Entered as well as Vacant land. [Issued by the Department of the Interior.] Edition of June 30, 1920.

1 inch to 24 miles. 20½ x 18. Published. Areas designated are shaded red. Also shows public land surveys. Filed as RG 49: New Mexico 7, Pub.

NEW YORK

601. A Map of the Province of New-York, Reduc'd from the large Drawing of that Province, Compiled from Actual Surveys by Order of His Excellency William Tryon, Esqr. . . . By Claude Joseph Sauthier; to which is added New-Jersey, from the Topographical Observations of C. J. Sauthier & B. Ratzer. . . . Engraved by William Faden . . . 1776. . . . Published . . . by Wm. Faden.

1 inch to ca. 16 miles. 31½ x 24. Published. Map includes the present States of New York, New Jersey, and Vermont with parts of adjoining States and areas of Canada. Counties in New York (Province of) shown in color. Only names of New Jersey counties are shown. Towns, military posts, manors, and roads. Filed as RG 77: US 3.

602. A Chorographical Map of the Province of New York in North America, Divided into Counties, Manors, Patents, and Townships; Exhibiting likewise all the private Grants of Land made and located in that Province; Compiled from Actual Surveys deposited in the Patent Office at New York, By Order of His Excellency Major General William Tryon, By Claude Joseph Sauthier, Esqr. . . . Engraved and Published by William Faden . . . January 1st, 1779.

1 inch to 5 miles. 4 sections, each 37½ x 28½. Published. Boundaries of military grants, manors, and townships shown in color. Also shows settlements, iron works, forts, names of grantees, and physical features. Map includes portions of New Hampshire, Massachusetts, Connecticut, and New Jersey as well as Vermont and part of Canada. Filed as RG 77: US 7.

603. A Map of the State of New York By Simeon DeWitt, Surveyor General. Contracted from his large Map of the State, 1804. Entered according to Act of Congress the 19th day March, 1804, by Simeon DeWitt of the State of New York.

1 inch to 15 miles. 23½ x 28½. Published. Also parts of Canada, Vermont, New Hampshire, Massachusetts, Connecticut, and New Jersey. Counties (some with boundaries shaded gray), civil divisions into towns and townships, cities, roads, and physical features. Filed as RG 77: US 96.

604. Map of the Northern Part of the State of New York. Compiled from actual Survey By Amos Lay, 1812.

1 inch to 7 miles. 2 sections, each 30½ x 24½. Published. County boundaries in color. Other civil divisions, cities, Indian reservations (shaded yellow), roads, and physical features. Part of Canada, but New York south of southern boundaries of Columbia, Greene, and Delaware counties is not shown. Filed as RG 77: US 19.

605. Map of the State of New-York with part of the States of Pennsylvania, New Jersey &c. Compiled, Corrected, & Published from the most recent Authorities and accurate Surveys, by Amos Lay, 1817. . . . Second edition revised & published, 1820.

1 inch to 7 miles. 4 sections, each 26½ x 25½. Published. County boundaries in color. Townships, towns, roads, courthouses, churches, colleges, forts, houses, mills, iron works, and Indian villages. Also shows adjoining part of Canada. Indian reservations colored yellow. Filed as RG 77: US 22-1.

606. Map of New York Exhibiting the Post Offices, Post Roads, Canals, Rail Roads, &c. By David H. Burr (Late Topographer to the Post Office). [1839]

1 inch to 10 miles. 4 sections, each 19 x 25½. Published. Also shows county boundaries (but not names), civil divisions within counties, mileages between post offices, forts, and parts of adjoining States and Canada. Filed as RG 28: Burr Atlas, map 3.

607. New York . . . Entered according to Act of Congress in the year 1842, by Sidney E. Morse and Samuel Breese in the Clerks Office of the Southern District of New York.

1 inch to ca. 28 miles. 14 x 18. Published. Counties, towns, roads, railroads, canals, and physical features. Also parts of adjoining States. New York is shaded green. Annotated apparently to show additional roads. Filed as Ref. Coll.: New York 1842.

608. Colton's Railroad & Township Map of the State of New York, With Parts of the Adjoining States & Canada. Published by J. H. Colton . . . 1852. . . . Drawn by Geo. W. Colton. J. M. Atwood, Sculp.

1 inch to 15 miles. 25 x 30. Published. Counties, minor civil divisions, settlements, roads, canals, and railroads. Population by county listed in table. Filed as RG 77: D 133.

NEW YORK

609. The State of New York from New and Original Surveys Under the Direction of J. H. French, C. E.; H. H. Lloyd & Co., Publishers . . . 1865.

1 inch to ca. 10 miles. 4 sections, each 35 x 37½. Published. County boundaries and civil divisions within counties shown in color. Cities, roads, railroads, physical features, and part of adjoining States and Canada. Inset city plans of Buffalo, Rochester, Syracuse, Oswego, Hudson, Schenectady, Poughkeepsie, Auburn City, Albany, Utica, Troy, and New York city. Inset maps showing the "Geology of the State and the bounds and names of all the Original Patent and Land Grants of more than 50,000 Acres" and "Meteorological Map of the State of New York . . . showing Average Mean Temperature, Depth of Rain and Direction of Winds at the several Meteorological Stations . . . ." Also illustrations of scenic points. Filed as RG 77: D 173.

610. Post Route Map of the State of New York and Parts of Vermont, Massachusetts, Connecticut, New Jersey, and Pennsylvania. Showing also the adjacent portions of the Dominion of Canada. . . . by W. L. Nicholson, Topographer of P. O. Dep't., 1868. . . . Engraved by D. McClelland . . . Paul Goepel, Draughtsman . . . [Revised] up to date of June 1, 1868.

1 inch to 6 miles. 4 sections, each 29 x 32. Annotated published. State boundaries in color. Frequency and types of mail service, mileages between post offices, counties, towns, and railroads. Post routes shown in color to illustrate frequency of service. Tables list statistical information. Note on map "Rec. for the files, from Gen'l Humphreys, June 1868." Inset map "Postal Service of Long Island with the principal mail connections of the city of New York." Scale 1 inch to 6 miles. Also inset map of northern boundary of New York and parts of adjoining Provinces in Canada. Filed as RG 28: series 1, folder I.

611. Colton's Railroad & Township Map of the State of New York, With Parts of the Adjoining States & Canada. Published by G. W. and C. B. Colton . . . 1873.

1 inch to 15 miles. 26 x 29. Published. Boundaries of counties and civil divisions within counties are shown in color. Settlements, roads, railroads, canals, and physical features. Population by county listed in table. Filed as Ref. Coll.: New York 1873.

612. Post Route Map of the State of New York and parts of Vermont, Massachusetts, Connecticut, New Jersey, and Pennsylvania. Also the adjacent portions of the Dominion of Canada, showing post offices with the intermediate distances and mail routes in operation on the 1st of February, 1887. Published . . . under the direction of W. L. Nicholson, Topographer, P. O. Dept.

1 inch to 6 miles. 4 sections, each 27½ x 31½. Published. Frequency and types of mail service, mileages between post offices, discontinued post offices, counties, towns, railroads, and physical features. Post routes in color to show frequency of service. Inset map of northern boundary of New York and adjacent areas of Canada. No scale indicated. Also inset map showing "Postal Service of Long Island with the principal mail connections of the city of New York." 1 inch to 6 miles. Filed as RG 28: series 1, folder XXIII.

613. Post Route Map of the State of New York and parts of Vermont, Massachusetts, Connecticut, New Jersey, and Pennsylvania. Also the adjacent portions of the Dominion of Canada, showing post offices with the intermediate distances and mail routes in operation on the 1st of August, 1890. Published . . . under the direction of C. Roeser Jr., Topographer, P. O. Dept.

1 inch to 6 miles. 4 sections, each 31 x 34. Published. Frequency and types of mail service, mileages between post offices, discontinued post offices, counties, towns, railroads, and physical features. Post routes in color to show frequency of service. Inset map of northern boundary of New York and adjacent areas of Canada. No scale indicated. Also inset map showing "Postal Service of Long Island with the principal mail connections of the city of New York." Scale 1 inch to 6 miles. In addition an inset map of the "Environs of New York." Scale 1 inch to 3 miles. Filed as RG 28: series 1, folder XXIV.

614. Post Route Map of the State of New York showing post offices with the intermediate distances on mail routes in operation on the 1st of March, 1901.

1 inch to 5 miles. 4 sections, each 34½ x 36½. Published. Frequency and types of mail service, discontinued post offices, counties, towns, railroads, physical features, and parts of adjoining States and

74 MAPS OF STATES AND TERRITORIES

Canada. Post routes in color to show frequency of service. Inset "Postal Service of Long Island . . . ." No scale indicated. Also inset "City of New York," at a scale of 1 inch to ca. 3¼ miles. Filed as RG 28: New York 1901.

615. [U.S. Geological Survey base map of New York. Compiled in 1913. Annotated to show locations of Indian reservations and boundaries of several "purchases."]

1 inch to ca. 15 miles. 23 x 29. Annotated published. Also shows number of acres in each Indian reservation and some information about treaties. Boundaries of purchases by Phelps-Gorman, Morris, and Holland Land Company are shown in color. Date of annotations is not shown. Filed as RG 75: map CA 261.

616. [Map of New York issued by the U.S. Geological Survey, 1916.]

1 inch to ca. 16 miles. 24 x 29. Published. County names and boundaries, towns and cities, steam and electric railroad lines, and drainage features. Filed as RG 57: New York 1916, Pub.

617. Post Route Map of the State of New York showing post offices with the intermediate distances on mail routes in operation on the 1st of January, 1917.

1 inch to 5 miles. 4 sections, each 34½ x 36. Published. Frequency and types of mail service, discontinued post offices, counties, towns, railroads, physical features, and parts of adjoining States and Canada. Inset map of part of Long Island with adjacent parts of the State and city of New York. Also an inset of "City of New York and Vicinity." Scale 1 inch to 2 miles. Filed as RG 28: New York 1917.

618. [Map of New York showing locations of Indian reservations. n.d.]

Scale not indicated. 23½ x 31. Manuscript on tracing cloth. Shows locations of reservations, and acreage and population of each. Also shown in color are boundaries of Morris, Holland, and Phelps purchases. Names and boundaries of counties in western New York are shown, but only a few settlements and place names appear. Filed as RG 75: map 7574.

NORTH CAROLINA

619. Map of the Province of North Carolina By Edward Moseley, late Surveyor General of the said Province, 1733.

1 inch to ca. 5 miles. 2 sections, each 44 x 28. Manuscript. Towns, Indian villages, ferries, roads, chapels, drainage features, and names of some residents. Inset map of "Port Brunswick or Cape Fear Harbour," "Port Beaufort or Topsail Inlet," and "Ocacock Inlet." Noted on map, "Engineer Department Topographical Office, September 5, 1822. Copy, T Roberdrau, Major, T. Engineers." Filed as RG 77: H 47.

620. An Accurate Map of North and South Carolina With Their Indian Frontiers, Shewing in a different manner all the Mountains, Rivers, Swamps, Marshes, Bays, Creeks, Harbours, Sandbanks and Soundings on the Coasts; with the Roads and Indian Paths; as well as the Boundary of Provincial Lines, the Several Townships and other divisions of the Land in Both the Provinces; the whole from Actual Surveys By Henry Mouzon and Others. Published by Laurie & Whittle . . . 12th May, 1794.

1 inch to ca. 8 miles. 2 sections, 40 x 28½ and 40 x 27. Published. Provinces shown in color. Also shows forts. Inset maps of "The Harbour of Port Royal," at a scale of 1 inch to 3 miles and "The Bar and Harbour of Charlestown," at a scale of 1 inch to a little more than 1 mile. Also shows part of Georgia. Filed as RG 77: US 11.

621. To David Stone and Peter Brown, Esqrs., This First Actual Survey of the State of North Carolina, Taken by the Subscribers, is respectfully dedicated By their humble Servants Jona. Price, John Strother. 1808. Engraved by W. Harrison, Philadelphia.

1 inch to ca. 8 miles. 2 sections, each 29½ x 30.

NORTH CAROLINA

Annotated published. Counties (in color), towns, roads, churches, iron works, physical features, and names of some residents. Filed as RG 77: US 16.

622. Map of North & South Carolina by H. S. Tanner. ... Published by H. S. Tanner, Philadelphia. [1823]

1 inch to ca. 18 miles. 24 x 31. Annotated published. Counties (in color), towns, roads, and physical features. Names of some towns are underlined in red, without explanation. "American Atlas" is printed at the top of the map. Filed as RG 77: US 166.

623. Map of the States of North & South Carolina. London. Published June 1, by I. T. Hinton & Simpkin & Marshall. [ca. 1830.] Engraved & Printed by Fenner Sears & Co.

1 inch to ca. 40 miles. 11½ x 17. Published. Counties, towns, roads, and physical features. Inset "Plan of Charleston" at a scale of ¾ inch to 2000 feet. Filed as Ref. Coll.: North Carolina 1830.

624. [Map of] Nth. Carolina. Drawn & Published by F. Lucas Jr., Baltimore. [ca. 1835]

1 inch to 28 miles 12 x 19½. Published. Counties (in color), towns, roads, and physical features. Filed as Ref. Coll.: North Carolina 1835.

625. Map of North and South Carolina Exhibiting the Post Offices, Post Roads, Canals, Rail Roads, &c. By David H. Burr (Late Topographer to the Post Office). ... Entered according to the Act of Congress, July 10th, 1839.

1 inch to 10 miles. 4 sections, each 19½ x 25½. Published. Also shows counties (in color), mileages between post offices, lighthouses, forts, physical features, and parts of adjoining States. Filed as RG 28: Burr Atlas, map 6.

626. [Map of] North Carolina ... Entered according to Act of Congress in the year 1843, by Sidney E. Morse and Samuel Breese in the Clerks Office of the Southern District of New York.

1 inch to ca. 32 miles. 14 x 18. Published. Counties, towns, roads, railroads, canals, and physical features. State is shaded yellow. Filed as Ref. Coll.: North Carolina 1843.

627. [Map of] North Carolina & South Carolina. U.S. Coast Survey, A. D. Bache, Supdt., 1865. ... Drawn by A. Lindenkohl. ... Chas. G. Krebs, Lith.

1 inch to 10 miles. 28 x 38. Published. Map includes all of North and South Carolina except the far extremities. Part of Georgia also included. Railroad lines in red. Shows towns, roads, and physical features. Filed as RG 23: Special Civil War Maps.

628. Map of North Carolina, By W. C. Kerr, State Geologist; Assisted by Capt. Wm. Cain, C. E. Published under the authority of the State Board of Agriculture. 1882. ... Embodying the surveys made by the State from 1820 to date, of swamplands, railroads, rivers, canals, and turnpikes.

1 inch to 10 miles. 2 sections, 26 x 27 and 26 x 29. Published. Counties (shown in color) and towns. Tables list railroads, population figures for major towns, and general information about the State. Filed as Ref. Coll.: North Carolina 1882.

629. Post Route Map of the States of North Carolina and South Carolina with adjacent parts of Georgia, Tennessee, Kentucky, West Virginia, and Virginia, showing post offices with the intermediate distances and mail routes in operation on the 1st of December, 1885. Published ... under the direction of W. L. Nicholson, Topographer, P. O. Dept. ... Engraved by D. McClelland. [Corrected to Feb. 1, 1886.]

1 inch to 8 miles. 4 sections, each 28½ x 34½. Published. Frequency and types of mail service, mileages between post offices, discontinued post offices, counties, towns, railroads, and physical features. Post routes in color to show frequency of service. Inset map of "Western Part of North Carolina." Scale not indicated. Filed as RG 28: series 1, folder XVI.

630. Post Route Map of the States of North Carolina and South Carolina with adjacent parts of Georgia, Tennessee, Kentucky, West Viriginia, and Virginia showing post offices with the intermediate distances and mail routes in operation on the 1st of February, 1887. Published ... under the direction of W. L. Nicholson, Topographer, P. O. Dept. ... .Engraved by D. McClelland.

1 inch to 8 miles. 4 sections, each 28½ x 34½.

Published. Frequency and types of mail service, mileages between post offices, discontinued post offices, counties, towns, railroads, and physical features. Post routes in color to show frequency of service. Inset map of "Western Part of North Carolina." Scale not indicated. Filed as RG 28: series 1, folder XXI.

631. Post Route Map of the State of North Carolina showing post offices with the intermediate distances on mail routes in operation on the 1st of January, 1917.

1 inch to 8 miles. 2 sections, each 35 x 25. Published. Frequency and types of mail service, discontinued post offices, counties, towns, railroads, physical features, and parts of adjoining States. Inset map of western North Carolina. No scale indicated. Inset of Ashe and Watauga counties and parts of adjacent counties. Scale 1 inch to 5 miles. Filed as RG 28: North Carolina 1917.

NORTH DAKOTA

(including Dakota Territory)

632. Reconnoisaance [sic] in the Dacota [sic] Country by G. K. Warren, Lieut: Top. Engrs., U.S.A. . . . 1855.

1 inch to 10 miles. 2 sections, each 37 x 33. Published. Includes present States of Nebraska and North and South Dakota. Settlements, military posts, Indian villages, general locations of Indian tribes, and routes of explorations. Also shown is a profile of the route from Fort Pierre to Fort Kearney. Filed as RG 77: 1855, Pub.

633. Map of the Ceded Part of Dakota Territory Showing also portions of Minnesota, Iowa, & Nebraska. Second Edition, July 1863. Compiled by B. M. Smith and A. J. Hill, 1861. Lith. by Louis Bueckner, St. Paul, Minnesota.

1 inch to 15.78 miles. 18½ x 24. Annotated published. Settlements, military posts, roads, trails, railroads, Indian reservations, explorers' routes, Indian treaty lines, and extent of public land surveys. "Second Edition, July 1863" added in red ink to the title block. Also noted in red ink: "Dennis Callahan Esq. with respects of A. J. Hill." Inset map, "Outline Map of Dakota Territory, &c." Scale 1 inch to ca. 150 miles. Filed as RG 77: Q 91.

634. [Map of] Dakota Territory [Issued by the General Land Office on Oct. 2, 1866].

1 inch to 18 miles. 25½ x 22. Published. Status of public land surveys, counties, settlements, Indian villages, military posts, "Yankton Cession," Indian reservations, and physical features. County boundaries in color. Includes North and South Dakota. Filed as RG 49: North Dakota 1, Pub.

635. Map of Public Surveys in Dakota Territory. [Dated July 27, 1868, Surveyor General's Office, Yankton, Dakota Territory.]

1 inch to 16 miles. 31 x 32½. Manuscript. County boundaries (in color) and names, status of public land surveys, towns, locations of coal mines, military posts, wagon roads, routes of several military expeditions, and physical features. Filed as RG 49: North Dakota 1.

636. Sketch of the Public Surveys in Dakota Territory [to] accompany annual report of Sur. Gen. [Dated Sept. 21, 1871, Yankton, Dakota Territory].

1 inch to 16 miles. 32½ x 13½. Manuscript. Status of public land surveys, towns, and Indian and military reservations. Boundaries of military reservations are shown in color. Filed as RG 49: North Dakota 2.

637. [Map of Dakota Territory] To Accompany Report of Surveyor General, 1872.

1 inch to 12 miles. 41 x 34. Manuscript. Status of public land surveys, Indian and military reservations, land district boundaries, roads, and railroad lines. Filed as RG 49: North Dakota 3.

638. [Map of the] Territory of Dakota. ... 1876. Compiled from the official Records of the General Land Office.
1 inch to 18 miles. 33 x 26½. Published. County boundaries, military and Indian reservations are shown in color. Also shows public land surveys, towns, locations of U.S. land offices, railroad lines, and railroad land-grant limits. Relief is shown by hachures. Filed as RG 49: Dakota Territory 1876, Pub. (Atlas).

639. [Map of the] Territory of Dakota. ... 1879. Compiled from the official Records of the General Land Office.
1 inch to 18 miles. 33 x 29. Published. Map includes present States of North and South Dakota. County boundaries, military and Indian reservations are shown in color. Also shows public land surveys, towns, location of U.S. land offices, railroad lines, and railroad land-grant limits. Relief is shown by hachures. Filed as RG 49: Dakota Territory 1879, Pub.

640. [Map of the] Territory of Dakota. ... 1879. Compiled from the official Records of the General Land Office.
1 inch to 18 miles. 33½ x 26½. Annotated published. Annotated to show land districts. Basic information is the same as that shown on entry 639. Filed as RG 49: North Dakota 7.

641. [Map of] Dakota Territory. Prepared [by] Order of Brig. Gen'l. A. H. Terry. ... 5th Ed., 1881, Revised & corrected under Capt. Edward Maguire, Corps of Engineers, by James E. Wilson, Topogl. Asst. Originally compiled under direction of Capt. D. P. Heap, Corps of Engrs., by W. H. Wood, 1872.
1 inch to 12 miles. 40½ x 23. Published. Shows settlements, military posts, public land surveys, railroad lines, routes of exploration, Indian reservations, and drainage features. Map includes present States of North and South Dakota. Filed as RG 77: Q 191-20.

642. [Map of the] Territory of Dakota. ... 1882. Compiled from the official Records of the General Land Office.
1 inch to 18 miles. 31 x 27. Published. Map includes present States of North and South Dakota. County boundaries, military reservations, and Indian reservations are shown in color. Also shows public land surveys, towns, locations of U.S. land offices, railroad lines, and railroad land-grant limits. Relief is shown by hachures. Filed as RG 49: Dakota Territory 1882, Pub.

643. [Map of the] Territory of Dakota. ... 1885. Compiled from the official Records of the General Land Office. ... Compiled by A. F. Dinsmore ... Drawn by Wm. Naylor.
1 inch to 12 miles. 2 sections, each 26½ x 33½. Published. Map includes present States of North and South Dakota. County boundaries, military reservations, railroad land-grant limits, and Indian reservations are shown in color. Also shows public land surveys, towns, locations of U.S. land offices, and railroad lines. Relief is shown in hachures. Filed as RG 49: Dakota Territory 1885, Pub.

644. [Map of the] Territory of Dakota. ... 1885. Compiled from the official Records of the General Land Office. ... Compiled by A. F. Dinsmore ... Drawn by Wm. Naylor.
1 inch to 12 miles. 43 x 33½. Annotated published. Annotated to show proposed extent of land surveys and change in Indian reservations. Marked "U.S. Surveyor General's Office, Huron, S. Dakota, Dec. 9, 1889. To accompany letter to Hon. Com'r dated December 9, 1889." See entry 643. Filed as RG 49: North Dakota 11.

645. Official Map Of The Territory Of Dakota, Showing The Two General Divisions of Dakota, South and North ... Copyright, 1885, by Rand, McNally & Co., Map Publishers, Chicago.
1 inch to ca. 30 miles. 22 x 14. Indian reservations, counties, towns, railroads. Land district boundaries and area not part of Indian reservations are shown in color. Note in lower margin states "This map has been thoroughly revised in my office, and corrected to date of March 1st, 1886. [Signed] Lauren Dunlap, Commissioner of Immigration, Territory of Dakota." Filed as Ref. Coll.: Dakota Territory 1885.

646. Post Route Map of the Territory of Dakota with adjacent parts of Montana, Wyoming, Nebraska, Iowa, and Minnesota and portions of the Dominion of Canada showing post offices with the intermediate distances and mail routes in operation on the 1st of October, 1885. Published ... under the direction of W. L. Nicholson, Topographer, P. O. Dept.
1 inch to 10 miles. 2 sections, each 29½ x 44.

Published. Frequency and types of mail service, mileages between post offices, discontinued post offices, counties, towns, railroads, military posts, and physical features. Post routes in color to show frequency of service. Filed as RG 28: series 1, folder X.

647. [Map of the] State of North Dakota. ... 1889. Compiled from the official Records of the General Land Office. . . . Compiled and Drawn by A. F. Dinsmore. ... Corrected to October 1st, 1889, by M. Hendges.

1 inch to 12 miles. 25 x 34½. Published. County boundaries and military and Indian reservations are shown in color. Also shows status of public land surveys, towns, railroad lines, railroad land-grant limits, and drainage features. Also a black and white base map for this date. 25 x 34½. Filed as RG 49: North Dakota 1889, Pub.

648. [Map of the] State of North Dakota. ... 1889. Compiled from the official Records of the General Land Office. ... Compiled and Drawn by A. F. Dinsmore. ... Corrected to October 1st, 1889, by M. Hendges.

1 inch to 12 miles. 26 x 36½. Annotated published. Annotated to show railroad land-grant limits. Basic information same as that shown on entry 647. Filed as RG 49: North Dakota 12.

649. [Map of the] State of North Dakota. ... 1892. Compiled for the official Records of the General Land Office. ... Compiled and Drawn by A. F. Dinsmore. Traced and Lettered by M. Hendges.

1 inch to 12 miles. 27 x 36½. Published. County names and boundaries, towns, locations of U.S. land offices, status of public land surveys, military and Indian reservations, and railroad lines proposed and completed. Drainage features in blue. Relief in brown. Filed as RG 49: North Dakota 1892, Pub.

650. [Map of the] State of North Dakota. Compiled from the official Records of the General Land Office ... 1903. ... Compiled and Drawn by M. Hendges. Lettered by Wm. Bauman, Jr.

1 inch to 12 miles. 27 x 34½. Published. County names and boundaries, towns, locations of U.S. land offices, Indian reservations, roads and trails, railroad lines, and physical features. Files as RG 49: North Dakota 1903, Pub.

651. [Map of the] State of North Dakota. Compiled from the official Records of the General Land Office ... 1910. ... Compiled and Drawn by M. Hendges. Lettered by Wm. Bauman, Jr.

1 inch to 12 miles. 29 x 36. Published. County names and boundaries, towns, locations of U.S. land offices, Indian reservations, railroad lines, and physical features. Filed as RG 49: North Dakota 1910, Pub.

652. [Map of the] State of North Dakota [showing] Lands designated by the Secretary of the Interior Under the provisions of the Enlarged Homestead Acts. Edition of June 30, 1916 [Issued by the Department of the Interior.]

1 inch to 24 miles. 15 x 19. Published. Areas designated are shaded red. Also shows public land surveys. Filed as RG 49: North Dakota 8, Pub.

653. Post Route Map of the State of North Dakota showing post offices with the intermediate distances on mail routes in operation on the 1st of January, 1917.

1 inch to 10 miles. 32 x 43. Published. Frequency and types of mail service, discontinued post offices, counties, towns, railroads, physical features, and parts of adjoining States. Filed as RG 28: North Dakota 1917.

654. [Map of the] State of North Dakota. Compiled from the official Records of the General Land Office . . . 1918. . . . Compiled by M. Hendges. : . . Traced and Lettered by Wm. Bauman, Jr.

1 inch to 12 miles. 28 x 32½. Published. County and land district boundaries, towns, Indian reservations, bird reservations and national monuments, military reservations, and reclamation projects are shown in color. Also shows public land surveys, towns, and railroad lines. Relief is shown in color. Also a black and white base map for this date. 28 x 35. Files as RG 49: North Dakota 1918, Pub.

655. [Map of the] State of North Dakota [showing] Lands designated as non-irrigable by the Secretary of the Interior under the provisions of the Enlarged Homestead Acts . . . Edition of June 20, 1920. [Issued by the Department of the Interior.]

1 inch to 24 miles. 15 x 19. Published. Areas designated are shaded red. Also shows public land surveys. Filed as RG 49: North Dakota 9, Pub.

See also entries 517 and 518.

OHIO

656. Map of Ohio in Connection with Pittsburg [sic], Erie, Detroit & [etc.], By G. Pease. [n.d.]
  1 inch to 10 miles. 38½ x 31. Manuscript. Early map. Map includes Ohio with part of western Pennsylvania, Lake Erie, and connection with Detroit. Settlements, forts, roads, physical features, and Connecticut Western Reserve. "Western Reserve" appears in pencil in that area. Filed as RG 77: P 11.

657. Map of Ohio and Indiana Exhibiting the Post Offices, Post Roads, Canals, Rail Roads, &c. By David H. Burr (Late Topographer to the Post Office). . . . Entered according to the Act of Congress, July 10th, 1839.
  1 inch to 10 miles. 4 sections, each 19¼ x 25½. Published. Also shows counties (in color), mileages between post offices, township and range numbers, physcial features, and parts of adjoining States. Filed as RG 28: Burr Atlas, map 10.

658. Ohio. [ca. 1840]
  1 inch to 20 miles. 18 x 14. Published. Counties, township lines but not township and range numbers, towns, railroads, and canals. State is shaded green. Filed as Ref. Coll.; Ohio 1840.

659. [Map of the] State of Ohio [Issued by the General Land Office on Oct. 2, 1866].
  1 inch to 18 miles. 17 x 19. Published. Public surveys, counties, county seats, railroads, military lands, purchases, and reserves. Map includes a note on the mineral resources. Boundaries of counties and various tracts and reserves are outlined in color. Filed as RG 49: Ohio 2, Pub.

660. [Map of] State of Ohio. . . . 1878. Compiled from the official Records of the General Land Office.
  1 inch to 10 miles. 27 x 34. Published. County boundaries are shown in color. Township and range numbers, towns, principal railroad stations, railroad lines, canals, and drainage features. Also a black and white base map for this date. 27 x 32½. Filed as RG 49: Ohio 1878, Pub.

661. Post Route Map of the States of Ohio and Indiana with adjacent parts of Pennsylvania, Michigan, Illinois, Kentucky, and West Virginia. Showing post offices with the intermediate distances and mail routes in operation on the 1st of December, 1885. Published . . . under the direction of W. L. Nicholson, Topographer, P. O. Dept.
  1 inch to 8 miles. 2 sections, each 44 x 30½. Published. Frequency and types of mail service, mileages between post offices, discontinued post offices, counties, towns, railroads, and physical features. Post routes in color to show frequency of service. Filed as RG 28: series 1, folder VII.

662. [Map of the] State of Ohio, 1887. Compiled from the official Records of the General Land Office. . . . Compiled and Drawn by A. F. Dinsmore, 1887.
  1 inch to 10 miles. 26½ x 34. Published. County boundaries and names and boundaries of military lands, purchases, and reserves are shown in color. Also shows public land surveys, towns and cities, boundaries of Indian reservations, canals, railroad lines, and drainage features. Also a black and white base map for this date. 27½ x 30½. Filed as RG 49: Ohio 1887, Pub.

663. Map of the State of Ohio. Compiled from the official Records of the General Land Office. . . . 1895. . . . Revised and Corrected by I. P. Berthong.
  1 inch to 12 miles. 25 x 28. Published. County names and boundaries, military lands, purchases, French land grants, Indian and other reservations, township and range numbers, towns and cities, military posts, railroad lines, and drainage features. Also a black and white base map for this date. 25 x 27. Filed as RG 49: Ohio 1895, Pub.

664. Post Route Map of the State of Ohio showing post offices with the intermediate distances on mail routes in operation on the 1st of March, 1901.
  1 inch to 8 miles. 47 x 34½. Published. Frequency and types of mail service, discontinued post offices, counties, towns, railroads, physical features, and parts of adjoining States. Post routes in color to show frequency of service. Small piece of eastern Ohio is missing. Inset map "City of Cincinnati and Environs." Scale 1 inch to ca. 2¼ miles. Filed as RG 28: Ohio 1901.

665. [Map of the] State of Ohio. Compiled from the official Records of the General Land Office ... 1910. ... Compiled and Drawn by A. F. Dinsmore.

1 inch to 12 miles. 23¾ x 26. Published. County boundaries are shown in color. Military lands, purchases, French land grants, towns and cities, military posts, Indian and other reservations, township and range numbers, railroad lines, and drainage features. Also a black and white base map for this date. 24½ x 26¾. Filed as RG 49: Ohio 1910, Pub.

666. [Map of Ohio issued by the U.S. Geological Survey, 1915.]

1 inch to ca. 16 miles. 20 x 18. Published. County names and boundaries, towns and cities, township and range numbers, steam and electric railroad lines, and drainage features. Also a copy of this map reprinted in 1918. Filed as RG 57: Ohio 1915, Pub.

667. [Map of the] State of Ohio ... Compiled in the U.S. Geological Survey in 1910 and 1911 ... [Issued in] 1918.

1 inch to ca. 8 miles. 31 x 32. Published. County names and boundaries, settlements, township and range numbers, steam and electric railroad lines, and drainage features. Noted: "Advance sheet. Subject to corrections." Filed as RG 57: Ohio 1918, Pub.

See also entries 259 and 264.

OKLAHOMA
(including Indian Territory)

668. Map of the Indian Territory corrected according to the latest surveys. By [I]saac McCoy, 1838. Drawn by J. C. McCoy.

1 inch to 20 miles. 30 x 31½. Manuscript. Includes present States of Oklahoma, Kansas, Nebraska, and Iowa. Settlements, Indian reservations and lands, and populations of tribes. Map is extremely faded. Filed as RG 75: map 216.

669. Map of the Indian Territory. Showing the Boundaries of the Choctaw and Chickasaw Nations, the Creek, Seminole and Leased Indian Country. ... By Daniel C. Major, U.S. Astronomer. Jones, Brown, Fairbanks, Surveyors. [1858-59.]

1 inch to 12 miles. 31 x 41. Manuscript. Map includes portions of Texas, Arkansas, and Missouri. Also shows settlements, military posts, and roads. Relief and timber areas shown in color. Almost illegible annotations relating to cessions by Creeks, Seminoles, and Chickasaws are dated 1866. Note signed by W. P. Dole, Commissioner of Indian Affairs, states, "This Map is strictly conformable to the field notes of the survey thereof on file in this Office which have been examined and approved." Filed as RG 75: map 495.

670. [Map of] Indian Territory with part of the adjoining State of Kansas &c. Prepared from the Map of Danl. C. Major, U.S. Astr., showing the Boundaries of the Choctaw and Chickasaw Nations, the Creek, Seminole, and Leased Indian Country ... Engineer Bureau, War Dept., October 1866.

1 inch to ca. 25 miles. 21 x 27½. Manuscript. Also shows settlements, military posts, and roads. Filed as RG 75: map 491.

671. [Map of] Indian Territory with parts of neighboring States and Territories. ... Compiled under direction of 1st Lieut. Henry Jackson, 7th U.S. Cavalry, September 1869. Drawn by Ado Hunnius.

1 inch to 18.94 miles. 26 x 37½. Annotated published. Map includes portions of adjoining States. Settlements, military posts, roads, routes of expeditions, and names of some residents. Filed as RG 77: Q 144.

672. Military Map of the Indian Territory Compiled under the direction of 1st Lieut. E. H. Ruffner, Engineers. ... Drawn and Engraved by Ado Hunnius ... Jan. 1875.

1 inch to ca. 8 miles. 4 sections, each 26 x 30.

Published. Includes portions of adjoining States and Territories. Settlements, military posts, Indian lands, roads, and railroad lines. Relief is shown by hachures. Inset ground plans of Forts Supply and Sill. Filed as RG 393: Dept. of Missouri 9.

673. Map of Indian Territory. Compiled by G. W. Ingalls, U.S. Indian Agent, 1875.

1 inch to 12 miles. 23 x 30. Manuscript. Indian cessions and reservations (boundaries in color), populations of tribes, settlements, military posts, railroad lines, roads, and extent of public land surveys. Filed as RG 75: map 191.

674. [Map of] Indian Territory. ... 1876. ... Compiled from the official Records of the General Land Office.

1 inch to 12 miles. 26½ x 33½. Published. Indian reservation boundaries are shown in color. Status of public land surveys, towns, military posts, stage stations, Indian agencies and missions, roads, and railroad lines. Relief is shown by hachures. Also a black and white base map for this date. 25 x 33. Filed as RG 49: Indian Territory 1876, Pub.

675. [Map of] Indian Territory. 1876.

1 inch to 12 miles. 24 x 29½. Annotated published. Indian cessions (in color) with dates of treaties, populations of Indian tribes, cities and towns, military posts and reservations, railroad lines, and extent of public land surveys. Filed as RG 75: map 850.

676. [Map of] Indian Territory ... 1879. Compiled from the official Records of the General Land Office.

1 inch to 12 miles. 24 x 32. Published. Indian reservation boundaries are shown in color. Status of public land surveys, towns, military posts, stage stations, Indian agencies and missions, roads, and railroad lines. Relief is shown by hachures. Also a black and white base map for this date. 27 x 34. Filed as RG 49: Indian Territory 1879, Pub.

677. [Map of] Indian Territory ... 1883. Compiled from the official Records of the General Land Office.

1 inch to 12 miles. 25 x 34. Published. Indian reservation boundaries are shown in color. Public land surveys, towns, military posts and reservations, stage stations, Indian agencies and missions, roads and trails, and railroad lines. Relief is shown by hachures. Filed as RG 49: Indian Territory 1883, Pub.

678. [Map of] Indian Territory ... 1887. Compiled from the official Records of the General Land Office.

1 inch to 12 miles. 25½ x 34. Published. Indian reservation boundaries are shown in color. Public land surveys, towns, military posts and reservations, stage stations, Indian agencies and missions, roads and trails, and proposed and completed railroad lines. Relief is shown by hachures. Filed as RG 49: Indian Territory 1887, Pub.

679. Map of the Indian Territory showing the Railways Built and Projected within its Boundaries. Prepared in compliance with letter from the chairman of the Senate Committee on Indian Affairs to the Secretary of the Interior, dated February 3, 1887. Paul Brodie, Draftsman.

1 inch to 14 miles. 24½ x 30½. Annotated published. Annotated in color to show the boundaries of "the Three Grand Divisions" (Creek, Choctaw and Chickasaw, and Cherokee country), Cherokee Strip in Kansas, and "Oklahoma." Note in pencil signed P. Brodie states, "Proof sheet Recd January 21-1888." Filed as RG 75: map 1250.

680. [Map of] Indian Territory Compiled under the direction of the Hon: John H. Oberly, Commissioner of Indian Affairs, by C. A. Maxwell, Chief, Law and Land Division, Indian Bureau. 1889. John Olberg, Draftsman.

1 inch to 12 miles. 25 x 33. Published. Indian cessions are outlined in color and numbered to correspond with the key on the map. Also shows extent of public land surveys, military reservations, and Fort Reno Timber Reserve. Filed as RG 75: map 613.

681. Outline Map of lands, known as Oklahoma Indian Ter. (including East and West Land Districts) Opened to Settlement by Executive Order, March 23, 1889.

1 inch to 4 miles. 29 x 24. Annotated published. Shows public land surveys and is annotated apparently to show correct location of railroad and stageline stations. (Published copy filed as RG 49: Oklahoma 1, Pub.) Filed as RG 49: Oklahoma 15.

682. [Map of] Indian Territory ... 1891. Compiled from the official Records of the General Land Office ... Compiled and Drawn by R. P. Lowe ... Traced and Lettered by Wm. Naylor. 1 inch to 9 miles. 30 x 28½. Published. Map

shows only lands occupied by the Chickasaws, Choctaws, Seminoles, Creeks, Cherokees, and the several small reservations in the northeastern corner of the Territory. Indian reservation boundaries are shown in color. Public land surveys in Chickasaw lands are shown, and towns, military posts and reservations, roads and trails, and railroad lines. Relief is shown in color. Also a black and white base map with drainage in blue for this date. 30 x 28. See entry 684. Filed as RG 49: Indian Territory 1891, Pub.

683. [Map showing] Judicial Districts of the Indian Territory . . . 1891. Compiled from the official Records of the General Land Office . . . Compiled and Drawn by R. P. Lowe . . . Traced and Lettered by Wm. Naylor.

1 inch to 9 miles. 32 x 29. Annotated published. Annotated to show judicial districts. "Judicial Districts of the" is added to the title (See entry 682). Filed as RG 75: CA 133.

684. [Map of] Oklahoma Territory, 1891. Compiled from the official Records of the General Land Office . . . Compiled and drawn by R. P. Lowe. Traced and Lettered by M. Hendges.

1 inch to 12 miles. 26½ x 39. Published. Status of public land surveys, Indian lands, towns, military posts and reservations, locations of U.S. land offices, roads and trails, railroads proposed and completed, and drainage features. Two copies of this map: one showing certain areas in color and a black and white base map. Filed as RG 49: Oklahoma 1891, Pub.

685. Map of Oklahoma and Indian Territory Showing the Railways Built and Projected within its Boundaries. 1892. [Issued by the Office of Indian Affairs.]

1 inch to ca. 18 miles. 17½ x 34. Annotated blue line print. Annotated to show additional railroad lines. Typed sheet listing names of railroads is attached to the map. A General Land Office map apparently was used as the base map. Filed as RG 75: map CA 311.

686. Map of Oklahoma Territory. Compiled from the official Records of the General Land Office . . . 1893. . . . Compiled by R. P. Lowe. Lettered and corrected for Re-issue by M. Hendges.

1 inch to 12 miles. 27½ x 36½. Published. Status of public land surveys, names and boundaries of existing counties, military posts and reservations, locations of U.S. land offices, roads and trails, towns, railroads proposed and completed, Indian lands, and drainage features. Relief is shown in color. County boundaries and some Indian lands also shown in color. Filed as RG 49: Oklahoma 1893, Pub.

687. Map of Oklahoma Territory. Compiled from the official Records of the General Land Office . . . 1894. . . . Compiled by R. P. Lowe. Lettered and corrected for Re-issue by M. Hendges.

1 inch to 12 miles. 29 x 40½. Published. Status of public land surveys, Indian Territory, names and boundaries of existing counties, military posts and reservations, locations of U.S. land offices, roads and trails, towns, railroads proposed and completed, Indian lands, and drainage features. Relief, county boundaries, and some Indian lands are shown in color. Also a black and white base map for this date. 27 x 40. Filed as RG 49: Oklahoma 1894, Pub.

688. Map of Oklahoma Territory. Compiled from the official Records of the General Land Office . . . 1898. . . . Revised and Drawn by M. Hendges.

1 inch to 12 miles. 28½ x 40. Published. County boundaries and some Indian lands are shown in color. Status of public land surveys, towns, Indian Territory, military posts and reservations, locations of U.S. land offices, roads and trails, railroads proposed and completed, and drainage features. Relief is shown in color. Filed as RG 49: Oklahoma 1898, Pub.

689. Map of Oklahoma Territory. Compiled from the official Records of the General Land Office . . . 1898 . . . Revised and Drawn by M. Hendges.

1 inch to 12 miles. 27½ x 39. Annotated published. Annotated to show land district boundaries. Basic information shown same as in entry 688. Filed as RG 49: Oklahoma 16.

690. [Map of] Indian Territory. Compiled from the official Records of the General Land Office . . . 1899. . . . Compiled, Drawn and Lettered by M. Hendges.

1 inch to 12 miles. 25 x 23. Published. Map shows lands occupied by the Chickasaws, Choctaws, Seminoles, Creeks, Cherokees, and the several small reservations in the northeastern corner of the territory. Also shows parts of adjoining States and Oklahoma Territory. Indian reservation boundaries

are shown in color. Public land surveys, towns, roads, and railroad lines. Relief is shown in color. Also a black and white base map with drainage shown in blue for this date. 24 x 19. Filed as RG 49: Indian Territory 1899, Pub.

691. Map of Oklahoma Territory. From the corrected map of the General Land Office of 1898 and from data on file in the Executive Office of the Territory, to accompany the Annual Report of the Governor of the Territory, 1901.

1 inch to 19 miles. 15½ x 23. Published. County boundaries, some Indian lands, military reservations, and national forests are shown in color. Status of public land surveys, towns, Indian Territory, locations of U.S. land offices, roads and trails, railroads proposed and completed, and drainage features. Relief is shown in color. Filed as RG 49: Oklahoma 1901, Pub.

692. [Map of] Proposed State of Oklahoma, Act of June 16, 1906. Compiled from the official Records of the General Land Office . . . 1906. . . . Compiled by A. F. Dinsmore and M. Hendges.

1 inch to 12 miles. 22 x 42. Published. County boundaries, land district boundaries, Indian and military reservations, national forests are shown in color. Public land surveys, towns and cities, locations of U.S. land offices, railroad lines, and drainage features. Relief is shown in color. Small scale inset plans of Lawton, Guthrie, Muskogee, McAlester. Also a black and white base map for this date. 22 x 44. Filed as RG 49: Oklahoma 1906, Pub.

693. Map of Indian Territory Showing Telegraph, Telephone, and Railroad Lines in operation July 1st, 1907, prepared in the office of The United States Indian Inspector for the Indian Territory.

1 inch to 8 miles. 35 x 31. Blueprint. Shows settlements and township and range numbers. Note states, "All lines designated by figures are operated by the Pioneer Telephone and Telegraph Company. All lines designated by letters are operated by other companies." Filed as RG 75: map 6042.

694. [Map of the] State of Oklahoma. Compiled from the official Records of the General Land Office . . . 1907. . . . Compiled by A. F. Dinsmore and M. Hendges. . . . Drawn by Charles J. Helm.

1 inch to 12 miles. 22 x 43. Published. County boundaries, land district boundaries, Indian and military reservations, national forests are shown in color. Public land surveys, towns and cities, locations of U.S. land offices, railroad lines, and drainage features. Relief is shown in color. Small inset plans of Lawton, Guthrie, Muskogee, and McAlester. Also a black and white base map for this date. 22 x 43. Filed as RG 49: Oklahoma 1907, Pub.

695. [Map of the] State of Oklahoma. Compiled from official Records of the General Land Office . . . 1914. . . . Compiled by A. F. Dinsmore and M. Hendges; Revised by D. O'H. Drawn by Chas. J. Helm and T. O. W.

1 inch to 12 miles. 24 x 45. Published. County boundaries, land district boundaries, Indian and military reservations, national forests, and national parks are shown in color. Public land surveys, towns and cities, locations of U.S. land offices, railroad lines, and drainage features. Relief is shown in color. Small inset plans of Muskogee, Guthrie, Tulsa, McAlester and vicinity, and Oklahoma City. Also a black and white base map for this date. 24 x 44½. Filed as RG 49: Oklahoma 1914, Pub.

696. Oklahoma Historical Chart, By George Rainey. Webb Publishing Company, Oklahoma City . . . Approved by Oklahoma State Board of Education . . . 1917.

Scale not indicated. 27 x 21. Published. A set of ten maps, each showing the present State of Oklahoma during a period of its history and containing brief statements of historical information. Maps show area now Oklahoma for the following periods: (1) 1820-1830, (2) 1830-1850, (3) 1850-1860, (4) 1860-1867, (5) 1867-1870, (6) 1870-1890, (7) 1890, (8) 1906, (9) 1917, and (10) Routes of explorers, railroads, and trails. Maps 1-8 show Indian cessions and lands; maps 8 and 9 show counties. Indian lands and counties are shown in color. The maps show very few towns. Filed as RG 75: map 9350.

See also entries 82, 314, and 779.

OREGON

697. Map of the Oregon Territory by the U.S. Ex.[ploring] Ex.[pedition], Charles Wilkes, Esqr., Commander. 1841. . . . [Published by] J. H. Young & Sherman & Smith.
1 inch to ca. 50 miles. 23 x 35½. Annotated published. Annotated to show within red lines the present States of Washington, Oregon, and Idaho with portions of Montana and Wyoming west of the Continental Divide. Also shown are military posts, names of Indian tribes and their general locations, physical features, and remarks about the land. Inset map of the Columbia River from Fort Walla Walla to its mouth. Scale 1 inch to ca. 12 miles. Filed as RG 77: W 22.

698. Map of the United States Territory of Oregon, West of the Rocky Mountains, Exhibiting the various Trading Depots or Forts occupied by the British Hudson Bay Company connected with the Western and northwestern Fur Trade. Engraved Expressly for W. Robertson's History of Oregon. Washington, D.C., 1846.
1 inch to ca. 18 miles. 12 x 18. Published. Map includes present States of Oregon, Washington, and Idaho with portions of adjoining States and Canada. Filed as Ref. Coll.: Oregon 1846.

699. Sketch Map of Oregon Territory, Exhibiting the Locations of the various Indian Tribes, The districts of Country ceded by them, with the dates of Purchases and Treaties, and the Reserves of the Umpqua and Rogue River Indians. [1855.]
1 inch to 10 miles. 2 sections, each 33½ x 36½. Manuscript. Includes area from 110° West to the Pacific Ocean between 42° and 46°30′ North. Also shows settlements, roads, and military posts. Filed as RG 75: map 234.

700. A Diagram of Oregon. (Dated August 31, 1859, Surveyor General's Office, Salem, Oregon.)
1 inch to 18 miles. 20 x 24½. Annotated published. Status of public land surveys, roads, and towns. Annotated to show standard parallels, status of public surveys, routes of exploration, and other roads including "General Harney's Proposed Road." Date of map is corrected in pencil to 1860. Filed as RG 49: Oregon 6.

701. Map of the State of Oregon, and Washington Territory, compiled in The Bureau of Topogl. Engrs. . . . 1859. Engraved by W. H. Donegal.
1 inch to ca. 25 miles. 28 x 38. Published. Settlements, military posts, and roads. Relief shown by shading. Filed as RG 77: 1859, Pub.

702. A Diagram of Oregon [Issued by Surveyor General's Office, Eugene City, Sept. 30, 1860].
1 inch to ca. 18 miles. 19½ x 24. Published. Shows status of public land surveys. Filed as RG 46: S. Ex. Doc. 1, 36th Cong., 2d sess.

703. A Diagram of Oregon [Issued by Surveyor General's Office, Eugene City, Aug. 16, 1861].
1 inch to ca. 20 miles. 19½ x 25. Published. Shows status of public land surveys. Filed as RG 46: S. Ex. Doc. 1, 37th Cong., 2d sess.

704. A Diagram of Oregon . . . Surveyor General's Office, Eugene City, July 20, 1865.
1 inch to 18 miles. 17½ x 23½. Published. Status of public land surveys, towns, roads, and physical features. Relief is shown by hachures. Filed as RG 49: Oregon 3, Pub.

705. [Map of] Oregon . . . Surveyor General's Office, Eugene City, July 20, 1866. [Issued by the General Land Office on Oct. 2, 1866.]
1 inch to 18 miles. 19½ x 23½. Published. County boundaries and gold deposits are shown in color. Also shows public surveys, county names, Indian reservations, military posts, "Oregon Central Military Road," and physical features. Filed as RG 49: Oregon 4, Pub.

706. Map of Oregon. [Dated Sept. 14, 1871. Surveyor General's Office, Eugene City, Oregon.]
1 inch to 12 miles. 26½ x 34½. Manuscript. Status of public land surveys, military roads, lighthouse and military reservations, and gold and coal mines. Filed as RG 49: Oregon 8.

707. [Map of the] State of Oregon. 1876. Compiled from the official Records of the General Land Office.
1 inch to 15 miles. 26½ x 33½. Published. County and land district boundaries, Indian reservations, and railroad land-grant limits are shown in color. Also shows status of public land surveys, towns and cities, locations of U.S. land offices, roads, and military posts. Relief is shown by hachures. Also a black and white base map for this date. 25½ x 33. Filed as RG 49: Oregon 1876, Pub.

708. [Map of the] State of Oregon. ... 1879. Compiled from the official Records of the General Land Office.
1 inch to 15 miles. 26½ x 33½. Annotated published. County and land district boundaries and Indian reservations are shown in color. Also shows status of public land surveys, towns and cities, locations of U.S. land offices, railroad lines and land-grant limits, and military reservations. Relief is shown by hachures. Annotated to show names of land districts. Filed as RG 49: Oregon 10.

709. [Map of the] State of Oregon, and Territories of Washington & Idaho, Prepared in the Office of the Chief of Engineers, U.S.A., 1879.
1 inch to ca. 8 miles. 33 x 35. Published. Settlements, military posts, roads, railroad lines, and drainage features. Relief shown by hachures. Filed as RG 77: 1879, Pub.

710. Post Route Map of the State of Oregon and Territory of Washington. ... W. L. Nicholson, Topographer of P. O. Dept., 1877. ... Drawn by A. F. Dinsmore ... [Revised] up to date of Jan. 1st, 1880.
1 inch to ca. 12 miles. 2 sections, each 23½ x 36. Annotated photoprocessed. Annotated to show additional post offices and post routes. Frequency and types of mail service, mileage between post offices, discontinued post offices, counties, towns, railroads, military posts, and physical features. Post routes in color to show frequency of service. Filed as RG 28: series 1, folder IV.

711. Post Route Map of the State of Oregon and Territory of Washington Showing post offices, with the intermediate distances between them and mail routes in operation on 1st August 1883. ... Under direction of C. Roeser Jr., Topographer of P. O. Dept., 1883. ... [Revised] up to date of Oct. 1st, 1883.
1 inch to 10 miles. 2 sections, each 30 x 43½. Frequency and types of mail service, mileages between post offices, counties, towns, military posts, and railroads. Post routes shown in color to illustrate frequency of service. Filed as RG 28: series 1, folder V.

712. [Map of the] State of Oregon. ... 1884. Compiled from the official Records of the General Land Office. ... Compiled by A. F. Dinsmore. Drawn by Wm. Naylor.
1 inch to 15 miles. 26½ x 34. Published. County boundaries and Indian and military reservations are shown in color. Also shows status of public land surveys, towns and cities, locations of U.S. land offices, roads, railroad lines, and railroad land-grant limits. Relief is shown by hachures. Also a black and white base map for this date. 25½ x 31. Filed as RG 49: Oregon 1884, Pub.

713. Post Route Map of the State of Oregon and Territory of Washington, showing post offices with the intermediate distances and mail routes in operation on the 1st of February, 1887. Published ... under the direction of W. L. Nicholson, Topographer, P. O. Dept.
1 inch to 10 miles. 2 sections, each 29 x 44. Published. Frequency and types of mail service, mileages between post offices, discontinued post offices, counties, towns, railroads, and physical features. Post routes in color to show frequency of service. Filed as RG 28: series 1, folder XXI.

714. [Map of the] State of Oregon. ... 1889. Compiled from the official Records of the General Land Office. ... Compiled and Drawn by A. F. Dinsmore.
1 inch to 12 miles. 29 x 41. Published. County boundaries and military and Indian reservations are shown in color. Also shows status of public land surveys, towns and cities, locations of U.S. land offices, roads, and railroad lines. Relief is shown by hachures. Also a black and white base map for this date. 30 x 38. Filed as RG 49: Oregon 1889, Pub.

715. Post Route Map of the States of Oregon and Washington with adjacent parts of Idaho, Nevada, California, and British Columbia. Showing post offices with the intermediate

distances and mail routes in operation on the 1st of June, 1891. Published ... under the direction of C. Roeser Jr., Topographer, P. O. Dept.

1 inch to 10 miles. 2 sections, each 28½ x 43. Published. Frequency and types of mail service, mileages between post offices, discontinued post offices, counties, towns, railroads, and physical features. Post routes in color to show frequency of service. Filed as RG 28: series 1, folder XXV.

716. Map of the State of Oregon. Compiled from the official Records of the General Land Office ... 1897. ... Compiled, Drawn, and Lettered by M. Hendges.

1 inch to 12 miles. 29½ x 37. Published. County boundaries, Indian reservations, and national forests are shown in color. Also shows status of public land surveys, towns and cities, locations of U.S. land offices, military roads, other roads and trails, lighthouses, lifesaving stations, and railroad lines proposed and completed. Relief is shown in color. Also a black and white base map for this date. Drainage in blue. 30 x 38. Filed as RG 49: Oregon 1897, Pub.

717. Post Route Map of the State of Oregon showing post offices with the intermediate distances on mail routes in operation on the 1st of June, 1897.

1 inch to 10 miles. 34 x 43½. Published. Frequency and types of mail service, discontinued post offices, counties, towns, railroads, physical features, and parts of adjoining States. Post routes in color to show frequency of service. Filed as RG 28: Oregon 1897.

718. [Map of the] State of Oregon. Compiled from the official Records of the General Land Office ... 1906. ... Compiled by M. Hendges, Revised by A. F. Dinsmore ... Traced and Lettered by Wm. Bauman, Jr.

1 inch to 12 miles. 30 x 38. Published. County and land district boundaries, military and Indian reservations, and national forests and parks are shown in color. Also shows status of public land surveys, towns and cities, locations of U.S. land offices, military roads, lighthouses, and railroad lines. Relief is shown in color. Small inset plan of Portland. Also a black and white base map for this date. 28 x 36. Filed as RG 49: Oregon 1906, Pub.

719. [Map of the] State of Oregon. Compiled from the official Records of the General Land Office ... 1906. ... Compiled by M. Hendges, Revised by A. F. Dinsmore ... Traced and Lettered by Wm. Bauman, Jr.

1 inch to 12 miles. 30½ x 39. Annotated published. Annotated to show U.S. location monuments for mineral surveys. Stamped No. 80531. Typed page listing monuments is attached to the map. Basic information is the same as that shown on entry 718. Filed as RG 49: Oregon 31.

720. [Map of the] State of Oregon [showing] Lands designated by the Secretary of the Interior, April 27, 1909, under the Enlarged Homestead Act of Feb. 19, 1909. [Issued by the Department of the Interior.]

1 inch to 24 miles. 16 x 20. Published. Areas designated are shaded red. Also shows public land surveys. Filed as RG 49: Oregon 11, Pub.

721. [Map of the] State of Oregon. Compiled from the official Records of the General Land Office ... 1910. ... Compiled by M. Hendges, Revised by A. F. Dinsmore. Traced and Lettered by Wm. Bauman, Jr.

1 inch to 12 miles. 31½ x 39. Published. County and land district boundaries, military and Indian reservations, national forests and parks, national monuments and bird reserves, and reclamation projects are shown in color. Also shows status of public land surveys, towns and cities, locations of U.S. land offices, military roads, lighthouses, and railroad lines. Relief is shown in color. Also a black and white base map for this date. 31½ x 39. Filed as RG 49: Oregon 1910, Pub.

722. [Map of the] State of Oregon [showing] Lands designated by the Secretary of the Interior As subject to entry under the provisions of the Enlarged Homestead Act of February 19, 1909. Edition of March 30, 1910. [Issued by the Department of the Interior.]

1 inch to 24 miles. 16 x 20. Published. Areas designated are shaded red. Also shows public land surveys. Filed as RG 49: Oregon 12, Pub.

723. [Map of the] State of Oregon [showing] Lands designated by the Secretary of the Interior As subject to entry under the provisions of the Enlarged Homestead Act of February 19, 1909. Edition of December 31, 1912. [Issued by the Department of the Interior.]

1 inch to 24 miles. 16 x 20. Published. Areas designated are shaded red. Also shows public land surveys. Filed as RG 49: Oregon 13, Pub.

724. [Map of the] State of Oregon ... Compiled [in the U.S. Geological Survey] in 1914.
1 inch to ca. 8 miles. 43 x 56. Published. County names and boundaries, towns and cities, township and range numbers, steam and electric railroad lines, and drainage features. Noted: "Advance sheet. Subject to corrections." Filed as RG 57: Oregon 1914, Pub.

725. [Map of Oregon issued by the U.S. Geological Survey, 1915.]
1 inch to ca. 16 miles. 22 x 28. Published. County names and boundaries, township and range numbers, towns and cities, steam and electric railroad lines, and drainage features. Filed as RG 57: Oregon 1915, Pub.

726. Post Route Map of the State of Oregon showing post offices with the intermediate distances on mail routes in operation on the 1st of January, 1917.
1 inch to 10 miles. 34 x 43½. Published. Frequency and types of mail service, discontinued post offices, counties, towns, railroads, physical features, and parts of adjoining States. Filed as RG 28: Oregon 1917.

727. [Map of the] State of Oregon [showing] Lands designated by the Secretary of the Interior Under the provisions of the Enlarged Homestead Act. Edition of June 30, 1918. [Issued by the Department of the Interior.]
1 inch to 24 miles. 16 x 20½. Published. Areas designated are shaded red. Also shows public land surveys. Filed as RG 49: Oregon 14, Pub.

PENNSYLVANIA

728. A Mapp of Ye Improved Part of Pensilvania [sic] in America, Divided into Countyes, Townships and Lotts Surveyed by Tho: Holme. [1681]
1 inch to ca. 3 miles. 21½ x 26. Published. Shows Bucks, Philadelphia, and Chester Counties with portion of Newcastle County and Manor of Rockland. Counties shown in color. Names of "inhabitants" are listed. Inset plan of Philadelphia. See entry 740. Filed as Ref. Coll.: Pennsylvania 1681.

729. To the Honourable Thomas Penn and Richard Penn, Esqrs. ... This map of the improved Part of the Province of Pennsylvania Is humbly dedicated by Nicholas Scull ... Engraved by Jas. Turner, and Printed by John Davis, for the Author. Published ... Jan. 1st, 1759.
1 inch to ca. 4 miles. 2 sections, each 34 x 31. Published. Map includes Pennsylvania from the eastern boundary north to Wyoming in Luzerne County and west to about 75 miles west of Shippensburg in Cumberland County. Shows counties, names of townships, settlements, roads, forges, furnaces, forts, mills, churches, Indian villages, and names of some residents. Filed as Ref. Coll.: Pennsylvania 1759.

730. To the Honourable Thomas Penn and Richard Penn, Esquires ... This Map of the Province of Pennsylvania Is humbly dedicated by ... W Scull ... Henry Dawkins, Sculp. ... Philadelphia, Printed by James Nevil for the Author, April 4th, 1770.
1 inch to 10 miles. 23½ x 34. Published. Most detail shown in southeastern part of the State, though area covered extends as far west as Fort Pitt. Counties (boundaries in color), settlements, roads, forts, furnaces, mines, and names of some residents. Filed as Ref. Coll.: Pennsylvania 1770.

731. A Map of Pennsylvania Exhibiting not only The Improved Parts of that Province, but also Its Extensive Frontiers: Laid down From Actual Surveys and Chiefly From the late Map of W. Scull, Published in 1770; And Humbly Inscribed to the Honourable Thomas Penn and Richard Penn, Esquires, True and Absolute Proprietaries & Governors of the Province of Pennsylvania And the Territories thereunto belonging. [1777]
1 inch to ca. 7 miles. 28½ x 49. Most detail

shown in southeastern Pennsylvania, although area covered extends as far west as Pittsburgh. Names and boundaries of existing counties, trails, settlements, forts, mills, township names, churches, meetinghouses, physical features, and names of a few residents. Filed as Ref. Coll.: Pennsylvania 1777.

732. A Map of the State of Pennsylvania, By Reading Howell, MDCCXCII. . . . Published 1 August 1792, for the Author, & Sold by James Phillips . . . London.

1 inch to 5 miles. 4 sections, each 28 x 29½. Published. Counties (in color), townships, towns, Indian villages, surveyors' districts, bridle paths, houses of worship, furnaces, forges, mills, roads, Indian paths, mineral deposits, physical features, and houses and names of residents. Map includes small portions of adjoining States. Map is inscribed to Governor Thomas Mifflin and to the Senate and House of Representatives of Pennsylvania. See entry 733. Filed as Ref. Coll.: Pennsylvania 1792.

733. A Map of the State of Pennsylvania. By Reading Howell. MDCCXCII.

1 inch to 5 miles. 2 sections, each 40½ x 33½. Published. Counties (boundaries in color), townships, surveyors' districts, Indian villages, forts, bridle paths, churches, furnaces, forges, mills, roads, Indian paths, mineral deposits, houses, names of some residents, and physical features. Map is inscribed to Governor Thomas Mifflin and to the Senate and House of Representatives of Pennsylvania. See entry 732. Filed as Ref. Coll.: Pennsylvania 1792.

734. A Map Exhibiting a General View of the Roads and Inland Navigation of Pennsylvania, and Part of the Adjacent States. Respectfully inscribed to Thomas Mifflin, Governor, and the General Assembly of the Commonwealth of Pennsylvania: by John Adlum, and John Wallis. [ca. 1792-5.]

1 inch to ca. 11 miles. 33 x 36½. Annotated published. Also shows settlements, forts, and physical features. Annotated to show additional roads and information about them. Inset illustrations of canal locks. Filed as RG 77: E 46.

735. A Map of the State of Pennsylvania By Reading Howell . . . 1817, Published by Kimber & Sharpless for Emmor Kimber.

1 inch to 10 miles. 23½ x 35½. Counties (boundaries in color), townships, towns, roads, churches, mineral deposits, physical features, and "Line limiting the purchase made of the Indians, November 1768." Map is inscribed to the Governor and Legislature of the Commonwealth of Pennsylvania. Map includes small portions of Maryland and Delaware. Filed as RG 77: US 10-2.

736. Map of Pennsylvania, Constructed from the County Surveys authorized by the State; and other original Documents, by John Melish. Engraved by B. Tanner. [1822.]

1 inch to 5 miles. 4 sections, each 26 x 38. Map shows counties (in color), townships, towns, roads, "Heads of Canoe Navigation" (and Boat Navigation), factories, mills, furnaces and forges, mineral deposits, churches, post offices, and physical features. Map includes parts of New York, New Jersey, Maryland, Delaware, and Virginia. Statistical table lists population, area, and other information concerning individual counties. Filed as RG 77: US 36.

737. Map of Pennsylvania, Constructed from the County Surveys authorized by the State; and other original documents, by John Melish. Engraved by B. Tanner. Corrected and Improved to 1832 . . . Published by B. Tanner.

1 inch to 5 miles. 4 sections, each 29½ x 38. Counties (in color), townships, towns, roads, "Heads of Canoe Navigation" (and Boat Navigation), factories, mills, furnaces and forges, mineral deposits, churches, post offices, canals, railroads, and physical features. Map includes parts of New York, New Jersey, Maryland, Delaware, and Virginia. Statistical table lists population, area, and other information concerning individual counties. Filed as RG 77: US 65.

738. Map of the State of Pennsylvania, and New Jersey. London. Published March 15, 1832, by Hinton & Simpkin & Marshall. Engraved & Printed by Fenner Sears & Co.

1 inch to ca. 35 miles. 11½ x 17. Published. Counties, settlements, roads, railroad, and physical features. Inset plan of Philadelphia. Filed as Ref. Coll.: Pennsylvania 1832.

739. [Map of] Pennsylvania . . . Entered according to Act of Congress in the year 1843, by Sidney E. Morse and Samuel Breese in the Clerks Office of the Southern District of New York.

1 inch to ca. 20 miles. 14 x 18. Published.

Counties, townships, major towns, railroads, canals, slack-water navigation, and physical features. Inset map of Philadelphia, Montgomery, and Delaware Counties and map of "Coal Region." Filed as Ref. Coll.: Pennsylvania 1843.

740. A Map of the Improved Part of the Province of Pennsilvania in America. ... Fac-simile of Holmes-Map of the Province of Pennsylvania with the names of the original purchasers from William Penn. Begun in 1681. Reproduced from the original in the Philadelphia Library by the Anastatic Process. 200 copies only printed. Published at the anastatic printing office ... and by Lloyd P. Smith. Philadelphia, 1846.

1 inch to 1 mile. 2 sections, each 34½ x 29½. Published. Inset plan of Philadelphia. See entry 728. Filed as Ref. Coll.: Pennsylvania 1846.

741. Post Route Map of the States of Pennsylvania, New Jersey, Delaware, and Maryland, and of the District of Columbia with adjacent parts of New York, Ohio, Virginia and West Virginia . . . by W. L. Nicholson, Topographer of P. O. Dep't., 1869. . . . Engraved by D. McClelland . . . Drawn by C. H. Poole ... [Revised] up to date of November 1st, 1869.

1 inch to 6 miles. 4 sections, each 30½ x 34½. State boundaries in color. Frequency and types of mail service, mileages between post offices, counties, towns, and railroads. Post routes shown in color to illustrate number of deliveries per week. Tables list statistical information. Note states "Presentation copy. Recd. Jany. 1870." Inset map showing postal service on Delmarva Peninsula and connections with the mainland of Virginia and the eastern shore of Maryland. Scale 1 inch to 10 miles. Filed as RG 28: series 1, folder I.

742. Post Route Map of the States of Pennsylvania, New Jersey, Delaware, and Maryland, and of the District of Columbia with adjacent parts of New York, Ohio, Virginia and West Virginia . . . by W. L. Nicholson, Topographer of P. O. Dep't., 1869. . . . Engraved by D. McClelland . . . Drawn by C. H. Poole ... [Revised] up to date of Feby. 1, 1873.

1 inch to 6 miles. 61 x 69. Frequency and types of mail service, mileages between post offices, counties, towns, and railroads. Post routes shown in color to illustrate frequency of service. Tables list statistical information. Inset map showing postal service on Delmarva Peninsula and connection with the mainland of Virginia and the eastern shore of Maryland. Scale 1 inch to 10 miles. Filed as RG 28: series 1, folder III.

743. Post Route Map of the States of Pennsylvania, New Jersey, Delaware, and Maryland, and of the District of Columbia with adjacent parts of New York, Ohio, Virginia and West Virginia. Showing post offices, with the intermediate distances between them and mail routes in operation on 1st, August 1883 ... under direction of C. Roeser Jr., Topographer of P. O. Dept., 1883 ... Engraved by D. McClelland.

1 inch to 6 miles. 4 sections, each 32½ x 28½. Frequency and types of mail service, mileages between post offices, counties, towns, and railroads. Post routes shown in color to illustrate frequency of service. Table lists distances between major eastern cities. Inset map of "City of Pittsburgh and Environs." Scale 1 inch to ca. 3 miles. Filed as RG 28: series 1, folder V.

744. Post Route Map of the States of Pennsylvania, New Jersey, Delaware, and Maryland, and of the District of Columbia with adjacent parts of New York, Ohio, Virginia, and West Virginia showing post offices with the intermediate distances and mail routes in operation on the 1st of April, 1885. Published ... under the direction of W. L. Nicholson, Topographer, P. O. Dept. [Corrected to June 1, 1885.]

1 inch to 6 miles. 4 sections, each 30½ x 33½. Published. Frequency and types of mail service, mileages between post offices, discontinued post offices, counties, towns, railroads, and physical features. Post routes in color to show frequency of service. Inset map of "City of Pittsburgh and Environs" at a scale of 1 inch to 3 miles. Inset map showing "Postal Service of the Eastern Shore of Virginia and Maryland and connections with Norfolk and with the lower peninsula of Virginia." Scale 1 inch to 10 miles. Filed as RG 28: series 1, folder XV.

745. Post Route Map of the States of Pennsylvania, New Jersey, Delaware, and Maryland, and of the District of Columbia with adjacent parts of New York, Ohio, Virginia, and West Virginia showing post offices with the intermediate distances and mail routes in operation on the

90   MAPS OF STATES AND TERRITORIES

1st of April 1885. Published ... under the direction of W. L. Nicholson, Topographer, P. O. Dept. [Corrected to Dec. 1, 1885.]

1 inch to 6 miles. 61 x 67. Published. Basic information same as that shown on entry 744. Filed as RG 28: Pennsylvania 1885.

746. Rail Road Map of Pennsylvania, Published by the Bureau of Railways of the Department of Internal Affairs of Pennsylvania, 1897. Drawn and compiled by J. Sutton Wall, Chief Draughtsman.

1 inch to 6 miles. 39 x 58. Published. Also shows counties (in color), cities and towns, and drainage features. Railroad systems are shown in color. Filed as Ref. Coll.: Pennsylvania 1897.

747. Post Route Map of the State of Pennsylvania showing post offices with the intermediate distances on mail routes in operation on the 1st of March, 1901.

1 inch to 5 miles. 4 sections, each 20½ x 36. Published. Frequency and types of mail service, discontinued post offices, counties, towns, railroads, physical features, and parts of adjoining States. Post routes in color to show frequency of service. Inset map of the "Environs of Philadelphia." Scale 1 inch to ca. 3 miles. Filed as RG 28: Pennsylvania 1901.

748. [Map of Pennsylvania issued by the U.S. Geological Survey, 1916.]

1 inch to ca. 16 miles. 18 x 25. Published. County names and boundaries, towns and cities, steam and electric railroad lines, and drainage features. Filed as RG 57: Pennsylvania 1916, Pub.

See also entry 562.

SOUTH CAROLINA

749. A Map of South Carolina and a Part of Georgia. ... Composed From Surveys taken by The Hon. William Bull, Esq., Lieutenant Governor, Captain Gascoign, Hugh Bryan, Esq., and William De Braham, Esqr., Surveyor General of the Southn. District of North America, Republished with considerable additions, from the Surveys made & collected by John Stuart, Esqr., His Majesty's Superintendant [sic] of Indian Affairs, By William Faden ... Charing Cross, 1780.

1 inch to 5 miles. 2 sections, each 27 x 48. Published. Parishes, townships, boroughs, roads, bridges, plantations, names of some residents, and physical features. Filed as RG 77: US 8.

750. [Map of] South Carolina. ... Entered according to Act of Congress in the year 1843, by Sidney E. Morse and Samuel Breese in the Clerks Office of the Southern District of New York.

1 inch to 20 miles. 14 x 18. Published. Counties, towns, roads, canals, and physical features. State shaded yellow. Filed as Ref. Coll.: South Carolina 1843.

751. [Map of South Carolina issued by the U.S. Geological Survey, 1916.]

1 inch to ca. 16 miles. 16 x 20. Published. County names and boundaries, towns and cities, steam and electric railroad lines, and drainage features. Filed as RG 57: South Carolina 1916, Pub.

752. [Map of the] State of South Carolina ... Compiled in the U.S. Geological Survey in 1913. ... Reprinted in 1917.

1 inch to ca. 8 miles. 32 x 20. Published. County names and boundaries, settlements, steam and electric railroad lines, and drainage features. Noted: "Advance sheet. Subject to corrections." Filed as RG 57: South Carolina 1917, Pub.

753. Post Route Map of the State of South Carolina showing post offices with the intermediate distances on mail routes in operation on the 1st of January, 1917.

1 inch to 8 miles. 31 x 39. Published. Frequency and types of mail service, discontinued post offices, counties, towns, railroads, physical features, and parts of adjoining States. Filed as RG 28: South Carolina 1917.

See also entries 620, 622, 623, 625, 627, 629, and 630.

SOUTH DAKOTA

754. [Map of the] State of South Dakota.... 1889. Compiled from the official Records of the General Land Office. ... Compiled by A. F. Dinsmore. Corrected to October 1st, 1889, by M. Hendges.

1 inch to 12 miles. 24½ x 37. Published. County names and boundaries, towns, locations of U.S. land offices, Indian reservations, military posts, status of public land surveys, railroad lines, and drainage features. Relief is shown by hachures. Filed as RG 49: South Dakota 1889, Pub.

755. Map of the State of South Dakota. Compiled from the Records of the General Land Office ... 1901. ... Compiled, Drawn, and lettered by M. Hendges.

1 inch to 12 miles. 24½ x 38. Published. County names and boundaries, towns, locations of U.S. land offices, military and Indian reservations, status of public land surveys, roads and trails, railroad lines, and physical features. (A copy of this map, annotated to show land districts, is filed as South Dakota 14, in RG 49.) Filed as RG 49: South Dakota 1901, Pub.

756. [Map of the] State of South Dakota. Compiled from the official Records of the General Land Office ... 1910. ... Compiled by M. Hendges, Revised by A. F. Dinsmore. Traced and Lettered by Wm. Bauman, Jr.

1 inch to 12 miles. 26 x 37. Published. County names and boundaries, towns and cities, status of public land surveys, locations of U.S. land offices, military and Indian reservations, national forests, and railroad lines. Filed as RG 49: South Dakota 1910, Pub.

757. [Map of the] State of South Dakota [showing] Lands designated by the Secretary of the Interior Under the provisions of the Enlarged Homestead Act. Edition of June 30, 1916. [Issued by the Department of the Interior.]

1 inch to 24 miles. 13½ x 19½. Published. Areas designated are shaded red. Also shows public land surveys. Filed as RG 49: South Dakota 8, Pub.

758. Post Route Map of the State of South Dakota showing post offices with the intermediate distances on mail routes in operation on the 1st of January, 1917.

1 inch to 10 miles. 32 x 42½. Published. Frequency and types of mail service, discontinued post offices, counties, towns, railroads, physical features, and parts of adjoining States. Filed as RG 28: South Dakota 1917.

759. [Map of the] State of South Dakota. Compiled from the official Records of the General Land Office ... 1918. ... Compiled by M. Hendges, Revised by G. A. Daidy. Traced and Lettered by Wm. Bauman, Jr.

1 inch to 12 miles. 26 x 36. Published. County boundaries, Indian reservations, military reservations, national forests and parks, and reclamation projects are shown in color. Also shows status of public land surveys, towns and cities, locations of U.S. land offices, land district boundaries, and railroad lines. Relief is shown in color. Also a black and white base map for this date. 26 x 36. Filed as RG 49: South Dakota 1918, Pub.

760. [Map of the] State of South Dakota [showing] Lands designated as non-irrigable by the Secretary of the Interior under the provisions of the Enlarged Homestead Acts . . . Edition of June 30, 1920. [Issued by the Department of the Interior.]

1 inch to 24 miles. 14 x 19. Published. Areas designated are shaded red. Also shows public land surveys. Filed as RG 49: South Dakota 9, Pub.

See also entries 517, 518, and 632-646.

TENNESSEE

761. A Map of the Tennassee [sic] Government, formerly part of North Carolina taken chiefly from Surveys by Genel. [sic] D. South & others. John Madert, Del. Engraved for Imlay's American Topography. June 1st, 1795.

1 inch to ca. 35 miles. 13 x 18½. Manuscript on tracing cloth. Roads, towns, Indian towns, and "Indian boundaries." Filed as RG 75: map 1237.

762. Map of Tennessee Constructed from the Surveys of the late John Strothers and other Documents, by John Melish. [Published by John Melish, 1819.]

1 inch to ca. 18 miles. 21 x 29. Published. Counties (in color), settlements, roads, and Indian lands. Also shows parts of adjoining States and Territories. Filed as RG 77: US 30.

763. Map of the State of Tennessee, Drawn from the Best Authorities by F. Lucas, Jr., Drawn & Published by F. Lucas, Jr . . . Entered according to Act of Congress the 21st day of June, 1823. . . . Engraved by B. T. Welch & Co.

1 inch to ca. 15 miles. 25 x 36. Annotated published. County names and boundaries, towns, colleges, roads, physical features, and parts of adjoining States. Also shows land districts and land surveys. Roads shown include part of the "Government road from Natchez to Nashville." Map is annotated to show segments of certain roads marked off. Table lists population of Tennessee by county, 1800-1820. Also included is a "View of the Chickasaw Bluff on the Mississippi River . . ." drawn by Lewis Brantz. Filed as RG 77: US 49.

764. Colton's Tennessee, Published J. H. Colton . . . New York. 1861.

1 inch to 25 miles. 14 x 25½. Published. Counties (in color), parts of adjoining States, towns, roads, railroads, and physical features. Illustration of State House. Filed as RG 77: T 16.

765. Map of Tennessee Representing Rail-Ways, Population, and Agricultural Productions. Prepared at the Census Office Under the Direction of Jos. C. G. Kennedy, Superintendent. [ca. 1861-65.]

Scale not indicated. 3 sections, each 20 x 17. Photoprocessed. Population for white, free-colored, and slaves. Filed as RG 77: T 215.

766. [Map of Tennessee issued by the U.S. Geological Survey, 1916.]

1 inch to ca. 16 miles. 11 x 34. Published. County names and boundaries, towns and cities, steam and electric railroad lines, and drainage features. Also a copy of this map reprinted in 1918. Filed as RG 57: Tennessee 1916, Pub.

See also entries 325, 327, 328, 331, 334, and 337-339.

TEXAS

767. Map of Texas With Parts of the Adjoining States. Compiled by Stephen F. Austin. Published by H. S. Tanner . . . Engraved by John & Wm. W. Warr . . . Entered according to Act of Congress the 17th day of March, 1830.

1 inch to ca. 25 miles. 20½ x 24½. Austin's Colony, Austin's Grant, Dewitt's Colony, towns, roads, military posts, sites and dates of battles, Indian villages, mines, missions, physical features, and information about characteristics of the land, and areas in which are found wild horses, cattle, and buffalo. Map shows Texas and parts of adjoining Mexican States. Filed as RG 77: Ama 12.

768. Plana Mayor Del Ejercito. Plano Geografico De Tejas . . . por orden del Exmo Senor Gefe del Cuerpo, General do Division. Dn. Gabriel Valencia. Mejico, Agosto 4 de 1841.

1 inch to 25 miles. 29½ x 24½. Manuscript. Colonies, "Concesion(s)," settlements, roads, and physical features. Includes portion of adjoining areas in Mexico. Filed as RG 77: Q 40.

769. [Map of] Texas. Entered according to Act of Congress in the year 1844, by Sidney E. Morse and Samuel Breese.

1 inch to 40 miles. 18 x 14. Published. County names and boundaries, settlements, military posts, and roads. Filed as Ref. Coll.: Texas 1844.

770. Genl. Austin's Map of Texas With Parts of the Adjoining States. Compiled by Stephen F. Austin. Published by H. S. Tanner . . . 1845.

1 inch to ca. 25 miles. 30 x 23½. Published. Counties, grants, roads, military posts, sites and dates of battles, Indian villages, mines, and remarks about characteristics of the land. Map shows parts of Mexico. Pieces of the map showing Mexican States are missing. Filed as RG 77: US 170.

771. A New & Correct Map of Texas, Compiled from the Most recent Surveys & Authorities to the Year 1845, By James T. D. Wilson, Published by R. W. Fishbourne.

1 inch to 30 miles. 22 x 28. Published. Counties, parts of adjoining States, Territories, and Mexico, in color. Grants and dates of them, towns, Indian villages, roads, Chihuahua Trail, military posts, missions, sites of battles, route of Santa Fe Expedition in 1841, route of "the Texian Prisoners from Santa Fe to the City of Mexico," silver mines, and physical features. Annotated apparently to show the route of an expedition from Presidio Rio Grande to a point on the Red River. Filed as Ref. Coll.: Texas 1845.

772. J. De Cordova's Map of the State of Texas. Compiled from the records of the General Land Office of the State by Robert Creuzbaur, Houston, 1849. Engraved by J. M. Atwood, New York.

1 inch to 20 miles. 34½ x 32. Counties (in color), boundaries of land districts, towns and cities, post offices, Indian villages, trading posts, roads, forts, ferries, missions, Fisher and Miller's Colony, and part of Fannin Land District, which includes no designated counties. Part of a road from Natchitoches to Presidio del Rio Grande is colored red without explanation. Inset map shows Texas in relation to adjoining States, Territories, and Mexico. Scale of inset map is 1 inch to ca. 150 miles. List of land districts and of which counties they are composed. Map signed by J. De Cordova and various officials of the Government of Texas. Filed as Ref. Coll.: Texas 1849.

773. J. De Cordova's Map of the State of Texas. Compiled from the records of the General Land Office of the State by Robert Creuzbaur, Revised & Corrected by Charles W. Pressler, Published by J. H. Colton & Co. . . . 1857.

1 inch to 20 miles. 37 x 34½. Published. Counties (in color), towns and cities, roads, post offices. List of land districts and counties of which they are composed. Inset map of area from western Texas to the Pacific Ocean, including California and New Mexico and Utah Territories. Filed as RG 77: Q 48.

774. Map of Texas and Part of New Mexico, compiled in the Bureau of Topographl. Engrs. chiefly for military purposes. 1857.

1 inch to ca. 23 miles. 35 x 40. Manuscript. Settlements, military posts, roads and trails, explorers' routes, and physical features. "Mail Route from California" is outlined in red. Map includes New Mexico east of the Rio Grande River. Note in bottom margin states "The principal Rivers, Portions of Towns &c. in the Eastern Part of the State are sketched in from 'De Cordova's Map of Texas.' " See entry 775. Filed as RG 77: Q 65-1.

775. Map of Texas and part of New Mexico, compiled in the Bureau of Topographl. Engrs. . . . 1857.

1 inch to ca. 25 miles. 2 sections, each 36 x 18½. Published. Shows only New Mexico east of the Rio Grande. Also shows part of Mexico. Settlements, military posts, and roads. Relief is shown by hachures. Filed as RG 77: 1857, Pub.

776. Pressler's Map of the State of Texas. Compiled from records of the General Land Office of the State and various other sources by Chas. M. Pressler, Principal Draftsman. Published by Jones, Root & Co. . . . 1858.

1 inch to 16 miles. 4 sections, 23 x 19½, 23 x 25½, 23½ x 32, 23 x 26. Counties (in color), "Territory of Young" (Panhandle), roads, railroads, towns, post offices, military posts, Staked Plain (Llano Estacado), and physical features. Table lists information about individual counties such as county seat, date created, land district to which it belongs, and judicial district to which it belongs. Inset maps showing "Original Land Districts" and "Map of the Old Colonies." Filed as RG 77: Q 94½A.

94   MAPS OF STATES AND TERRITORIES

777. Preliminary Post Route Map of the State of Texas with adjacent parts of Louisiana, Arkansas, and Indian Territory ... by W. L. Nicholson, Topographer of P. O. Dept., 1874 ... N. Peters, Photo-Lithographer ... E. D. Boyd, del. . . . The mail service on this map (Jan'y 1st 1875) has been in many parts absent or superseded by later arrangements. [Note about service added in manuscript.]

1 inch to 15 miles. 2 sections, 22 x 41 each. Frequency and type of mail service (but no key to explain them), mileages between post offices, counties, towns, military posts, and railroads. Inset map of Texas west of the Pecos River. Scale 1 inch to 25 miles. Filed as RG 28: series 1, folder III.

778. [Map of Texas by Frank A. Gray, 1875. Specimen sheet of atlas of the United States, being prepared.]

1 inch to 45 miles. 28 x 21½. Published. Counties, Bexar and Young Territories. Staked Plain (Llano Extacado), military posts, railroads, major towns, physical features, and Indian reservations in Indian Territory (Oklahoma). Map includes Indian Territory, Kansas, and part of New Mexico. Filed as RG 77: US 373-61.

779. Colton's New Map of the State of Texas, The Indian Territory, and adjoining portions of New Mexico, Louisiana, and Arkansas. Compiled from the Official County Maps of the General Land Office, the personal reconnaisances and geological explorations of Prof. A. R. Roessler ... Published by G. W. & C. B. Colton & Co. . . . 1876.

1 inch to 24 miles. 32½ x 38. Counties (in color), towns, roads, railroads, military posts, locations of mineral deposits, Staked Plain, and physical features. Shows Indian reservations in New Mexico and Indian Territory. Table lists population by county for 1870. Filed as RG 77: Q 292.

780. Map of the State of Texas. Compiled from the records on file in the General Land Office of the State, the U.S. Coast Surveys, the reports of the Mexican & U.S. boundary commissions & topographical maps of Army officers, by Chas. M. Pressler & A. B. Langermann ... 1879.

1 inch to 16 miles. 4 sections, each 25½ x 26½. Counties (in color), towns, roads, railroads, railroad land grants, military posts, post offices, and physical features. Table lists counties, county seats, areas of counties, date county was created, and land district to which county belongs. Small pieces of map are missing. Filed as RG 77: Q 412.

781. Post Route Map of the State of Texas, with adjacent parts of Louisiana, Arkansas, Indian Territory, and of the Republic of Mexico, showing post offices with the intermediate distances and mail routes in operation on the 1st of October, 1885. Published ... under the direction of W. L. Nicholson, Topographer, P. O. Dept.

1 inch to 15 miles. 2 sections, each 44 x 29½. Published. Frequency and types of mail service, mileages between post offices, discontinued post offices, counties, towns, railroads, and physical features. Post routes in color to show frequency of service. Inset map of "North-western portion of Texas" [in "Panhandle"]. Scale 1 inch to 20 miles. Filed as RG 28: series 1, folder XII.

782. History of the Geography of Texas, By Z. T. Fulmore. ... Copyrighted 1897, by Z. T. Fulmore.

Scales not indicated. 4 sections, each 34 x 26. Published. This includes five maps of about 13 x 15 inches showing boundaries of 1) Spanish Province of Texas, 2) Colonial Texas, 3) Republic of Texas as claimed by Texas, Dec. 19, 1836, to Nov. 25, 1850, 4) Texas in 1835, and 5) Texas since 1850. Maps show boundaries of counties and other civil divisions, but little other detail. Also included is a variety of statistical information as well as lists of public officials with their terms of office and a brief history of Texas. Filed as Ref. Coll.: Texas 1897.

783. Map of Texas and parts of Adjoining Territories. Compiled by and under the direction of Robert T. Hill. Drawn by Henry S. Selden and Willard D. Johnson ... 1899.

1 inch to 25 miles. Contour interval 250 feet. 31 x 35½. Counties, Indian reservations, major towns, and railroads. Drainage in blue. Contours in brown. Map includes parts of Oklahoma and New Mexico. Indian reservations shown are in Oklahoma. Filed as Ref. Coll.: Texas 1899.

See also entry 314.

UTAH

784. Map Showing the extent of Surveys in the Territory of Utah, 1856.
 1 inch to 30 miles. 35 x 17½. Published. Filed as RG 46: S. Ex. Doc. 5, 34th Cong., 3d sess.

785. Map of Utah Territory showing the Routes connecting it with California and the East. Compiled in the Bureau of Topogl. Engrs. of the War Departmt. . . . 1858.
 1 inch to ca. 25 miles. 34 x 46. Published. Military posts, wagon roads, proposed roads, and exploration routes of Frémont, Stansbury, Gunnison, and Beckwith. Relief shown by hachures. Filed as RG 77: 1858, Pub.

786. Map of the Territory of Utah. To accompany the annual Report of the Commissioner of the General Land Office. [Issued by the General Land Office on Oct. 2, 1866.]
 1 inch to 18 miles. 27½ x 19½. Published. Public surveys, counties, military posts, Indian reservations, towns, and physical features. County boundaries and areas of mineral deposits are shown in color. Filed as RG 49: Utah 1, Pub.

787. Map of the Territory of Utah, Showing the extent and progress of the Public Surveys. To accompany Annual Report of the Surveyor General, 1874.
 1 inch to 8 miles. 2 sections, 26½ x 38 and 23 x 38. Annotated published. County boundaries, mining district boundaries, and types of mineral deposits are shown in color. Also shows status of public land surveys, towns, Indian reservations, roads, telegraph lines, explorers' routes, and proposed and completed railroad lines. Map includes census table showing population by county. Filed as RG 49: Utah 8.

788. [Map of the] Territory of Utah. . . . 1876. Compiled from the official Records of the General Land Office.
 1 inch to 12 miles. 34 x 26½. Published. County boundaries, Indian reservations, and railroad land-grant limits. Also shows status of public land surveys, towns, military reservations, and roads and trails. Relief is shown by hachures. Also black and white base map for this date. 33½ x 25. Filed as RG 49: Utah 1876, Pub.

789. [Map of the] Territory of Utah. . . . 1884. Compiled from the official Records of the General Land Office . . . Compiled by A. F. Dinsmore. Drawn by W. Naylor & G. P. Strum.
 1 inch to 15 miles. 33½ x 22. Published. County boundaries, Indian and military reservations, and railroad land-grant limits are shown in color. Also shows status of public land surveys, towns and cities, and completed railroad lines. Relief is shown by hachures. Also a black and white base map for this date. 31 x 24. Filed as RG 49: Utah 1884, Pub.

790. [Map of the] Territory of Utah. . . . 1889. Compiled from the official Records of the General Land Office . . . Compiled and drawn by A. F. Dinsmore.
 1 inch to 12 miles. 36 x 26½. Published. County boundaries and military and Indian reservations are shown in color. Also shows status of public land surveys, towns and cities, and completed railroad lines. Relief is shown by hachures. Also a black and white base map for this date. 35 x 26½. Filed as RG 49: Utah 1889, Pub.

791. [Map of the] Territory of Utah. . . . 1893. Compiled from the official Records of the General Land Office . . . Compiled and drawn by R. H. Morton. Lettered by M. Hendges.
 1 inch to 11 miles. 38 x 29½. Published. County and Indian reservation boundaries are shown in color. Also shows status of public land surveys, towns and cities, military reservations, and railroad lines. Relief is shown in color. Also a black and white base map for this date. Drainage in blue. 38 x 29. Filed as RG 49: Utah 1893, Pub.

792. Map of the State of Utah. Compiled from the official Records of the General Land Office . . . 1902. . . . Compiled and drawn by J. Ulke.
 1 inch to 12 miles. 36 x 26½. Published. County names and boundaries, towns and cities, Indian and military reservations, status of public land surveys, and railroad lines. Drainage features. Filed as RG 49: Utah 1902, Pub.

793. [Map of the] State of Utah. Compiled from the official Records of the General Land Office . . . 1908. . . . Compiled by A. F. Dinsmore. . . . Traced and lettered by Wm. Bauman, Jr.

1 inch to 12 miles. 34 x 29. Published. County and land district boundaries, Indian and military reservations, and national forests are shown in color. Also shows status of public land surveys, towns and cities, locations of U.S. land offices, and railroad lines. Relief is shown in color. Also a black and white base map for this date. 36 x 28. See entry 794. Filed as RG 49: Utah 1908, Pub.

794. [Map of the] State of Utah. Compiled from the official Records of the General Land Office ... 1908. ... Compiled by A. F. Dinsmore. ... Traced and lettered by Wm. Bauman, Jr.
1 inch to 12 miles. 36 x 29. Annotated published. Annotated to show mining districts. Filed separately is an "Index giving Approximate Location of Mining Districts and Number of U.S. Location Monuments Established Therein." See entry 793. Filed as RG 49: Utah 35 (a and b).

795. [Map of the] State of Utah [showing] Lands designated by the Secretary of the Interior, April 27, 1909, under the Enlarged Homestead Act of Feb. 19, 1909. [Issued by the Department of the Interior.]
1 inch to 24 miles. 19 x 14½. Published. Lands designated under the act are shaded red. Map also shows public land surveys. Filed as RG 49: Utah 3, Pub.

796. [Map of the] State of Utah. Compiled from the official Records of the General Land Office ... 1915. ... Compiled by A. F. Dinsmore. Traced and lettered by Wm. Bauman, Jr. and Thos. O. Wansleben.
1 inch to 12 miles. 35 x 27½. Published. County and land district boundaries, Indian and military reservations, national forests, national monuments and bird reservations, and reclamation projects are shown in color. Also shows status of public land surveys, towns and cities, locations of U.S. land offices, and railroad lines. Relief is shown in color. Also a black and white base map for this date. 36 x 28½. Filed as RG 49: Utah 1915, Pub.

797. [Map of the] State of Utah [showing] Lands designated by the Secretary of the Interior Under the provisions of the Enlarged Homestead Act. [Issued by the Department of the Interior.] Edition of June 30, 1916.
1 inch to 24 miles. 18½ x 15½. Published. Areas designated under Enlarged Homestead Act, Sections 1 to 5, are shaded red, and those designated under Section 6 are shaded blue. Also shows public land surveys. Filed as RG 49: Utah 5, Pub.

798. Post Route Map of the State of Utah showing post offices with the intermediate distances on mail routes in operation on the 1st of January, 1917.
1 inch to 10 miles. 42½ x 31½. Published. Frequency and types of mail service, discontinued post offices, counties, towns, railroads, physical features, and parts of adjoining States. Filed as RG 28: Utah 1917.

799. Post Route Map of the State of Utah showing post offices with the intermediate distances on mail routes in operation on the 1st of January, 1918.
1 inch to 10 miles. 42½ x 31½. Published. Frequency and types of mail service, discontinued post offices, counties, towns, railroads, physical features, and parts of adjoining States. Filed as RG 28: Utah 1918.

800. [Map of the] State of Utah [showing] Lands designated as non-irrigable by the Secretary of the Interior under the provisions of the Enlarged Homestead Acts. Includes Patented and Entered as well as Vacant land. [Issued by the Department of the Interior.] Edition of June 30, 1920.
1 inch to 24 miles. 18 x 15½. Published. Areas designated under general provisions shown in red and those designated under non-residence provisions (section 6) are shaded blue. Also shows public land surveys. Filed as RG 49: Utah 7, Pub.

See also entries 101 and 131.

VERMONT

801. A Topographical Map of the State of Vermont from actual Survey. . . . Engrav'd and Printed for William Blodget by Amos Doolittle. . . . 1789.
1 inch to ca. 4½ miles. 39½ x 31. Published. Counties (in color), townships, roads, meetinghouses, forts, mills, iron works, and physical features. "Most Humbly Dedicated to his Excellency Thomas Chittenden, Esqr., Governor and Commander in Chief; The Honorable the Council and the Honorable the Representatives of said State; By their Most Obedient and Devoted Humble Servant, William Blodget." Filed as RG 77: US 107.

802. A Map of the State of Vermont. Drawn under the Direction of Ira Allen, Esqr., late Surveyor Genl. of the said State, for his History thereof. London, March 28th, 1798 . . . Engraved by I. Pabner.
1 inch to ca. 17 miles. 18½ x 22½. Published. Counties, towns, forts, colleges, physical features, and parts of New York, New Hampshire, Maine, and Canada. Filed as RG 77: US 13.

803. Vermont. From Actual Survey With all the late Additions & Improvements, by James Whitelaw, Esq., Late Surveyor General. To His Excellency Richard Skinner, Esq., This Map Is Respectfully Dedicated By The Publishr., Ebeneezer Hutchinson, Hartford, Vt., A.D. 1821.
1 inch to ca. 7 miles. 46½ x 32½. Annotated published. County names and boundaries, township names and boundaries, roads, meetinghouses, courthouses, grammar schools, dwelling houses, various types of mills, forts, iron works. Also shown are populations and dates of grants of townships. Filed as RG 77: US 48.

804. Vermont. From Actual Survey With all the late Additions & Improvements, by James Whitelaw, Esq., Late Surveyor General. M. M. Peabody, sc. To his Excellency Richard Skinner, Esq., This Map Is Respectfully Dedicated By The Publishr. . . . 1824. Ebeneezer Hutchinson.
1 inch to 3¾ miles. 47 x 32. Published. Counties (boundaries in color), townships, dates of grants and 1820 population of townships, roads, meetinghouses, courthouses, grammar schools, names of some residents, mills, iron works, ferries, post towns, forts, and physical features. Tables listing population by county in Vermont for 1820 and population of States of the Union in 1810 and 1820. Inset illustration "View of the Village of Montpelier Taken from Mill Point in Berlin." By Mrs. S. I. Watrous. Filed as RG 77: US 92.

805. [Map of] Vermont and New Hampshire. [ca. 1840.]
1 inch to ca. 14 miles. 18 x 14. Published. Counties, townships, major towns, roads, railroads, canals, and physical features. States shaded yellow. Annotated to show a few additional roads and towns. Filed as Ref. Coll.: Vermont 1840.

806. Map of the State of Vermont, from Surveys under the Direction of H. F. Walling. Drawn, Engraved, Printed, Colored, and Mounted at H. F. Walling's Map Establishment . . . Published by Johnson & Browning. [1859]
1 inch to ca. 2½ miles. 4 sections, each 31 x 31. Published. County boundaries and townships in color. Dates of charters and population of townships, railroads, roads, towns, churches, cemeteries, forts, mills, quarries, mineral deposits, sites and dates of battles, schools, and physical features. List of "subscribers" with their addresses and occupations. Inset map: "Geological Map of the State of Vermont, Compiled by Albert D. Hager, 1859." Geological formations shown in color. Inset plans of Proctorsville (Cavendish), Middleton, St. Albans, Winooski Village, Burlington, Middlebury, Montpelier, St. Johnsbury, Rutland, West Rutland, Bennington, Bennington Centre, Rutland Centre, West Rutland Marble Quarries, Manchester, Factory Point (Manchester), Bakersfield, Wells Corners, Woodstock, Bellows Falls, Vergennes, Benson, Fair Haven, Danbyborough, Castleton, East Poultney, West Poultney, West Pawlet, Hydenville (Castleton), Fayetteville, Scotch Hill (Fair Haven), and Brattleborough. Inset "View of the Capitol at Washington" and view of "New State Capitol [at] Montpelier." Small pieces of map are missing. Filed as Ref. Coll.: Vermont 1859.

807. Map of the State of Vermont from Surveys under the Direction of H. F. Walling. Drawn, Engraved, Printed . . . at H. F. Walling's Map Establishment . . . Published by Albert D. Hager, Proctorsville, Vt. [n.d.]
1 inch to ca. 2½ miles. 2 sections, each

98   MAPS OF STATES AND TERRITORIES

32½ x 42½. Published. County boundaries and townships are shown in color. Railroads, roads, settlements, churches, cemeteries, grist and saw mills, quarries, mineral deposits, sites and dates of battles, schools, and physical features. Also shows population figures for 1850 and 1860 and dates of charter and settlement for each township. It is noted on the map that 1850 population figures are according to the 1850 census and those for 1875 (?) are according to the 1860 census. Inset map: "Geological Map of the State of Vermont Compiled by Albert D. Hager." Geological formations are shown in color. Filed as RG 77: U 4.

See also entries 158, 159, 161, 371, 372, 556, 558.

VIRGINIA

808. [Map of] Virginia ... Descouvered and Described by Captayn John Smith, 1606 [sic].
1 inch to ca. 15 miles. 25 x 31½. Photoprocessed. In lower right corner, "Page 41 Smith." Shows King's houses and ordinary houses, and names. Filed as Ref. Coll.: Virginia 1606.

809. A Map of the most Inhabited part of Virginia containing the whole Province of Maryland with Part of Pensilvania, [sic] New Jersey, and North Carolina. Drawn by Joshua Fry & Peter Jefferson in 1775 ... Publish'd 12th May 1794, by Laurie & Whittle.
1 inch to 10 miles. 2 sections, each 34 x 26. States (colonies) in color. County names, towns, roads, and physical features. Bears inscription, "To the Right Honourable, George Dunk, Earl of Halifax, First Lord Commissioner; and to the Rest of the Right Honourable and Honourable Commissioners, for Trade and Plantations. This Map is most humbly Inscribed to their Lordship's, By their Lordships' Most Obedient & most devoted humble Servt., Thos. Jefferys." Filed as Ref. Coll.: Virginia 1794.

810. [Map of] Virginia, Maryland, and Delaware. By H. S. Tanner ... (from the American Atlas) ... Engraved & Published by H. S. Tanner, Philadelphia. Entered according to Act of Congress, 20th day of Dec. 1820.
1 inch to ca. 18 miles. 22 x 31. Annotated published. Map includes present State of West Virginia and parts of adjoining States. Counties in Virginia and West Virginia (in color), roads, towns, and physical features. Map is annotated to show additional towns and certain roads in red ink. Filed as RG 77: US 161.

811. Map of Virginia, Maryland, and Delaware Exhibiting the Post Offices, Post Roads, Canals, Rail Roads, &c. By David H. Burr. (Late Topographer to the Post Office.) ... Entered according to the Act of Congress, July 10th, 1839.
1 inch to 10 miles. 4 sections, each 19 x 25½. Published. Also shows counties, mileages between post offices, forts, physical features, and parts of adjoining States. Filed as RG 28: Burr Atlas, Map 5.

812. [Map of] Virginia [including West Virginia]. [ca. 1840.]
1 inch to 30 miles. 14 x 18. Published. Counties, major towns, railroads, canals, and physical features. State shaded yellow. Filed as Ref. Coll.: Virginia 1840.

813. Map of the State of Virginia, Containing the Counties, Principal Towns, Railroads & All Other Internal Improvements. Lithographed & Published by Ritchie & Dunnavant ... 1858.
1 inch to ca. 12 miles. 27 x 38½. Counties shown in color. Map includes Maryland and Delaware as well as parts of Pennsylvania, New Jersey, and North Carolina. Virginia includes present State of West Virginia. "Internal improvements" include canals, different types of roads, and railroads completed and in progress. Filed as Ref. Coll.: Virginia 1858.

814. A Map of the State of Virginia, Reduced from the Nine Sheet Map of the State, in conformity to Law: by Herman Boye. 1828. Corrected by order of the Executive, by L. v Buchholtz. 1859.
1 inch to 10 miles. 32 x 49½. Counties in

VIRGINIA

Virginia (in color), railroads, canals, towns, mills, mineral deposits, factories, iron works, academies and colleges, churches, roads (stage, turnpike, common), ferries, courthouses, "places remarkable for military incidents," and physical features. Virginia includes present State of West Virginia. Map also includes Maryland, Delaware, and parts of Pennsylvania, New Jersey, Tennessee, and North Carolina. Tables list steamboat routes, altitudes of mountains, and population (of "whites, slaves, free blacks") of State in 1790, 1800, 1810, and 1859. Filed as Ref. Coll.: Virginia 1859.

815. Map of Virginia, Showing the distribution of its Slave Population from the Census of 1860 ... Washington, June 13, 1861.

1 inch to 20 miles. 22 x 30. Includes present state of West Virginia. Names and boundaries of counties. Counties shaded according to slave population, with those counties having the lowest slave populations left unshaded. Tables list additional population information. Map "Sold for the benefit of the sick and wounded of the U.S. Army." Note in lower right corner states "Presented to Lt. Col. Bache, Corps Topogl Engineers, by his friend & Sert W R Palmer, Augt 31, 1861." Filed as RG 77: G 103.

816. Lloyd's Official Map of the State of Virginia. From Actual surveys by order of the Executive, 1828 & 1859. Corrected and Revised by J. T. Lloyd to 1862, from Surveys made by Capt. W. Angelo Powell, of the U.S. Topographical Engineers of Gen. Rosencrans' Staff.

1 inch to 10 miles. 30¾ x 47¼. Counties in Virginia (in color), railroads, canals, towns, mills, mineral deposits, factories, iron works, academies and colleges, churches, roads, ferries, courthouses, "places remarkable for military incidents," and physical features. Virginia includes present State of West Virginia. Map also includes Maryland, Delaware, and parts of Pennsylvania, New Jersey, Tennessee, and North Carolina. Tables list steamboat routes, altitudes of mountains, and population (of "whites, slaves, free blacks") of State in 1790, 1800, 1810, and 1859 Filed as Ref. Coll.: Virginia 1862.

817. A Map of the State of Virginia, Reduced from the Nine Sheet Map of the State, in conformity to Law: by Herman Boye. 1828. Corrected by order of the Executive, by L. v Buchholtz. 1859. [Annotated to show geological formations, 1862.]

1 inch to 10 miles. 30½ x 47. Annotated photoprocessed. Geological formations in color, keyed to a list added to the map. Key also tells what type of road results from the various geological formations. Letters A, B, C, and D show the general locations of four coalfields. (Map) "Made for Maj. A. A. Humphreys, Topgl Engineers, by Tho. S. Ridgway, formerly of the Geological Survey of Va., March 1862." Map includes present State of West Virginia, Maryland, Delaware, and parts of Pennsylvania, New Jersey, Tennessee, and North Carolina. Geological formations are shown in Virginia, some in West Virginia, and western Maryland (Garrett County). Also shows counties, railroads, canals, towns, mills, mineral deposits, roads, churches, factories, iron works, ferries, courthouses, academies and colleges, and "places remarkable for military incidents." Tables list steamboat routes, altitudes of mountains, and population (of "whites, slaves, free blacks"). Filed as RG 77: G 74.

818. Map of the State of Virginia, Compiled from the best authorities, and printed at the Coast Survey Office. A. D. Bache, Supdt., 1862.... Lith. by Chas. G. Krebs.

1 inch to ca. 14 miles. 26 x 39. Published. Map includes Maryland, Delaware, and parts of adjoining States. Virginia includes present State of West Virginia. Railroad lines are shown in red. Table lists distances between principal eastern cities via railroad. Also shows towns, roads, canals, railroad stations, and physical features. Filed as RG 23: Special Civil War Maps.

819. Map of the State of Virginia, Compiled from the best authorities, and printed at the Coast Survey Office. A. D. Bache, Supdt., August 1863 ... Lith. By Chas. G. Krebs.

1 inch to ca. 14 miles. 26 x 39. Published. Basic information same as that shown in entry 817. Drainage in blue. State boundaries shaded red. West Virginia shown as a separate State. Also a December 1863 edition of this map. Filed as RG 23: Special Civil War Maps.

820. Gray's New Topographical Map of Virginia and West Virginia, By Frank A. Gray.... Copyright, 1877, by O. W. Gray & Son.

1 inch to 15.78 miles. 18½ x 37. Published. Counties (in color), towns, railroad lines, and physical features. Small inset maps of the West Virginia "Pan-handle," southwestern Virginia, "Environs of

Harpers Ferry," "Hampton Roads and the Approaches," "Hypsometric Sketch of Virginia and West Virginia," and Norfolk Harbor. Filed as RG 77: US 373-51.

821. Preliminary Post Route Map of the States of Virginia and West Virginia, together with Maryland and Delaware [and adjoining states] ... by W. L. Nicholson, Topographer of P. O. Dept., 1879 ... Drawn by C. H. Poole ... [revised] up to date of Aug. 1, 1879.

1 inch to 8 miles. 4 sections, each 30 x 34. (2 copies of each of the eastern sections.) Frequency and types of mail service, mileage between post offices, discontinued post offices, counties, towns, railroads, and physical features. Post routes shown in color to illustrate frequency of service. Filed as RG 28: series 1, folder IV.

822. [Map of the] State of Virginia ... Compiled [in the U.S. Geological Survey] in 1914 in cooperation with the State of Virginia.

1 inch to ca. 8 miles. 29½ x 63. Published. County names and boundaries, towns and cities, steam and electric railroad lines, and drainage features. Noted: "Advance sheet. Subject to corrections." Filed as RG 57: Virginia 1914, Pub.

WASHINGTON

823. Map of Washington Territory, Showing the Indian Nations and Tribes. Copied from the original preliminary sketch compiled from the archives of the N.P.R.R. Exploration and survey, under the direction of Gov. I. I. Steve[ns] by J. Lambert, topographer of the expedition; Indian names and boundaries by G. Gibbs, 1853-4.

1 inch to 20 miles. 29 x 36. Manuscript on tracing cloth. Note on map states, "San Francisco, California, April 14th, 1884. Forwarded to Maj. Genl Wool, Commanding the Division of the Pacific..." Filed as RG 77: US 324-57.

824. Map of Public Surveys in the Territory of Washington, to accompany Report of Surv. Genl., 1865.

1 inch to 12 miles. 25 x 33½. Manuscript. Military and Indian reservations are shown in color. Also shows status of public land surveys, towns, roads and trails, and railroad lines. Relief is shown by hachures. For published copy, see entry 825. Filed as RG 49: Washington 6.

825. Map of Public Surveys in the Territory of Washington, To Accompany Report of Surveyor General. 1865.

1 inch to 12 miles. 25 x 33½. Published. Shows status of public land surveys, roads, trails, settlements, and railroad lines. See entry 824. Filed as RG 49: Washington 3, Published.

826. Map of Public Surveys in the Territory of Washington, To Accompany Report of Surveyor General ... Surveyor General's Office, Olympia, W. T., July 15th, 1865. [Issued by the General Land Office with additions on Oct. 2, 1866.]

1 inch to 12 miles. 25 x 33. Published. County boundaries, military and Indian reservations, and mineral deposits are shown in color. Also shows status of public surveys, projected and completed railroads, roads and trails, military posts, physical features, county names, and boundaries of Puget Sound Agricultural Company's claims. Filed as RG 49: Washington 4, Pub.

827. Map of Public Surveys in Washington Territory, to accompany Report of Surveyor General, 1868.

1 inch to 12 miles. 27 x 34. Manuscript. County boundaries, military and Indian reservations, and locations of lighthouses and mineral deposits are shown in color. Also shows status of public land surveys, towns, Puget Sound Agricultural Company claims, roads and trails, and proposed and completed railroad lines. Relief is shown by hachures. Filed as RG 49: Washington 9.

828. Map of Public Surveys in Washington Territory, to accompany Report of Surveyor General, 1870.

1 inch to 12 miles. 27 x 34. Manuscript.

County boundaries, military and Indian reservations, and locations of lighthouses and mineral deposits are shown in color. Also shows status of public land surveys, towns, roads and trails, and railroad lines. Relief is shown by hachures. Filed as RG 49: Washington 10.

829. Map of Public Surveys in Washington Territory, to accompany Report of Surveyor General, 1874.
1 inch to 12 miles. 27 x 34. Manuscript. Status of public land surveys, towns and cities, military reservations, missions, railroad land-grant limits, and railroad lines completed and proposed. Relief is shown by hachures. Filed as RG 49: Washington 11.

830. [Map of the] Territory of Washington.... 1876. Compiled from the official Records of the General Land Office.
1 inch to 12 miles. 26½ x 33. Published. County and land district boundaries, Indian reservations, and railroad land-grant limits are shown in color. Also shows status of public land surveys, towns and cities, military reservations, and railroad lines. Relief is shown by hachures. Filed as RG 49: Washington 1876, Pub. (Atlas).

831. [Map of] Washington Territory ... 1883. Compiled from the official Records of the General Land Office.
1 inch to 15 miles. 27 x 34. Published. County boundaries, Indian and military reservations, and railroad land-grant limits are shown in color. Also shows status of public land surveys, towns and cities, locations of U.S. land offices, and railroad lines. Relief is shown by hachures. Also a black and white base map for this date. 24 x 33. Filed as RG 49: Washington 1883, Pub.

832. [Map of] Washington Territory ... 1884. Compiled from the official Records of the General Land Office.
1 inch to 14 miles. 24 x 31½. Published. County boundaries, Indian and military reservations, and railroad land-grant limits are shown in color. Also shows status of public land surveys, towns and cities, locations of U.S. land offices, and railroad lines. Relief is shown by hachures. Filed as RG 49: Washington 1884, Pub.

833. [Map of] Washington Territory ... 1887. Compiled from the official Records of the General Land Office ... Compiled and Drawn by Robert H. Morton.
1 inch to 15 miles. 23 x 29½. Published. County boundaries and Indian and military reservations are shown in color. Also shows status of public land surveys, towns and cities, locations of U.S. land offices, and railroad lines. Relief is shown by hachures. Filed as RG 49: Washington 1887, Pub.

834. [Map of the] State of Washington.... 1891. Compiled from the official Records of the General Land Office ... Compiled and Drawn by Robt. H. Morton.
1 inch to 11 miles. 29 x 39. Published. County boundaries and Indian and military reservations are shown in color. Also shows status of public land surveys, towns and cities, locations of U.S. land offices, and railroad lines. Relief is shown in color. Also a black and white base map for this date. Drainage in blue. 27¼ x 40. Filed as RG 49: Washington 1891, Pub.

835. Map of State of Washington, Compiled by Washington State Immigration Association, Issued by Secretary of State, 1896.... Geo. H. Plummer, Del., The Blatchly Co., Lith., Tacoma.
1 inch to 15 miles. 21 x 27. Counties, towns, railroads, Indian reservations, developed coalfields, and physical features. Natural resources and products of areas within the State are noted. Filed as Ref. Coll.: Washington 1896.

836. Map of the State of Washington. Compiled from the official Records of the General Land Office ... 1897.... Revised and Drawn by Daniel O'Hare. Compiled by Robt. H. Morton.
1 inch to 12 miles. 26 x 37. Published. County boundaries, Indian and military reservations, and forest reserves are shown in color. Also shows status of public land surveys, towns and cities, locations of U.S. land offices, lighthouses, lifesaving stations, and railroad lines. Relief is shown in color. Also a black and white base map for this date. Drainage in blue. 23½ x 34. Filed as RG 49: Washington 1897, Pub.

837. [Map of the] State of Washington. Compiled from the official Records of the General Land Office ... 1905. ... Compiled and drawn by Daniel O'Hare. Lettering by Wm. Bauman, Jr.
1 inch to 12 miles. 25 x 36. Published. County names and boundaries, towns and cities, locations of U.S. land offices, status of public land surveys, forest reserves, Indian and military reservations, and railroad lines. Drainage partly in blue. Filed as RG 49: Washington 1905, Pub.

838. [Map of the] State of Washington. Compiled from the official Records of the General Land Office ... 1909. ... Compiled and drawn by Daniel O'Hare. Lettered by Wm. Bauman, Jr.
1 inch to 12 miles. 25 x 37. Published. County names and boundaries, towns and cities, locations of U.S. land offices, status of public land surveys, forest reserves, Indian and military reservations, and railroad lines. Drainage features. Filed as RG 49: Washington 1909, Pub.

839. [Map of the] State of Washington, [showing] Lands designated by the Secretary of the Interior, April 27, 1909, under the Enlarged Homestead Act of Feb. 19, 1909. [Issued by the Department of the Interior.]
1 inch to 24 miles. 13½ x 19. Published. Areas designated are shaded red. Also shows public land surveys. Filed as RG 49: Washington 6, Pub.

840. [Map of the] State of Washington ... Compiled in 1914 in cooperation with the State of Washington [Issued by the U.S. Geological Survey].
1 inch to ca. 8 miles. 35 x 50. Published. County names and boundaries, township and range numbers, towns and cities, steam and electric railroad lines, and drainage features. Noted: "Advance sheet. Subject to corrections." Filed as RG 57: Washington 1914, Pub.

841. [Map of the] State of Washington [showing] Lands designated by the Secretary of the Interior, Under the provisions of the Enlarged Homestead Act. Edition of June 30, 1916. [Issued by the Department of the Interior.]
1 inch to 24 miles. 13½ x 19½. Published. Areas designated are shaded red. Also shows public land surveys. Filed as RG 49: Washington 7, Pub.

842. [Map of the] State of Washington [showing] Lands designated as non-irrigable by the Secretary of the Interior, under the provisions of the Enlarged Homestead Acts ... Edition of June 30, 1920. [Issued by the Department of the Interior.]
1 inch to 24 miles. 13½ x 19½. Published. Areas designated are shaded red. Also shows public land surveys. Filed as RG 49: Washington 9, Pub.

See also entries 697, 698, 701, 709-711, 713, and 715.

WEST VIRGINIA

843. Map of Western Virginia, Compiled from the best authorities, and printed at the Coast Survey Office ... 1862.
1 inch to 14 miles. 23½ x 21. Annotated published. Map includes southwestern Virginia and Pennsylvania. Settlements, railroad lines, roads, and physical features. Filed as RG 75: map 987.

844. White's County and District Map of the State of West Virginia, From the most recent Surveys & Authentic sources. Published by M. Wood White. Grafton, W. Va., 1875.
1 inch to 5 miles. 38 x 53. Annotated published. Counties (in color), towns, roads, railroad lines, mills, post offices, general locations of coal deposits, and drainage features. Relief is shown by hachures. Filed as RG 77: G 244.

845. [Map of West Virginia issued by the U.S. Geological Survey, 1916.]
1 inch to ca. 16 miles. 18 x 19. Published. County names and boundaries, towns and cities, steam and electric railroad lines, and drainage features. Filed as RG 57: West Virginia 1916, Pub.

846. [Map of West Virginia issued by the U.S. Geological Survey, 1918.]
1 inch to ca. 16 miles. 18 x 19. Published. County names and boundaries, towns and cities, steam and electric railroad lines, and drainage features. Filed as RG 57: West Virginia 1918, Pub.

See also entries 810-821.

WISCONSIN

847. Map of Wiskonsin [sic] Territory, Compiled from the Public Surveys. [1839]
1 inch to ca. 9 miles. 37 x 26. Annotated published. Shows ledges, natural and artificial mounds, lead and copper mines, towns and villages, and roads and canals. An unidentified grid has been added in red ink, similar to the township grid, but at an angle to and with squares numbered differently from the townships shown on the published map. This map (without annotations), is published in S. Doc. 140, 26th Cong., 1st sess., Serial 357. Filed as RG 77: O 112-2.

848. Sketch [map] of the Public Surveys in Wisconsin Territory. [n.d.]
1 inch to 18 miles. 15 x 24. Published. "Notes" of explanation concerning the status of township surveys as indicated by colors and symbols are given on the map. Filed as RG 46: 26th Cong., 2d sess.

849. Sketch [map] of the Public Surveys in Wisconsin Territory. [n.d.]
1 inch to 18 miles. 15 x 21. Published. Shows status of public land surveys. Filed as RG 46: 27th Cong., 2d sess.

850. Sketch [map] of U.S. Roads in Wiskonsan [sic] Territory, October, 1842.
1 inch to 9 miles. 16 x 21. Manuscript on tracing paper. Note: "To/J. J. Abert. Col., T. E. (signed) T. J. Cram, Capt. T. E., Oct. 14, 1842." Filed as RG 77: O 122-10.

851. Geological Map of Wisconsin, Iowa, and Minnesota, Exhibiting, also, the extension of the Iowa Coal-field into Missouri, and its relation to the Illinois Coal-field. Constructed ... By David Dale Owen, M. D., Principal Geologist. ... 1851.
1 inch to 20 miles. 45½ x 28. Published. Also shows settlements. Inset map "Geological Map of the North Shore of Lake Superior ..." at a scale of 1 inch to 10 miles. Filed as RG 49: Iowa 3, Pub.

852. (No. 1.) Sketch of the Public Surveys in Wisconsin and Territory of Minnesota [Issued by Surveyor General's Office, Dubuque, Oct. 21, 1853].
1 inch to 18 miles. 19 x 22. Published. Status of public land surveys. Filed as RG 49: Wisconsin 2, Pub.

853. (No. 1) Sketch [Map] of the Public Surveys in Wisconsin and Territory of Minnesota [Issued by Surveyor General's Office, Dubuque, Oct. 21, 1854].
1 inch to 18 miles. 19 x 23. Published. Shows status of public land surveys. Filed as RG 46: S. Ex. Doc. 1, Pt. 3, 33d Cong., 2d sess.

854. A Geological Map of Wisconsin, By I. A. Lapham. Based on the Geographical Map of J. H. Colton & Co., New York, 1855.
1 inch to ca. 25 miles. 17 x 14. Published. Geological formations shown in color. Counties, extent of public land survey, major towns, roads, railroads, canals, and physical features. Filed as Ref. Coll.: Wisconsin 1855.

855. (No. 1) Sketch [map] of the Public Surveys in Wisconsin and Territory of Minnesota [Issued by Surveyor General's Office, Dubuque, Oct. 13, 1856].
1 inch to 18 miles. 19 x 21. Published. Shows status of public land surveys. Filed as RG 46: S. Ex. Doc. 5, 34th Cong., 3d sess.

104 MAPS OF STATES AND TERRITORIES

856. (No. 1) Sketch [map] of the Public Surveys in the State of Wisconsin and Territory of Minnesota [Issued by Surveyor General's Office, Dubuque, Oct. 13, 1857].

1 inch to 18 miles. 20½ x 24. Published. Shows status of public land surveys. Filed as RG 46: S. Ex. Doc. 11, 35th Cong., 1st sess.

857. (No. 1) Sketch [map] of the Public Surveys in State of Wisconsin and Territory of Minnesota [Issued by Surveyor General's Office, Dubuque, Oct. 10, 1860].

1 inch to 18 miles. 20 x 24. Published. Shows status of public land surveys. Only southeastern Minnesota is shown. Filed as RG 46: S. Ex. Doc. 1, 36th Cong., 2d sess.

858. Sketch of the Public Surveys in the State of Wisconsin. [Issued by the General Land Office on Oct. 2, 1866].

1 inch to 18 miles. 18½ x 18½. Annotated published. County boundaries, locations of land offices, and mineral deposits are shown in color. Also shows names of counties, public land surveys, Indian reservations, railroad lines and land-grant limits, and wagon roads. Filed as RG 49: Wisconsin 18.

859. A New Geological Map of Wisconsin, Prepared mostly from original observations by I. A. Lapham, 1869, Milwaukee ... Lith. by L. Lipman, Milwaukee.

1 inch to 15 miles. 28 x 22. Published. Geological formations shown in color. Red lines and figures "show the probable depth in feet below the level of Lake Michigan at which the azoic or primary rocks may be reached by artesian wells." Also shows county names, township and range numbers, towns, railroads. Inset. "Geological Section, from Prairie du Chien to Milwaukee." Filed as RG 77: O 233.

860. [Map of the] State of Wisconsin ... 1878. Compiled from the official Records of the General Land Office.

1 inch to 12 miles. 30 x 27. Published. County boundaries and Indian reservations are shown in color. Also shows public land surveys, towns and cities, principal railroad stations, locations of U.S. land offices, railroad lines, and railroad land-grant limits. Drainage features. Filed as RG 49: Wisconsin 1878, Pub.

861. [Map of the] State of Wisconsin .... 1886. Compiled from the official Records of the General Land Office.

1 inch to 12 miles. 34 x 27. Published. County boundaries and Indian reservations are shown in color. Also shows public land surveys, towns and cities, locations of U.S. land offices, railroad lines, and railroad land-grant limits. Drainage features. Also a black and white base map for this date. 31 x 26½. Filed as RG 49: Wisconsin 1886, Pub.

862. Map of the State of Wisconsin. Compiled from the official Records of the General Land Office ... 1895.... Compiled, Drawn, and Lettered by M. Hendges.

1 inch to 12 miles. 30½ x 27. Published. County boundaries and Indian reservations are shown in color. Also shows public land surveys, towns and cities, locations of U.S. land offices, military reservations, lighthouses, lifesaving stations, and railroad lines proposed and completed. Drainage shown in blue. Also a black and white base map for this date. Drainage in blue. 31 x 28. Filed as RG 49: Wisconsin 1895, Pub.

863. Map of the State of Wisconsin. Compiled from the official Records of the General Land Office ... 1896.... Compiled, Drawn, and Lettered by M. Hendges.

1 inch to 12 miles. 30½ x 28. Published. County boundaries and Indian reservations are shown in color. Also shows public land surveys, towns and cities, locations of U.S. land offices, military reservations, lighthouses, lifesaving stations, and railroad lines proposed and completed. Drainage shown in blue. Also a black and white base map for this date. Drainage in blue. 31½ x 28. Filed as RG 49: Wisconsin 1896, Pub.

864. [Map of the] State of Wisconsin. Compiled from the official Records of the General Land Office ... 1912.

1 inch to 12 miles. 32 x 27. Published. County boundaries, Indian and military reservations, and bird reservations are shown in color. Also shows public land surveys, towns and cities, lighthouses, lifesaving stations, and railroad lines. Drainage features. Also a black and white base map for this date. 31 x 29. Filed as RG 49: Wisconsin 1912, Pub.

865. Relief Map of Wisconsin Accompanying "The Physical Geography of Wisconsin," By Lawrence Martin. Reproduced from a model prepared by W. O. Hotchkiss and F. T. Thwaites and Modelled by E. H. J. Lorenz, in 1910 ... 1915. A. Hoen & Co., Baltimore, Md.
1 inch to ca. 15 miles. 29½ x 20½. Counties, major towns, and some roads. Table lists "Elevation of Important Points in Wisconsin." In upper margin this map is identified as Plate 1, Bulletin No. XXXVI, of Wisconsin Geological and Natural History Survey. Filed as Ref. Coll.: Wisconsin 1915.

866. [Map of the] State of Wisconsin ... Compiled in 1910 and 1911 [Issued by the U.S. Geological Survey in 1913 and reprinted in 1915].
1 inch to ca. 8 miles. 2 sections, each 22 x 41. Published. Counties, towns and cities, steam and electric railroad lines, and drainage features. Noted: "Advance sheet. Subject to corrections." Filed as RG 57: Wisconsin 1915, Pub.

867. [Map of Wisconsin issued by the U.S. Geological Survey, 1918.]
1 inch to ca. 16 miles. 24½ x 22. Published. County names and boundaries, township and range numbers, towns and cities, steam and electric railroad lines, and drainage features. Filed as RG 57: Wisconsin 1918, Pub.

See also entries 394, 396, 408, 411, and 414.

WYOMING

868. Map of the Territory of Wyoming, Accompanying the Annual Report of the Commissioner of the General Land Office for 1869.
1 inch to ca. 12 miles. 26½ x 43. Manuscript. Towns, military posts, roads, and route of the Union Pacific Railroad. Relief is shown by hachures. Filed as RG 49: Wyoming 1.

869. [Map of Wyoming. Military Department of the Platte.] Compiled under the direction of Captain Wm. A. Jones ... 1874. Drawn by Louis von Froben.
1 inch to 18.94 miles. 21 x 31. Published. Includes portions of adjoining States and Territories. Settlements, military posts, roads, and railroad lines. Relief shown by hachures. Filed as RG 393· Dept. of the Platte 2.

870. [Map of the] Territory of Wyoming. 1876. ... Compiled from the official Records of the General Land Office.
1 inch to 15 miles. 24 x 30¼. Published. County names and boundaries, towns, status of public land surveys, military and Indian reservations, and railroad land-grant limits. Relief is shown by hachures. Filed as RG 49: Wyoming 1876, Pub.

871. [Map of the] Territory of Wyoming. ... 1879. Compiled from the official Records of the General Land Office.
1 inch to 15 miles. 26 x 34. Published. County boundaries and military and Indian reservations are shown in color. Also shows national park, status of public land surveys, towns and cities, and railroad lines and land-grant limits. Relief is shown by hachures. Also a black and white base map for this date. 26 x 34. Filed as RG 49: Wyoming 1879, Pub.

872. [Map of] Wyoming. Compiled, by permission, from official records in U.S. Land Office. Published by G. L. Holt, Cheyenne, Wyo. Frank & Fred. Bond, Draftsmen. Entered according to Act of Congress in the year 1883 by Geo. L. Holt ... N. Peters, Photo-Lithographer, Washington, D.C.
1 inch to 16 miles. 23 x 27. Counties (boundaries in color), township and range numbers, towns, ranches, roads, railroads, telegraph lines, and physical features. Filed as Ref. Coll.: Wyoming 1883.

873. [Map of the] Territory of Wyoming. ... 1883. Compiled from the official Records of the General Land Office. ... Drawn by M. Hendges.
1 inch to 15 miles. 26 x 31. Published. County

boundaries, military and Indian reservations, Yellowstone National Park, and railroad land-grant limits are shown in color. Also shows status of public land surveys, towns and cities, and railroad lines. Relief is shown by hachures. Also a black and white base map for this date. 24½ x 29. Filed as RG 49: Wyoming 1883, Pub.

874. [Map of the] Territory of Wyoming. . . . 1888. Compiled from the official Records of the General Land Office. . . . Compiled and Drawn by A. F. Dinsmore, 1887.
1 inch to 12 miles. 30 x 36. Published. County boundaries, military and Indian reservations, boundaries of Yellowstone National Park, and railroad land-grant limits are shown in color. Also shows status of public land surveys, towns and cities, roads and trails, and railroad lines. Relief is shown by hachures. Also a black and white base map for this date. 28½ x 34. Filed as RG 49: Wyoming 1888, Pub.

875. [Map of the] Territory of Wyoming. . . . 1888. Compiled from the official Records of the General Land Office. . . . Compiled and Drawn by A. F. Dinsmore, 1887.
1 inch to 12 miles. 30 x 36. Published. Overprinted to show Wyoming Oil Belt, oil and coal fields, and mining areas. "Geological Features from surveys by Gilbert E. Bailey, E. M., Ph. D., late Geologist of Wyoming." Basic information is the same as that shown on entry 874. Filed as RG 49: Wyoming 1, Pub.

876. Map of the State of Wyoming. Compiled from the official Records of the General Land Office . . . 1900. . . . Compiled, Drawn, and Lettered by I. P. Berthong.
1 inch to 12 miles. 29 x 34. Published. County boundaries, military and Indian reservations, Yellowstone National Park boundaries, and national forest boundaries are shown in color. Also shows status of public land surveys, towns and cities, locations of U.S. land offices, and railroad lines. Relief is shown in color. Also a black and white base map for this date. 30½ x 34. Filed as RG 49: Wyoming 1900, Pub.

877. Map of the State of Wyoming. Compiled from the official Records of the General Land Office . . . 1900. . . . Compiled, Drawn, and Lettered by I. P. Berthong.
1 inch to 12 miles. 29 x 34. Published. Overprinted to show boundaries of water divisions and water districts. Basic information is the same as that shown on entry 876. Filed as RG 49: Wyoming 6, Pub.

878. Map of the State of Wyoming. Compiled from the official Records of the General Land Office . . . 1900. . . . Compiled, Drawn and Lettered by I. P. Berthong.
1 inch to 12 miles. 31 x 35½. Annotated published. Annotated to show Indian reservations and land cessions with references to U.S. statutes. Basic information is the same as that shown on black and white base map in entry 876. Filed as RG 49: Wyoming 21.

879. [Map of the] State of Wyoming. Compiled from the official Records of the General Land Office . . . 1905. . . . Compiled, and Drawn by I. P. Berthong. Traced and Lettered by I. P. Berthong.
1 inch to 12 miles. 30 x 35. Published. County and land district boundaries, military and Indian reservations, and national forests are shown in color. Also shows status of public land surveys, towns and cities, locations of U.S. land offices, and railroad lines. Relief is shown in color. Also a black and white base map for this date. 30 x 35. Filed as RG 49: Wyoming 1905, Pub.

880. [Map of the] State of Wyoming. Compiled from the official Records of the General Land Office . . . 1905. . . . Compiled and Drawn by I. P. Berthong. Traced and Lettered by I. P. Berthong.
1 inch to 12 miles. 31 x 35½. Annotated published. Annotated to show mining districts and U.S. mineral or location monuments. Basic information is the same as that shown on black and white base map in entry 879. Filed as RG 49: Wyoming 29.

881. [Map of the] State of Wyoming. Compiled from the official Records of the General Land Office . . . 1907 [Compiled, traced and lettered by I. P. Berthong].
1 inch to 12 miles. 31 x 37. Published. County and land district boundaries, military and Indian reservations, and national forests are shown in color. Also shows status of public land surveys, towns and cities, locations of U.S. land offices, Yellowstone National Park, and railroad lines. Relief is shown in color. Also a black and white base map for this date. 32 x 36½. Filed as RG 49: Wyoming 1907, Pub

WYOMING

882. [Map of the] State of Wyoming. [Showing] Lands designated by the Secretary of the Interior, March 3 and April 27, 1909, under the Enlarged Homestead Act of Feb. 19, 1909. [Issued by the Department of the Interior.]
1 inch to 24 miles. 16 x 19. Published. Areas designated are shaded red. Also shows public land surveys. Filed as RG 49: Wyoming 16, Pub.

883. [Map of the] State of Wyoming. [Showing] Lands designated by the Secretary of the Interior As subject to entry under the provisions of the Enlarged Homestead Act of February 19, 1909. Edition of March 30, 1910. [Issued by the Department of the Interior.]
1 inch to 24 miles. 16½ x 19. Published. Areas designated are shaded red. Also shows public land surveys. Filed as RG 49: Wyoming 17, Pub.

884. [Map of the] State of Wyoming. Compiled from the official Records of the General Land Office . . . 1912 [Compiled, traced, and lettered by I. P. Berthong.]
1 inch to 12 miles. 30½ x 37. Published. County and land district boundaries, military and Indian reservations, and national forests and parks are shown in color. Also shows status of public land surveys, towns and cities, locations of U.S. land offices, and railroad lines. Relief is shown in color. Also a black and white base map for this date. 30 x 36. Filed as RG 49: Wyoming 1912, Pub.

885. [Map of Wyoming compiled in the U.S. Geological Survey in 1913.]
1 inch to ca. 8 miles. 40 x 49. Published. County names and boundaries, towns and cities, township and range numbers, steam and electric railroad lines, and drainage features. Noted: "Advance sheet. Subject to corrections." Filed as RG 57: Wyoming 1913, Pub.

886. [Map of the] State of Wyoming. [Showing] Lands designated by the Secretary of the Interior Under the provisions of the Enlarged Homestead Acts. Edition of June 30, 1916. [Issued by the Department of the Interior.]
1 inch to 24 miles. 16½ x 19. Published. Areas designated are shaded red. Also shows public land surveys. Filed as RG 49: Wyoming 18, Pub.

887. [Map of the] State of Wyoming. [Showing] Lands designated as non-irrigable by the Secretary of the Interior, under the provisions of the Enlarged Homestead Acts . . . Edition of June 30, 1920. [Issued by the Department of the Interior.]
1 inch to 24 miles. 16½ x 19. Published. Areas designated are shaded red. Also shows public land surveys. Filed as RG 49: Wyoming 19, Pub.

See also entries 495, 496, 498-501, and 512.

Index

This is an index to names of cartographers, surveyors, publishers, and other persons and companies connected with the production of the maps. References are to entry numbers in this special list.

Abert, J. J., 566
Abrahams, J. F., 279
Adlum, John, 734
Allen, Ira, 802
Anderson, Allen L., 575
Annin, W. B., 370, 371
Atwood, J. M., 608, 772
Austin, Stephen F., 767, 770
Bache, A. D., 627, 815, 818, 819
Bailey, Gilbert E., 875
Balch, V., 393
Banks, N. P., 354
Barcroft, E., 459
Barker, Elihu, 324
Barnes, R. L., 200, 279
Barralet, J. J., 556
Bauman, William, Jr., 60, 62, 83, 119, 121, 148, 150, 190, 228, 367, 511, 534, 593, 594, 596, 597, 650, 651, 718, 719, 721, 756, 759, 793, 794, 796, 837, 838
Bayley, G. W. R., 346
Berthong, I. P., 25, 118, 206, 207, 208, 210, 211, 223, 224, 319, 320, 322, 434, 435, 502, 505, 589, 590, 663, 876, 877, 878, 879, 880, 881, 884
Besley, E., & Co., 144
Bien, Julius, & Co., 335, 336
Blake, J. E., 169
Blatchly Co., 835
Blodget, William, 801
Bond, Frank, 872
Bond, Fred., 872
Bonner, William G., 199
Bonneville, B. L. E., 570
Boos, George E., 497
Bosnan, D. M., 356
Boyd, E. D., 777
Boyd, R. W., 344
Boye, Herman, 814, 817
Bradley, Burr, 257
Brantz, Lewis, 763
Breese, Samuel, 8, 68, 173, 197, 241, 261, 277, 328, 343, 401, 465, 607, 626, 739, 750, 769
Brisbane, A. H., 198

Brodie, Paul, 679
Brooks, Alfred H., 35
Brown, C. T., 425
Brown, Peter, 621
Browne, E., 459
Bruff, J. Goldsborough, 175, 176
Bryan, Hugh, 749
Buchholtz, L. von, 814, 817
Bueckner, Louis, 633
Buell, Don Carlos, 331
Bull, William, 749
Burr, David H., 170, 196, 237, 327, 373, 396, 443, 562, 606, 625, 657, 811
Butts, James R., 200
Cain, William, 628
Callender, Joseph, 388
Carleton, James H., 575
Carleton, Osgood, 368, 369, 388
Carrigain, Philip, 556
Chapman, Silas, 424
Clark, Rawdon & Co., 394
Clark, Richard, 161
Colton, G. W. & C. B., & Co., 245, 246, 356, 490, 497, 611, 779
Colton, George W., 608
Colton, J. H., & Co., 89, 91, 163, 234, 262, 330, 395, 415, 476, 608, 764, 773, 854
Corey & Fairbank, 326
Cram, D. H., 10
Cram, T. J., 850
Craven, A., 104
Creuzbaur, Robert, 772, 773
Croker, L. V., 378
Cummings & Hilliard, 370
Cunningham, E. E., 525
Daidy, George A., 16, 228, 292, 457, 759
Dall, W. H., 19
Darby, William, 341
David, P. S., 557
Davis, Jefferson, 180
Davis, John, 729
Dawkins, Henry, 730
De Brahm, William, 749

De Cordova, J., 772, 773
De Lacy, W. W., 483, 490
De Werthern, H., 131
De Witt, Simeon, 603
Degroot, 536
Dinsmore, A. F., 51, 53, 81, 117, 119, 121, 135, 143, 145, 146, 147, 148, 150, 188, 190, 224, 268, 362, 364, 367, 410, 432, 433, 437, 511, 534, 543, 593, 594, 596, 597, 643, 644, 647, 648, 649, 662, 665, 692, 694, 695, 710, 712, 714, 718, 719, 721, 754, 756, 789, 790, 793, 794, 796, 874, 875
Donegal, W. H., 701
Doniat & Zastrow, 424
Doolittle & Munson, 326
Douglas, H. T., 77
Drew, Columbus, 177
Du Bois, Charles, 310
Durage, Julius J., 493
Early, Eleazer, 193
Eastman, S., 516
Ebert, Frederick J., 126
Eddy, O. T., 555
Eddy, R. A., 89
Eddy, W. M., 89
Faden, William, 554, 560, 601, 602, 749
Farmer, John, 393, 394, 395, 402
Farnham, T. J., 87
Fenner Sears & Co., 259, 325, 372, 460, 623, 738
Fiala, John T., 471, 475
Fishbourne, R. W., 771
Franklin, W. B., 175
French, J. H., 609
Friend & Aub, 161, 279
Froben, Louis von, 869
Fry, Joshua, 809
Fulmore, Z. T., 782
Gascoign, 748
Gast, Leopold, 519
Gedney, Joseph F., 310
Gibbons, R., 102
Gibbs, G., 823
Gillet, George, 156
Gilman, E., 442
Gilpin, William, 126, 129
Gird, Richard, 42
Goepel, Paul, 250, 375, 610
Goldthwait, J. H., 160
Goodwin, John N., 42
Gordon, T., 563
Gray & Crawford, 475
Gray, Frank A., 11, 79, 334, 358, 384, 390, 454, 778, 820

Gray, O. W., 11, 79, 265, 334, 358, 384, 390, 454, 820
Greene & McGowran, 167
Greenleaf, Moses, 370, 371
Griffith, Dennis, 379
Gunn, O. B., & D. T. Mitchell., 307
Haake, A. von, 558
Hager, Albert D., 806, 807
Hale, Nathan, 157
Halsall, John, 299
Hardee, T. S., 452
Harrison, Samuel, 193, 232
Harrison, W., 556, 621
Haviland, William, 326
Hayden, F. V., 134
Hazzard, J. L., 284
Heap, D. P., 641
Heberlein, Alexander, 569
Helm, Charles J., 32, 224, 225, 226, 227, 253, 412, 437, 545, 546, 548, 592, 694, 695
Hendges, M., 32, 53, 54, 141, 146, 147, 188, 269, 320, 480, 481, 529, 530, 532, 543, 544, 646, 647, 648, 649, 650, 651, 684, 686, 687, 688, 689, 690, 694, 695, 716, 718, 719, 721, 754, 755, 756, 759, 791, 862, 863, 873
Henn, Williams & Co., 284, 285
Herrick, S. W., 382
Hill, A. J., 633
Hill, Robert T., 783
Hill, Samuel, 388
Hinton & Simpkin & Marshall, 4, 325, 372, 460, 623, 738
Hoeing, J. B., 335, 336
Hoelcke, William, 576
Hoen, A., & Co., 383, 865
Hoffmann, John D., 553
Holland, Samuel, 554
Holme, Thomas, 728, 740
Holt, George L., 872
Holt, Warren, 536, 537
Holtz, H., 576
Hopkins, G. M., Jr., 161
Hotchkiss, W. O., 865
Howell, Reading, 732, 733, 735
Hudson & Goodwin, 156
Humphreys, A. A., 174, 175, 817
Humphreys, Thomas H., 112
Hunnius, Ado, 579, 671, 672
Hutawa, Edward, 466
Hutawa, Julius, 466
Hutchinson, Ebenezer, 803, 804
Ingalls, G. W., 673

INDEX

Jackson, Henry, 671
Jackson, Sheldon, 20, 21, 23, 26, 31
Jefferson, Peter, 809
Jefferys, Thomas, 809
Jennings, Herrick & Dearborn, 382
Jocelyn, N. & S. S., 158
Johnson & Browning, 806
Johnson, Willard D., 783
Jones, Brown, Fairbanks, 669
Jones, Root & Co., 776
Jones, W. A., 526, 869
Karl, Anton, 580, 581
Kearney, James, 256
Kearney, S. W., 566
Keeler, W. J., 310
Keen & Lee Co., 284, 285
Keen, W. B., 285
Kelsey, C. E., 120
Kelsey, Fletcher F. S., 116
Kennedy, Joseph C. G., 201, 765
Kern, Richard H., 567, 568
Kerr, W. C., 628
Kilp, A., 250
Kimber & Sharpless, 735
Kimber, E., 735
Knauer, J., 415
Krebs, Charles G., 627, 818, 819
Lambert, J., 823
Langermann, A. B., 780
Langtree, C., 71, 76
Lapham, I. A., 854, 859
La Tourrette, John, 5, 10, 347
Laurie & Whittle, 155, 620, 809
Lay, Amos, 388, 604, 605
Lee, Edmund F., 329, 330
Leicht, F. v.,104
Leonhardt, Theodore, 284
Lichtenberg, C. A., 580, 581
Linderkohl, H., 22
Lipman, L., 859
Lippincott, Grambo & Co., 516
Lloyd, J. T., 332, 474, 861
Lockett, S. H., 356
Lorenz, E. H. J., 865
Loring, B., 369
Loring, J., 369
Lowe, R. P., 682, 683, 684, 686, 687
Lucas, F., Jr., 166, 381, 624, 763
Lyon, Sidney S., 329
McClellan, J., 174, 175
McClelland, D., 375, 408, 429, 431, 557, 610, 629, 630, 741, 742, 743

McCoy, Isaac, 668
McCoy, J. C., 668
McJilton, 383
MacLean & Lawrence, 300
Mackay, John, 169
Madert, John H., 324, 761
Magny, X., 344
Maguire, Edward, 641, 493
Mahony, F. E., 188
Major, D., 568
Major, Daniel C., 669, 670
Major, J., 568
Manson, Marsden, 116
Martin, Lawrence, 865
Mathewson, A. J., 245
Matthews, J. N., & Co., 321, 533
Maxwell, C. A., 680
Mayer, Ferd.,& Co., 285
Mayer, J.,& Co., 333
Meigs, M. C., 576
Melish, John, 2, 3, 232, 233, 257, 341, 440, 441, 736, 737, 762
Mendenhall, E., 472, 520
Merrill, William E., 131
Messinger, John, 234, 245
Michler, N., 331
Middleton, Stroridge, & Co., 472
Middleton, Wallace, & Co., 520
Milne, C. R., 329
Moll, H., 154
Monk, Jacob, 126
Morrison, C. C., 580, 581
Morse, Sidney E., 8, 68, 173, 197, 241, 261, 277, 328, 343, 401, 465, 607, 626, 739, 750, 769
Morton, Robert H., 24, 54, 221, 222, 223, 434, 435, 504, 505, 588, 589, 590, 791, 833, 834, 836
Moseley, Edward, 619
Mouzon, Henry, 620
Mullan, John, 102
Munsell, Luke, 326
National Survey Co., 378
Naylor, William, 145, 589, 590, 643, 644, 682, 683, 712, 789
Nell, Louis, 138, 139, 144
Nevil, James, 730
Newton, H. E., 213
Nicholson, W. L., 186, 250, 360, 361, 363, 375, 376, 408, 431, 496, 498, 499, 557, 587, 610, 612, 629, 630, 646, 660, 661, 710, 712, 741, 742, 744, 745, 777, 781, 821
Nicollet, J. N., 277
Oberly, John H., 680

O'Hare, Daniel, 16, 34, 57, 58, 59, 60, 62, 117, 228, 292, 366, 506, 508, 509, 545, 546, 695, 836, 837, 838
Olberg, John, 680
Olney, E. B., 83
Overland Publishing Co., 139
Owen, David Dale, 851
Pabner, I., 802
Palmer, W. R., 815
Parke, Jno. G., 567, 568
Paul, R., 256
Peabody, M. M., 804
Pease, G., 656
Peck, J. M., 234, 245
Peck, W. G., 566
Peters, N., 777, 872
Phillips, James, 732
Pierce, Justin, 158
Plummer, George H., 835
Pohlers, A., 317
Poole, C. H., 408, 741, 742, 821
Powell, W. Angelo, 816
Powers, R. C., 452
Pressler, Charles W., 773, 776, 780
Price, Jonathan, 621
Procter, John R., 335, 336
Quin, Smith, & Van Zandt, 519
Rainey, George, 696
Rand, McNally & Co., 645
Ratzer, B., 601
Ream, Robert L., 520
Reed, Abner, 156
Reed, Edwin O., 76
Ridgway, T. S., 817
Riecker, Paul, 50
Ritchie & Dunnavant, 813
Roberdrau, T., 619
Robert, Henry M., 101
Robertson, W., 698
Robyn, Charles, & Co., 471, 475
Roeser, C., 82, 429, 495, 500, 501, 613, 711, 715, 743
Roessler, A. R., 779
Royce, C. C., 267
Ruffner, E. H., 579, 672
Ruggles, Edward, 555
Sauthier, Claude Joseph, 601, 602
Scull, Nicholas, 729
Scull, W., 730, 731
Searcy, I. G., 166
Searcy, J. G., 166
Selden, Henry S., 783

Sewall, J. S., 418
Shaler, N. S., 333
Simpson, J. H., 421
Smith, A. E., 483
Smith, B. M., 633
Smith, Fred A., 50
Smith, J. C., 43
Smith, John, 808
Smith, Lloyd P., 740
Snow, William P., 497
South, D., 761
Stansbury, Howard, 421
Stanton, W. S., 529
Stevens, I. I., 823
Stiles, S., 393
Stiles, S., & Co., 234, 395
Stone, David, 621
Strother, John, 621
Strothers, John, 762
Strum, G. P., 187, 362, 364, 455, 789
Stuart, John, 749
Sturges, Daniel, 193
Sullivan, Judge, 368
Swann, Charles E., 331
Swett, C. A., 418
Tackabury, Robert M., & George N., 161
Tanner, B., 736, 737
Tanner, H. S., 165, 195, 468, 622, 767, 770, 810
Tassin, J. B., 88
Taylor, Z., 169
Terry, A. H., 641
Thackara, J., 379
Thayer, H. L., 137
Thom, George, 214, 421
Thomas & Anderson, 368
Throop, J. V. N., 157
Towson, R. M., 54
Thwaites, F. T., 865
Trouvelot, L., 333
Troy, Henry W., 134
Tryon, William, 601, 602
Turner, James, 729
Ulke, J., 792
Valencia, Gabriel, 768
Vallance, J., 379
Venable, Richard M., 77
Vignoles, Charles, 165
Wagner, Ernst, 529
Wagner, Thomas S., 177
Wall, J. Sutton, 746
Walling, H. F., 806, 807
Wallis, John, 734

INDEX

Wansleben, Thomas O., 481, 796
Warner & Foote, 290
Warr, John, 381, 459, 767
Warr, William W., 767
Warren, G. K., 517, 518, 519, 632
Warren, Moses, 156
Watrous, S. I., 804
Watson, William, 561
Webb Publishing Co., 696
Welch, B. T. & Co., 763
White, M. Wood, 844
Whitelaw, James, 803, 804

Wiggin, C. P., 300
Wilkes, Charles, 697
Willcox, O. B., 50
Williams, C. S., 468
Williams, Henry T., 134
Williams, J. Lee, 167
Wilson, James E., 641
Wilson, James T. D., 771
Winstanley, C., 112
Wood, W. H., 641
Worth, W. I., 174
Young, Sherman, & Smith, 697

www.ingramcontent.com/pod-product-compliance
Lightning Source LLC
Chambersburg PA
CBHW070510100426
42743CB00010B/1801